INSIDE THE BOTTLE:

Exposing the Bottled Water Industry

by Tony Clarke

Inside the Bottle: Exposing the Bottled Water Industry (Revised Edition)
by Tony Clarke

Canadian Centre for Policy Alternatives
410-75 Albert Street, Ottawa, ON K1P 5E7
Tel (613) 563.1341 Fax (613) 233.1458

info@policyalternatives.ca
www.policyalternatives.ca

Polaris Institute
180 Metcalfe St. Suite 500
Ottawa, Ontario, Canada
Tel (613) 237.1717 Fax (613) 237.3359

polaris@polarisinstitute.org
www.polarisinstitute.org
www.insidethebottle.org

Published by Canadian Centre for Policy Alternatives
Inside the Bottle: Exposing the Bottled Water Industry
Printed and bound in Canada
National Library of Canada Cataloguing in Publication Data

ISBN 978-0-88627-536-5
Library and Archives Canada Cataloguing in Publication

Clarke, Tony
Inside the Bottle : Exposing the bottled water industry / Tony Clarke.

1. Bottled water industry-United States. 2. Bottled water industry-Canada. 3. Bottled
water industry-Corrupt practices-United States. 4. Bottled water industry-Corrupt
practices-Canada.
I. Polaris Institute. II. Title.

HD9349.M542C53 2005 338.4'766361'0973 C2004-907276-5

CCPA
CANADIAN CENTRE
for POLICY ALTERNATIVES
CENTRE CANADIEN
de POLITIQUES ALTERNATIVES

Acknowledgements

AT THE POLARIS INSTITUTE, we want to convey a special thanks to everyone involved in the second publication of *Inside the Bottle.* This has been a remarkable team effort. Initially, the extensive background research for this book was provided by **Marc-Antoine Fleury** and his associate **Olivier De Champlain** of Interica Environnement.

Richard Girard from Polaris contributed additional research about the main corporate players and worked diligently in compiling data for the updates and coordinating the revisions for this edition. And **Verda Cook** from Polaris reviewed the final manuscript for edits.

Community activists engaged in struggles concerning local bottled water operations in both the United States and Canada enriched the text by providing the stories and profiles on what is taking place in their own communities.

Originally, **Susan Wright** edited the entire manuscript and **Stephen Perry** engagingly illustrated the text with his wonderful graphics, while **Shelagh Corbett** did a fine job in originally laying out the book for printing. For this revised and updated version, **Ed Finn** and **Kerri-Anne Finn** of the Canadian Centre for Policy Alternatives both added their expertise in editing and preparing the manuscript for publication.

Karl Flecker, our Water Program Director at Polaris, worked closely with the entire team, coordinating their diverse inputs. We are also grateful to **Maude Barlow** and **Paul Hawken** for providing insightful comments and suggestions on the manuscript through the peer review process. To each and all of you, we express our deep appreciation and gratitude.

TABLE OF CONTENTS

Foreword

A GREAT DEAL HAS HAPPENED since we launched the first edition of **Inside the Bottle**.

The formal launch took place in February 2005 when bottled water activists from across the United States and Canada came together to share their experiences, analysis, and strategies. The gathering took place in Michigan at a place called Traverse City, where one of the campaigns has been ongoing against Nestlé for its bottled water takings. Using the book as an organizing tool, the participants began to map out plans for education and action to be undertaken with key constituencies in relation to various bottled water issues.

During the course of 2005, bottled water started to emerge as an issue for education and action in several sectors of society. Consumer groups began to look at the price gouging that goes on in the bottled water industry. Health activists started to focus attention on the chemical and bacteriological contaminants in bottled water. Environmental networks began to address the greenhouse gas emissions and chemical leaching associated with the use of plastic bottles. And, in some instances, poor urban communities started to see how bottled water creates a new rich-poor divide in terms of water as a human right.

At the same time, public sector unions began to actively defend public water services by questioning the promotion of bottled water in public places. In schools, colleges, and universities, student groups started to openly challenge the exclusivity contracts signed between their administrations and major corporate players in the bottled water industry. And many faith-based communities began to focus public attention on the ethics of bottled water as a prime example of the commodification of the building blocks of life itself on this planet.

Since the publication of the first edition of the book, there have also been numerous community-based campaign activities around bottled water issues. The Polaris Institute and other allied organizations in the U.S. like Corporate Accountability International have tried to encourage and strengthen these initiatives in a variety of ways. An *Awareness to Action* kit has been developed providing tools for campaign activities on bottled water issues and the main corporate players. An Internet news service called *News Bytes* has been developed to provide strategic information on what is happening in the industry. A "rapid response" mechanism has also been put in place so that community groups can get answers to questions needed for their local education and action programs. And an "alliance building" list-serve has helped bottled water activists network with one another in both the U.S. and Canada.

Moreover, the book has become a bit of a catalyst for research, education, and action on bottled water issues outside North America. In early 2005, for example, the book was featured at events in Plachimada, India, marking the 1,000 Days of Protest against the local Coca-Cola plant for its water takings in that community. Similarly, in Brazil, the book has been used in the community campaign against Nestlé's mineral water takings in Sao Lourenço, as well as by civil society groups in Switzerland who have been actively challenging the operations of Nestlé on a variety of issues. Educational events have also been organized around the contents of the book at the World Social Forum in Porto Alegre, Brazil [2005], and at the alternative assembly to the World Water Forum in Mexico City [2006].

As a result, the book generated a fair amount of media attention for bottled water issues. Dozens of television, radio, and print media have featured the book in both the U.S. and Canada, including several national networks. Indeed, since bottled water has become so personally fashionable in North America, journalists found it to be a good entry point into other issues such as the privatization of water services.

For all these reasons, it made sense to come out with an updated version of the book. We are pleased that the Canadian Centre for Policy Alternatives agreed to co-publish this revised version with the Polaris Institute. This new edition of *Inside the Bottle* contains a revised chapter format, data and information updates for each of the sections, plus two new sections [one on the "Global Reach" of the Big-Four corporations and one on "Industry Responses" to the first edition of the book]. We hope that this revised and expanded edition will stimulate further education and action on bottled water issues as a public policy priority for democratic social change.

Tony Clarke
May, 2007

Introduction

OF ALL THE NATURAL RESOURCES ON EARTH, drinking water is arguably the most precious. It is essential to life. As recently as 10 years ago, most people living in the United States and Canada took their drinking water directly from the tap or the water cooler in their workplace. Today, close to one-fifth of the population relies exclusively on bottled water for their daily hydration. Over the past decade, sales in bottled water have exploded in North America. It is now the fastest-growing segment of the entire beverage industry.

Between 1993 and 2004, the consumption of bottled water more than doubled in the U.S. alone—from 10.5 gallons (40 litres) per capita to 23.8 gallons (90 litres). (Source: *Beverage Marketing Corp*). The following chart shows the rate of market growth in single-serve bottles of water during this period:

U.S. BOTTLED WATER ANNUAL GROWTH, 1994-2005	
1994	10.0%
1995	11.3%
1996	8.9%
1997	10.1%
1998	10.5%
1999	13.9%
2000	15.0%
2001	12.6%
2002	14.8%
2003	7.9%
2004	7.5%
2005	7.8%

Source: Beverage Marketing Corporation

Today, bottled water ranks as the second-largest commercial beverage sold in the United States on a volume basis. In Canada, it now outpaces the consumption of each of these beverages: coffee, tea, apple juice, and milk. In the United States, per capita consumption has grown by at least one gallon (3.8 litres) annually, and has doubled in the past decade.

Although bottled water began as a fad, it has rapidly become a part of daily diets in both the U.S. and Canada. To be sure, bottled water does have an important role to play during emergencies when municipal water systems are temporarily disrupted. And in some major cities and countries of the world, bottled water may be the only available source of safe drinking water. Bottled water can provide important short-term substitutes in these cases. But this does not mean that bottled water should become the long-term solution to people's daily hydration needs.

As the dean of a network of water scientists in Switzerland, Dr. Joan Davis, puts it: "water is meant to flow freely. In flowing freely, it cleanses and purifies itself. But, once you put water in a bottle and trap it there, it can have all sorts of implications in terms of quality, safety and human health.'"

In 1999, the U.S. Natural Resources Defense Council (NRDC) published a major study called *Bottled Water: Pure Drink or Pure Hype?* After conducting a survey of the bottled water industry, and testing 103 brands, the NRDC came to the conclusion that bottled water was more "pure hype" than "pure drink." Among its findings, the study showed that one-third of the brands tested contained levels of contamination (including traces of arsenic and E-coli); that one-quarter of all bottled water is actually taken from the tap, filtered, and then sold back to the consumer; and that bottled water is generally subject to less-rigorous testing and lower purity standards than tap water.

The closer we look inside the bottle water industry, the more accurate the NRDC assessment—that bottled water is more "pure hype" than "pure drink"—becomes. Two specific industry manipulations expose the hype.

First, the "Get hydrated or Die" campaign message promoted by the bottled water industry uses questionable science to boost sales. For years now, people in the U.S. and Canada have been diagnosed as "dehydrated" and instructed to drink at least eight eight-ounce glasses of water a day to remedy the problem. The industry's trade association in the U.S. even provides a "hydration calculator" on its website at www.bottledwater.org/public/hydratio.htm to assist people in determining whether or not they need more than the "eight-by-eight" recommendation.

Yet little is known about either the origins or the basis for the "eight-by-eight" rule. Nobody knows for certain where it came from, and health experts are now questioning its validity. In a nine-month study published by the American Journal of Physiology in late 2004, Dr. Heinz Valtin of Dartmouth Medical School concludes that, although the "eight-by-eight" idea "is being promoted terrifically by the bottled water industry... I have found no scientific evidence that supports the claim." Indeed, nutrition specialist Ann Grandjean of the University of Nebraska says the only studies researchers have been able to find that support this rule are those performed on soldiers in high altitudes, hospitalized patients, or people in other "non-typical environments." In other words, the "eight-by-eight" rule may prove to be more than enough, or even too much, daily water intake for most adults.

The second industry manipulation can be seen in the way the bottled water industry, in collusion with the plastics industry, has created a devious marketing device that implies their plastic bottles are recyclable. The logo used by the plastics industry—three chasing arrows in a triangle–is an obvious imitation of the well-known symbol associated with recycling. Yet the symbol is used as an industry sorting device only, and has nothing to do with recycling. The bottled water industry liberally applies this misleading logo to its beverage containers, thereby implying that bottled water is environmentally friendly. This is particularly important, since the bottled water industry has worked hard to link its product to good health and the natural world.

It is now time to revisit this NRDC study, and to go beyond it. During the intervening period, the bottled water industry has become more concentrated as smaller, independent water bottlers have been swallowed up by the major conglomerates. Today, the bottled water market is dominated by four big players: the European food-processing corporations Nestlé and Groupe Danone, and the American soft drink giants PepsiCo and Coca-Cola.

The Big-Four are ubiquitous in many communities, either as a retail presence or by having a bottling or distribution plant. The Polaris Institute has begun the process of mapping the locations of these plants in the U.S. and Canada. A map of the locations can be found at www.insidethebottle.org.

In this publication, we have developed a set of questions designed to elicit grassroots information about how the industry is operating in North America. We invite readers to participate in this initiative by applying these questions to their own communities, and then submit the knowledge they gather by sending an email to insidethebottle @polarisinstitute.org.

Information gathered in this way will contribute to a mapping of the industry and enhance our collective understanding of the bottled water industry and its operations at the local level. We hope this project will also help to bring together activists to jointly develop strategies that can be used to regulate the industry and to protect our water systems.

Inside the Bottle has been written to stimulate public discussion and debate about bottled water issues in communities within the U.S. and Canada. We have identified 10 issues that we believe are central to this discussion. These are examined in detail in this book. A summary of which can be found below.

What follows are 10 of the most frequently raised concerns about the production and sale of bottled water today:

1. Price Gouging: What kind of price mark-ups do we find in the bottled water market?

Single serving bottles of water range in price from $1.00 to $1.75 U.S. The same amount of tap water costs a fraction of this price. The U.S. Natural Resources Defense Council has estimated that bottled water is between 240 and 10,000 times more expensive than tap water. For Coca-Cola or Pepsi, who draw the water for their products directly from municipal taps, this price mark-up is astonishing. But it is even more shocking in the case of Danone or Nestlé, because they pay little or nothing for the water they take out of groundwater streams and aquifers. This section explores the issue of price gouging in depth.

2. Water Takings: When the label on the bottle says "pure spring water," where does the water really come from, who owns it, and how is it regulated?

In the U.S., bottled water companies are not required by law to disclose the source and geographical location of their water takings on their labels. In Canada they are, but only for takings from underground water. Water takings are also largely unregulated in both countries, which have more laws governing surface waters than groundwater. Where groundwater regulations do exist, they differ, often dramatically, from state to state and from province to province. As a result of the lax regulatory environment, bottled water labels are often very misleading. This section explores some of the issues raised by these gaps in legislation.

3. Transforming Water: What kinds of filtering and processing methods do companies use to turn "real" water into bottled water? What's the difference between bottled water and tap water?

The Big-Four bottled water companies imply that their elaborate "proprietary" treatment processes are the justification for the higher cost of their products. Yet, unlike other raw materials such as timber, minerals, oil, and gas, which are transformed into identifiably new products, bottled water is simply *water transformed into water*. The industry's treatment processes do not guarantee that bottled water is safer than tap water; in fact, a number of studies have demonstrated that bottled water is often *less* safe than tap water. Consider that one treatment process uses bromate, which is considered to be a carcinogen. This section examines these issues in detail.

4. Contaminating Water: What evidence is there to support the industry's claim that bottled water is superior to tap water?

The International Bottled Water Association proclaims that bottled water is superior to tap water. Yet several peer-reviewed scientific studies have found disturbing concentrations of toxic ingredients, such as arsenic and mercury, in their bottled water samplings. When Coca-Cola launched its Dasani product in the UK in March 2004, it had to withdraw nearly half a million bottles due to bromate contamination. Bottling plants face inspections only once every three to six years, depending on the country, and regulations governing tap water are often stricter than those governing bottled water. In this section we take a closer look at these regulations, and at industry claims about their product.

5. Marketing Schemes: What kinds of marketing and advertising schemes are used by the companies to sell what is really "water transformed into water"?

The tag-line for Pepsi's Aquafina has changed from: *"So pure we promise nothing"* to *"Pure Water, Pefect Taste"* and *"Make your body happy, drink more water."*

Through relentless advertising, the Big-Four companies have turned bottled water into "America's most affordable status symbol". Using images that evoke "activity," "health," "relaxation," "pureness" and "replenishment," the bottled water giants dupe consumers into buying something that largely exists in an imaginary environment. Industry slogans like "get hydrated or die" expose internal corporation contradictions, such as the fact the same companies that sell dehydrating soft drinks are promoting bottled water as a solution to dehydration. This section makes the case that the value of bottled water is more perceived than real.

6. Eco-Threatening: What environmental damage is caused by the escalating use and disposal of plastic bottles?

Bottled water containers labelled with images of pristine natural environments are rapidly becoming a major threat to the environment and to our health. These containers release highly dangerous toxic chemicals and contaminants into the air and water when they are manufactured, and again when they are burned or buried. Yet these same plastic packages are becoming the fastest-growing form of municipal solid waste in the U.S. and Canada. This section asks the question: Are the real environmental costs of bottled water worth the imaginary benefits?

7. Recycling Record: What is the track record of the Big-Four when it comes to recycling?
Recycling rates for plastic bottles has been in steady decline since 1995, despite the explosion in plastic-bottle use. Not only has the industry promoted the shift from glass to plastic containers, and failed to live up to promises about using more recycled material in its containers, but it also actively opposes legislation aimed at improving recycling rates for plastic bottles and requiring beverage container deposits. More sinister still is the use of a deceptive logo that misleads consumers into thinking the product can be recycled, when the opposite is often true. This section exposes the reality of the industry's *commitment* to recycling.

8. Manipulating Consumers: Why are people turning from tap water to bottled water? What's really fuelling this new bottled water culture?
Ten years ago, most people relied on their municipal system for all their drinking water. Today, close to one-fifth of the population in Canada and the U.S. drinks bottled water exclusively—demonstrating how extraordinarily successful the industry has been in luring people away from tap water. The industry is surgical, targeting the young, the affluent, the athletic, and the hip. It capitalizes on North America's fear and fashion factors to convince consumers to purchase its products. This section examines the manipulative strategies used by the industry to create a new bottled-water culture.

9. School Contracting: What marketing devices have the bottled water companies used in cash-strapped schools, colleges, and universities?
Across the U.S. and Canada, there is now a growing number of kindergarten to Grade 12 schools, universities, and colleges that have signed contracts with Pepsi or Coca-Cola. "Exclusive beverage contracts" give these companies long-term high profit access to students in captive environments. Skillful management of these exclusivity contracts turn students into life-long consumers of their products. Resistance to the deals is made nearly futile under secretive contracts that are cloaked from public scrutiny. This section examines the social consequences of selling public space and access to young people's minds.

10. Water Privatizing: What role and impact does the bottled water industry have on the privatization of public water utilities in the U.S. and Canada?

The world's largest for-profit water service corporations have set their sights on North America: Suez and Veolia Environment from France and Thames Water in the UK are eager to deliver privatized water services. The bottled water industry's marketing of "safe, clean water" undermines citizens' confidence in public water systems, and paves the way for the water companies to take over underfunded local utilities. In return, public willingness to pay premium prices for bottled water enables water service corporations to establish a top dollar price. This section shines some light on the parasitic relationship between these two water industries.

The mountain of evidence gathered in these chapters points to one word: scam.

Like the snake oil salesmen of the frontier days in the American West, today's bottled water peddlers are trying to put one over on an unsuspecting public by promoting their products as the pathway to pure, healthy living. Our evidence suggests that people are not only being misled, but are also being swindled and defrauded. And, although it will be argued that the practices of the bottled water industry are perfectly legal and that no laws have been broken, the issues raised by this book go beyond narrow legal definitions. Ultimately, citizens will have to decide for themselves whether they are being manipulated, lied to, or bamboozled.

In some parts of the U.S. and Canada, resistance to bottled water production has begun to surface. Nestlé has been facing organized community resistance in places like Waushara County, Wisconsin; Mecosta County, Wisconsin; and Pasco County, Florida. In Canada, community groups have been actively opposing independent bottled water companies, and students in both countries have begun to challenge exclusive beverage contracts in their schools.

These examples of community resistance are early skirmishes in what we hope will become *full-scale national and even international campaigns aimed at stopping water companies from gaining complete control over a resource that is essential to life.*

Resistance alone, however, is not sufficient. New public policies and laws are needed, outlining rules for governing the production and marketing of bottled water. Throughout the U.S. and Canada, we have found public policy initiatives and legislative action designed to:

rebuild public tap water systems;
control corporate water takings;
ensure water quality and safety;
recycle plastic water bottles;
establish public right-to-know rules;
certify safe bottled water brands; and
overhaul regulatory agencies and tools.

In addition, effective public policy tools must be created to curb the power of the Big-Four corporate players in the industry and their increasing concentration and control over water. Communities must regain control over their water supplies, and over these industries.

Access to clean drinking water is a universal human right. People must act to safeguard this right and to ensure that no person in any country is asked to live without it. Today, it is clear the role of bottled water, and the bottled water industry, must be brought under the public policy microscope. We hope this book will stimulate the public discussion, debate, and action that is so urgently needed.

1

THE BOTTLED WATER INDUSTRY

IT IS CONSIDERED QUITE FASHIONABLE these days to drink bottled water. Although water is often described as the *essence of life* itself, it contains many non-essential properties, such as minerals, which have made it highly marketable. Indeed, there is nothing really new about the commodification of mineral water. It has been going on for more than 500 years. As historian Christopher Hamlin observed:

> *By the early modern period, mineral waters were clearly part of the domain of capitalism. Royal or noble patronage could convert a bucolic backwater into a center of fashion, raising property values and providing a lucrative living for the medical practitioner who could claim to know the secrets of the local spring.*[1]

In the U.S. and Canada, water has been bottled and sold for over a century. For most of this period, the industry was dominated by dozens of small companies selling local brands. This changed in the mid-1970s when sales of bottled water began to take off in North America. At that point, Perrier was the most renowned brand of bottled water and the number-one bestseller in the world. Within two decades, Nestlé, the international food and beverage conglomerate, bought out Perrier, along with dozens of other brands, including Vittel and San Pellegrino. Soon after, U.S. soft drink giants PepsiCo and Coca-Cola were competing with Nestlé with products such as Aquafina and Dasani. The European-based food processing company Danone, producers of Evian, also battled for market share. A global bottled water industry had emerged.

During this period, bottled water sales more than doubled, from 300 million U.S. gallons per year (about 1 billion litres) in the 1970s, to 650 million U.S. gallons per year (over 2 billion litres) by 1980. By the end of the 1980s, two billion U.S. gallons of bottled water (about 7.5 billion litres) were being consumed annually around the world.[2] Once the global economy recovered from the economic recession of 1989-90, sales in bottled water skyrocketed again. By 2000, 22.3 billion U.S. gallons (84 billion litres) were being bottled and sold.[3] In 1999-2000, bottled water sales translated into a $22 billion (U.S.) industry[4]; by 2003, annual world-wide bottled water sales had reached $35 billion (U.S.).[5]

According to Datamonitor Market Research, in 2005 bottled water sales totalled $62.9 billion U.S., which represents a compound annual growth rate (CAGR) of 7.4% for the five-year period spanning 2001-2005. According to the Beverage Marketing Corporation, global consumption of bottled water reached 40.75 billion gallons. This is an increase of 32% since 1999 when 25.99 billion gallons were consumed worldwide.

In early 2006, the UK research group Zenith International forecasted that more bottled water will be drunk per person than carbonated soft drinks within five years. The group said global bottled water consumption would reach 217 billion litres in 2009, up from 163 billion in 2004. Asia is the fastest-growing region for bottled water, comprising 24.5% of the global market in 2004, and is expected to overtake Western Europe as the world's biggest regional market.[6]

Bottled water has quickly emerged as one of the fastest-growing and least-regulated industries in the world. As Gustave Levin, past chairman of Perrier, once remarked, it is also one of the most lucrative: *"It struck me... that all you had to do is take the water out of the ground and then sell it for more than the price of wine, milk, or for that matter, oil."*[7]

Today, bottled water ranks as the second largest commercial beverage sold in the United States by volume.[8] The situation is similar in Canada, where, according to the Canadian Food Bureau, the consumption of bottled water now outpaces each of these beverages: coffee, tea, apple juice, and milk. From 1993 to 2003, growth in bottled water consumption averaged over 8% per year in the United States.

As the chart above illustrates, the consumption of bottled water doubled between 1993 and 2003—from nearly 40 litres to 86 litres per capita. Meanwhile, in Canada, the compounded annual growth rate in

YEAR	MILLIONS OF GALLONS	ANNUAL CHANGE (%)	PER CAPITA (LITRES)
1993	2,689.4	8.2	39.8
1994	2,966.4	10.3	43.5
1995	3,226.9	8.8	48.2
1996	3,495.1	8.3	49.6
1997	3,794.3	8.6	53.4
1998	4,130.7	8.9	57.9
1999	4,583.4	11.0	63.6
2000	4,904.4	7.0	67.4
2001	5,372.1	9.5	73.1
2002	5,950.7	10.8	80.3
2003	6,395.9	7.5	85.6
2004	6,806.7	8.6	90.1
2005	7,357.1	10.7	
2006	8,267.0	9.7	

Beverage Marketing Corporation U.S. Bottled Water Market, Gallonage, Growth and Per Capita Consumption, 1993-2006

bottled water sales between 1996 and 2002 was 6.4%.[9] Although the rate of growth was lower than in the U.S., the per capita consumption of bottled water by Canadians rose steadily during this period as well, with the highest rate being in Quebec.[10]

While bottled water may have started out as a fad, these numbers show that it now figures prominently in the daily diets of many North Americans. There are several social factors that explain this explosive growth. One is the bottled water industry's ability to tap into the baby-boomers' drive to maintain a youthful image. The industry also benefited from the education campaign waged during the 1990s by physicians and nutritionists anxious to address issues such as proper hydration and obesity. And the industry's massive marketing campaigns have also been a major factor.

There's no denying that fashion has also played a big role in selling bottled water, which has become associated with an active and healthy lifestyle. It has also become a means of social distinction—between those who can afford it and those who cannot.

At the same time, the news media, wittingly or unwittingly, have become allies of the bottled water industry. According to U.S. law, any violation of the drinking water regulations and standards of the Environmental Protection Agency must be reported to the media so the public can be informed. As a result, the bottled water industry has benefited from this free negative advertising, especially since one of its main objectives has been to promote suspicion of tap water, its main competitor.[11]

YEAR	WHOLESALE $ IN BILLIONS
1994	3.164
1995	3.521
1996	3.835
1997	4.222
1998	4.666
1999	5.314
2000	6.113
2001	6.880
2002	7.901
2003	8.526
2004	9.169
2005	10.01
2006	10.98

Source: Beverage Marketing Corporation data on U.S. bottled water sales since 1994

Even so, the real success of the industry lies in the fact that, through clever marketing, it has turned an easily obtained and relatively free resource into a fashionable, high price consumer product. The chart above illustrates resulting trends in market sales within the U.S.

And the prospects for the bottled water industry look very promising. According to forecasts conducted by the industry-wide publication Packaged Facts, the fastest growing segment of the bottled water industry has been single-serve bottles. In 2004, rates of market growth for these bottles were pegged at 19%, which is considered to be very positive.[12] And, even though this growth rate is expected to taper off to 12% by 2008,[13] revenues from single-serve bottled water in the U.S. alone are expected to reach a high of $9 billion (U.S.) by 2008, an increase of 50% over four years.[14] Another major component of the bottled water industry, home and office delivery, known as HOD, is also expected to maintain a steady rate of growth. Industry projections also suggest that other product lines will soon be leading the way. So called "functional water brands," which include oxygenated water, herbal water, and vitamin-added water, are forecast to be the "next big thing" in bottled water.

As market sales continue to soar, the bottled water industry has consolidated. In the North American market, the four major players can be divided into two camps: the European food-processing conglomerates Nestlé and Groupe Danone, and the American soft drink giants PepsiCo and Coca-Cola. Together, these Big-Four have come to dominate the bottled water industry in North America.

U.S. Market Projection of All Bottled Water, 2004-2008. Adapted from *Packaged Facts*: A market study by the Bottled Water Industry

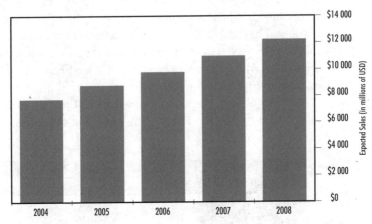

The preceding chart illustrates the growth trend line for all bottled water over the next four years.

During the 1980s and 1990s, bottled water was barely on the radar screen for the American and Canadian food and beverage industry. It was the European bottled water makers who led the way in building and consolidating the industry in North America. Nestlé, formerly known as the Perrier Group of America, and Groupe Danone, whose major brand of bottled water was Evian, began to expand into North American markets and to establish their own production sites on this continent.

In the U.S., Nestlé took the lead in purchasing well-established local and regional bottling companies. In 1980, it acquired Poland Spring and Ozarka, in 1987 Zephyrhills, in 1989 Quebec-based Montclair, and in 1993 Deer Park. Danone followed suit in Canada by purchasing seven bottling companies in Quebec between 1995 and 2002, including Naya, Larochelle, Boischatel, and Naturo. In 2002, Danone struck a deal with Coca-Cola for the distribution of its North American bottled water brands.

Once bottled water sales really began to soar, the two major soft drink giants entered the scene. PepsiCo introduced Aquafina into test markets in 1994, taking the brand to a national level in 1997. While Coke had made two previous attempts to enter the American market, with Belmont Springs in the early 1980s and Mendota Springs in the 1990s, it finally succeeded with the launch of the Dasani brand in 1999. Both PepsiCo and Coca-Cola were spurred on by the relative stagnation of the soft drink market in the 1990s as soft drinks were coming to be associated with the growing problem of obesity.

Yet, unlike Nestlé and Danone, PepsiCo and Coca-Cola did not have to build their home market in North America by purchasing local or regional bottling companies. They each had their own networks of bottlers. They also had ready-made access to water supplies, namely, municipal water systems themselves. Asia and Latin America are the only places where Coca-Cola and PepsiCo have had to make acquisitions to expand their bottled water interests.[15]

The following provides a summary of the market share currently (2005) held by the Big-Four in the U.S. (Note that Danone's sales are combined with Coke's):

RANK	COMPANY	2005 MARKET SHARE
1	Nestlé Waters NA	29.2%
2	Coca-Cola/Danone	9.7%
3	PepsiCo	6.4%

Source: Beverage Marketing Corporation

The Big-Four Corporate Players

In order to understand how the bottled water industry has developed and how it operates, it's useful to take a closer look at the four major corporate players that dominate the industry in the U.S. and Canada. Although Coca-Cola has recently taken over much of the North American distribution of Danone's products, thereby reducing the Big-Four to the Big-Three corporate players, we maintain that Danone is still a key player in the global bottled water industry and needs to be included in this overview.

1) Nestlé

Nestlé is the largest food processing and packaging company in the world. With annual sales of over $80.78 billion (U.S.) in 2006, it consistently ranks among the top ten corporations worldwide.[1] It manufactures and sells a wide range of food and related products, including water, juices, a variety of other beverages, roasted and ground coffee, baby food, dairy products, breakfast cereals, chocolate products, pet care products, cosmetics, and pharmaceutical products.[2]

Nestlé was first known as the Anglo-Swiss Condensed Milk Company in Switzerland, where it started in 1866. It specialized in the production of various chocolate and milk-related products. Through a series of acquisitions and mergers, the company grew larger, expanding its product lines until it became a food-processing corporation. In May 1977, the name was changed to Nestlé, remaining registered in both Switzerland and the United Kingdom. Today, as the world's largest food manufacturer, Nestlé has operations in all regions of the globe and has nearly 250,000 employees worldwide.[3]

Nestlé's foray into the bottled water industry began in 1969 with its acquisition of a 30% stake in a company called Société Générale des Eaux Minérales de Vittel.[4] As noted earlier, Nestlé went on a buying spree in the 1980s, purchasing a string of regionally based bottled water companies in Europe and in North America. Then, in 1992, Nestlé acquired its flagship bottled water company, The Perrier Group. Perrier's sparkling water was already well established as the leading brand of bottled water on the market. During its golden era of the 1980s, The Perrier Group itself had acquired several bottling companies in North America, building an impressive brand portfolio in all price segments.

Today, Nestlé owns and sells a broad range of bottled water brands through its North American operations:

Bottled water brands in North America owned by Nestlé	Perrier	San Pellegrino	Aqua Pana	Vitell
	Arrowhead	Calistoga	Deer Park	Ice Mountain
	Montclair	Poland Spring	Zephyrhills	Ozarka
	Santa Maria	Great Bear (discont.)	Aberfoyle-Nestlé Pure Life	

In 2002, Nestlé's Perrier Group of America changed its name to Nestlé Waters North America. Nestlé's main marketing strategy in the U.S. and Canada was to combine sales of nationally and internationally known brands such as Perrier, San Pellegrino, Vittel, and Aqua Panna, with the local and regionally known brands it had already acquired. As a result, Nestlé established tremendous depth in all categories and price segments of this market. In 2005, Nestlé Waters led the American bottled water market with a one-third share of total sales, or $3.13 billion (U.S.).[5]

Since 1997, Nestlé's chief executive officer has been Peter Brabeck-Letmathe, an Austrian who was also appointed vice-chairman of the board of directors in 2001. In addition to serving on the board of Credit Suisse Bank and the Foundation Board of the World Economic Forum, he is a member of the powerful European Roundtable of Industrialists. As CEO, Brabeck-Letmathe was responsible for Nestlé's "brand strategy, consisting of a clear hierarchy of strategic brands on the global, regional, and local level."[6]

Like other global corporations, Nestlé is organized in such a way as to wield considerable political clout over governments. The company's board of directors includes influential people like Kaspar Villiger, former president of the Swiss Confederation (1995-2001), who also served as the Swiss Minister of Defence (1989-1995) and Minister of Finance (1996-2003). Nestlé USA invests on average $1.5 million (U.S.) a year on industry lobbying activities, and makes substantial "soft money" contributions to political parties and candidates.[7]

Certainly, Nestlé has been no stranger to political controversies. The long-standing battle over Nestlé's marketing of infant formula to new mothers in developing countries has drawn worldwide attention. Nestlé has been accused of breaking the World Health Organization (WHO) code regarding the marketing of substitution products such as Cerelac, NAN, and Alsoy for breastfeeding.[8] Advocacy groups like

INFACT, now known as Corporate Accountability International, have for years argued that children are dying in many developing countries from waterborne diseases because, in part, the water used in the infant formula substitutions contains contaminants. Meanwhile, Nestlé continues to aggressively promote its infant formula products by lobbying national governments in developing countries to relax their breastfeeding programs, by supplying hospitals with free stock of infant formula, and by television advertising campaigns in the countries concerned.[9]

Now Nestlé's water-use practices are emerging as a controversial issue. In 2003, it is estimated that Nestlé Waters withdrew a total of 1,862,486,080 gallons (this equals 2820 Olympic sized swimming pools) for its bottled water production in the U.S. alone. Since Nestlé takes most of its water from underground sources, the company claims that it "collect[s] as much as the spring can safely support."[10] But rising demand for bottled water compelled Nestlé to double its production capacity between 1999 and 2002.[11] Since Nestlé companies use boreholes to tap water from springs, more water is withdrawn than the natural flow of the spring.

In particular, serious concerns have been raised about Nestlé's water takings in areas that are prone to drought conditions. In Pasco County, Florida, for example, Nestlé bottles its Zephyrhills product with water taken from the Crystal Springs that feeds the Hillsborough River, one of Tampa's main sources of drinking water. In 2000-2001, when a drought hit the region, Nestlé continued to push for a permit to increase its water takings from 301,000 gallons to 1.8 million gallons per day. Elsewhere, in Brazil, where Nestlé bottles its Pure Life brand, the company reportedly was responsible for drying up the Magnesiana, one of the main springs in the Agulhas Negras (Black Needles).[12]

"Since it started increasing production in 1999," reports *Packaged Facts*, "Nestlé has faced battles over their water takings in six states: California, Florida, Maine, Michigan, Pennsylvania, and Texas."[13] So far, Nestlé has prevailed in these battles of corporate vs. community rights. But, because Nestlé must continue to seek out new sources to meet production demands, it keeps running into new resistance. Citizens and local government officials are beginning to realize the economic benefits of welcoming a major bottling company like Nestlé into their communities are often surpassed by the price their communities must pay in terms of potential harm to the environment and to their quality of life.

2) Coca-Cola

The red and white Coca-Cola label is *the* most recognized logo in the entire world. Unlike its competitors, Coca-Cola is first and foremost a soft drink and beverage company, specializing in the sale of non-alcoholic beverages, and the manufacture, distribution and marketing of concentrates and syrups. Indeed, Coca-Cola's primary business is the selling of concentrates and syrups to bottlers who, in turn, add water, and then sell the final product to retail outlets.

The entire Coca-Cola venture dates back to 1886, when the famous Coke syrup was first mixed with carbonated water in an Atlanta pharmacy. Within 10 years, Coca-Cola was being bottled and sold through a network of bottlers and retail stores across the U.S. In 1906, the Coca-Cola Company extended its operations into Canada, Cuba, and Panama.[1]

In 2006, the Coca-Cola Company boasted revenues of $24.08 billion (U.S.) and employed nearly 55,000 employees worldwide (down from 56,000 in 2002)[2]. Coke sells nearly 400 beverage brands in close to 200 countries. In 2005, the North American and European regions alone provided close to 60% of Coke's total operating revenues (28.9% and 29.4%, respectively). Coke's sister company and largest bottler, Coca-Cola Enterprises, Inc., has 74,000 employees and provides annual revenues of close to $19 billion (U.S.)[3]

Coke entered the European bottled water market in 1970 with the launch of BonAqua in Austria. The brand is now sold in nearly 50 countries, most of those in Europe.[4] As noted above, Coca-Cola tried to enter the U.S. bottled water market on two previous occasions: at the beginning of the 1980s with Belmont Springs (which was sold to Suntory in 1989), and again in the 1990s with Mendota Springs. It was not until April 1999, however, that Coca-Cola was successful in launching its Dasani bottled water brand in North America.

Prior to the mid-1990s, the bottled water market was relatively small. Coke and Pepsi's early forays into this market had modest results, likely because health-conscious trends had not taken root and neither product line was accompanied by intensive marketing support.

Coke's later entry into the North American bottled water market was due, in part, to an internal debate within the company. Since Coke makes its revenues and profits by selling syrup and concentrate to bottlers, bottled water presented a particular problem: there was no syrup to sell.[5] Coke found a way to circumvent this by developing a special mineral package to be sold to bottlers who could then add tap water to produce the Dasani bottled water product.

During its first year on the U.S. market, Dasani was ranked 13th in sales, but by 2002 it had become the second best-selling brand behind Pepsi's Aquafina.[6] Coke's biggest move, however, occurred in 2002 when it joined forces with its competitor Danone to form Coca-Cola Danone Waters. Under this joint venture, Coke, a 51% shareholder, manufactured and distributed Danone's water brands in North America. With this deal, Coca-Cola greatly expanded its bottled water portfolio to include premium-priced brands like Evian and Volvic, along with lower-priced brands like Sparkletts and Pure American. Today, Coca-Cola is ranked second to Nestlé in overall bottled water sales in North America, and boasts ownership and/or licence to sell the following brands.

Bottled water brands in North America owned by Coca-Cola

Dasani	Dannon
Dasani Sensations	Spring! By Dannon
Dasani Flavors	Spring! By Dannon Fluoride to go
Dasani Nutriwater	Ciel [Mexico]

Coke also expanded its bottled water operations internationally in 2003. That year, Coke bought brands or license rights to the Cosmos brands in the Philippines, the Multivita spring water brand in Poland, the Neverfail Springwater trademark in Australia, the Chaudfontaine water brand in Belgium, and the Valpre water trademark in South Africa.[7] In addition, it owns rights to other well-established brands in

GEOGRAPHICAL AREA (COCA COLA COMPANY)	% OF REVENUE (2005)
European Union	29.4
North America	28.9
North Asia, Eurasia and Middle East	19.5
Latin America	10.9
Africa	5.5
East and South Asia, Pacific Rim	5.4
Corporate	0.4

large markets such as Kinley in India, Mount Franklin in Australia, and Malvern in Great Britain.

Although most of Coke's revenues are not based directly on the number of cases they sell, Coke acknowledges the unit case volume is one measure of the underlying strength of the corporation, because "it measures trends at the consumer level"[8] In 2005, Coca-Cola sold over 20 billion unit cases, approximately 19.8 billion unit cases in 2004, and 19.4 billion unit cases in 2003.[9] In its North American operations, the increased sales were "primarily related to Dasani, Coca-Cola Zero, and non-carbonated beverages, along with growth in the warehouse juice and warehouse water operations."[10]

In June 2004, Douglas Daft, Coca-Cola's long-time CEO and chair, was replaced by E. Neville Isdell. Coke's board has included business titans like Warren Buffet, CEO and chair of Berkshire Hathaway Inc., and Robert Nardelli, president and CEO of The Home Depot. In addition, the former President of Mexico, Vincente Fox, was himself previously president of Coca-Cola Mexico. The complete and current list of board members can be found at http://www2.coca-cola.com/ourcompany/board.html. As of 2006, the board members include Ronald Allen, CEO of Delta Airlines; and Cathleen Black, president of Hearst Magazines, a unit of The Hearst Corporation. The company's top lobbyists include Barclay Resler, Vice-President of Government Affairs, and John Brownlee Jr., Manager of Federal Government Affairs, both with track records as legislative aides in Washington.

Coca-Cola maintains a well-oiled machine when it comes to political donations and influence. During the U.S. election cycle, Coca-Cola and its subsidiaries and joint-ventures are generous contributors to both Republican and Democratic parties (although more to the former than to the latter).[11] Like PepsiCo, Coke also makes Political Action Committee (PAC) donations. During the 2004 and 2006 election cycles, Coke made donations to 13 out of 18 senators on the Senate Committee on Agriculture, Nutrition, and Forestry.[12] And, like its main competitor, it donates to its own corporate lobbying associations, like the Grocery Manufacturers Association and the National Soft Drink Association, both of which wield considerable political influence.

In other countries, however, Coke's extensive political influence has not always prevented the company from getting into hot water. In India, for example, after having been asked to leave the country in 1977, Coke returned in 1993 only to find itself embroiled in a number of cases where the company was accused of draining groundwater resources. In the town of Plachimada in the Indian State of Kerala, for instance, Coke became the prime target of mass protests by farmers and villagers for drying up valuable groundwater supplies. This caused the local government to cancel Coke's water-use permit in February of 2004.[13] At the same time, a parliamentary committee of the Indian government found that Coke's beverages "contained unacceptable amounts of pesticide residue."[14] The pesticide issue resurfaced again in 2006 when Indian public interest organization, Center for Science and the Environment, released a report that showed high levels of pesticides in Coke and Pepsi products.[15]

Some of Coke's "independent" bottlers have had their own troubling track record. In Colombia, for example, two of Coke's bottlers, Bebidas y Alimentos and Panamerican Beverages (Panamco), have been accused of using right-wing paramilitary death squads linked to the Colombian Army to break up unions at bottling plants. Since 1989, eight union leaders from Colombian plants have been murdered, while hundreds of other workers and their family members have been tortured, kidnapped, or illegally detained by the paramilitaries.[16] In 2001, both the bottlers and Coke were charged in a Miami Federal Court.[17] A federal judge dismissed the case in October 2006 admitting the appellate court was better suited to clarify the law upon which he based his dismissal of the cases. An appeal was filed later the same month.

In 1980, Coke and its bottlers faced similar court charges in Guatemala, igniting a worldwide boycott against the company.

In the U.S., employees from the Atlanta headquarters of Coca-Cola filed a lawsuit charging the company with a pattern and practice of racial discrimination against African-American employees. After a protracted legal battle, Coca-Cola agreed to pay over $190 million in order to end the litigation, the largest settlement in a U.S. race-discrimination lawsuit.[18]

3) PepsiCo

PepsiCo is more than a soft drink company. With annual revenues around $35.14 billion (U.S.),[1] PepsiCo is ranked as the fourth largest food and beverage company in the world. It owns and produces six of the 15 largest selling brand products in supermarket chains across the United States.[2]

The original Pepsi-Cola Company was established in the early 1900s by a North Carolina pharmacist. Through a series of acquisitions and mergers in the first half of the 20th century, PepsiCo expanded its operations to include other foods and beverages. In the late 1960s, Pepsi-Cola merged with Frito-Lay, a chips and snack company. It then proceeded to gobble up a variety of restaurant chains, including Kentucky Fried Chicken, Pizza Hut, Taco Bell, East Side Mario's, and D'Angelo Sandwich Shops. In 1997, PepsiCo began to sell off these restaurant chains, and in 1998 it bought out Tropicana Products, its biggest acquisition to date. In 2001, PepsiCo negotiated a merger with Quaker Oats, thereby securing its position as one of the largest food and beverage companies in the world.

Today, PepsiCo has four major business units—Frito-Lay North America, Quaker Foods North America, PepsiCo Beverages and Foods, and PepsiCo Beverages International[3]—and in 2006 Pepsi had 157,000 employees around the world. In addition to its North American division, which operates in both Canada and the U.S., PepsiCo's international divisions operate in 200 countries, the largest being in Mexico and the United Kingdom.[4]

PepsiCo made two modest attempts to enter the bottled water market, in 1987 and in 1991, and maintained a low marketing profile. It was not until 1994, when PepsiCo launched Aquafina in Wichita, Kansas, that the company became a major player in the bottled water industry. Its marketing tag line was "Take me to the water."[5] Over the next three years, the marketing of Aquafina spread into the southern and western states of the U.S. In 1997, Pepsi's recycled tap water went eastward to Chicago, where it reached into markets throughout the midwest. By that time, close to 75% of the Pepsi bottling system was producing and selling Aquafina.[6] Aquafina was quietly introduced to Canada in 1996.

Unlike Nestlé's bottled water products, which use spring water, Aquafina is tap water taken from municipal water distribution systems in cities like Denver or Detroit. It is then put through a seven-step purification process, which Pepsi refers to as "HydRO-7."[7] Selling little more than doctored tap water, Pepsi chose Aquafina as a name that would give the product a natural "feel," appealing to consumer desire for pure, clean water.[8] Incredibly, by 2001, Aquafina had become the best selling single-serve bottled water product in North America. By 2005, Pepsi had cornered 6.4% of the total U.S. bottled water market,[9] with U.S. sales of Aquafina approaching $1 billion.

At first glance, Pepsi's position may seem a bit vulnerable because, unlike Nestlé and Danone, it has only one brand-name product for sale. But Pepsi's share of U.S. bottled water market and sales of Aquafina show that a company like Pepsi does not have to promote several brands of bottled water to be successful. It can make it with one single product, provided its marketing is effective.

Pepsi has since decided to diversify and expand its market options by investing in the industry's latest trend, namely, functional waters, and they are paying off.

According to PepsiCo's third quarter 2005 financial report, "net revenues increased by 17%, reflecting volume growth of 8%. The volume increase was driven by a 24% increase in non-carbonated beverages, while carbonated soft drink volume was unchanged from 2004. The non-carbonated beverage growth was fuelled by double-digit growth in Gatorade, Trademark Aquafina, and Propel."

As a global corporation, PepsiCo is well placed to exercise political influence. Under the direction of CEO Indra K. Nooyi, Pepsi's management team includes a former legal advisor to the U.S. Department of State, and Pepsi's board boasts such business and government heavyweights as John Akers, former chair and CEO of International Business Machines Corporation (IBM); Robert Allen, former chair and CEO of AT&T Corp.; and Ray Hunt, chair and CEO of Hunt Oil Company and Hunt Consolidated Inc.[10]

PepsiCo, along with its subsidiaries and joint-venture partners, also donates large sums of money to candidates during election campaigns. While the company does not invest the millions of dollars that some corporate giants do, its donations are strategically invested in congressional and senatorial campaigns through their Political Action Committees (PACs), which are political committees organized for the purpose of raising money to elect and defeat candidates. For example, during the 2004 and 2006 election cycles, PepsiCo made donations to 10 out of the 18 senators on the Senate Committee on Agriculture, Nutrition and Forestry, which studies and proposes legislation affecting nutrition, diet, and food safety.[11]

Internationally, PepsiCo has not always been successful in exercising its considerable influence. It faced difficulties in Burma, now known as Myanmar, where the company set up a bottling operation under a military dictatorship. Its joint-venture partner, a local businessman who was affiliated with the military junta, was known for promoting the use of "forced" labour.[12] In order to import the required supplies for its bottling plants, PepsiCo bought farm goods allegedly produced by forced labor and exported them in exchange for hard currency. As a result, Pepsi became the target of a national and international boycott, and in 1996-97 the company decided to leave Burma altogether.[13]

Meanwhile, back home, despite its best efforts to present itself as an environmentally friendly company, Pepsi has been the target of environmental groups over its use of recycled plastic. In 2002, the GrassRoots Recycling Network and the Container Recycling Institute said that Pepsi, along with Coke, is "responsible for a dramatic increase in packaging waste over the last 10 years,"[14] and that the two companies are "trashing America." Industry statistics show that waste from aluminum cans, plastic, and glass bottles in the United States doubled between 1992 and 2000. In 1990, Pepsi committed to using 25% recycled material in its plastic bottles, but quickly decided that this level would be too costly. In the wake of Coke's 2002 announcement that it was using 10% recycled plastic in its bottles, Pepsi committed to the same 10% figure.[15]

Environmentalists, however, say that neither Pepsi nor Coke has lived up to this commitment so far, and the quota itself is inadequate in light of the damage caused by plastic bottle waste.

4) Danone

Groupe Danone is a European food manufacturing and processing corporation based in France, the smallest and perhaps least known of the Big-4. Danone's major product lines fall into three categories: fresh dairy products, cereal snacks and biscuits, and bottled water.

Groupe Danone was initially established in 1966 as Boussois Souchon Neuvesel, a manufacturing company that produced glass containers and flat glasses. Commonly known as BSN, in 1973 the company merged with Gervais-Danone, a food manufacturer, and changed its name to BSN-Gervais. During the 1970s and 1980s, the company rapidly established itself as a leader in the French foods and beverage market, and during this period it made numerous acquisitions. By the mid-1980s, it had abandoned the flat glass industry and entered the biscuit market with the purchase of General Biscuit and the acquisition of Nabisco's European biscuit division. In 1994, BSN-Gervais became Groupe Danone and Franck Riboud took over from his father to run the company as president and general manager in 1996.[1]

Today, Groupe Danone operates in 120 countries and has 90,000 employees. Danone's portfolio of brands and products include the world's number-one dairy brand, Danone (Dannon in the United States), the world's leading retail water brand, Evian, and the world's second largest cereal and biscuits products brand, LU'S. In 2006, Groupe Danone's annual revenue was $18.69 billion (U.S.)—27% generated by its bottled water products, 47% by its dairy products, and 23% by its biscuits.[2]

Danone's participation in the bottled water industry dates back to 1966 when, as BSN, it acquired the Evian brand. Later, in the 1990s, Danone went on a buying spree, purchasing a number of other bottled water brands, particularly in North America.

Bottled Water brands in North America owned by Danone Waters:

Naya	Bonafont (Mexico)
Naya Go	Naya Aquakids
Naya Aquakids	

By 2000, Groupe Danone was the number-two player in the North American bottled water market through its purchase of the Quebec-based Naya and McKesson, bottler of both Sparkletts and Alhambra.

In early 2000, Coke forged a joint venture with Danone Waters of North America (DWNA) for the production, marketing, and distribution of DWNA bottled spring and source water business in the US. In August 2005, Coke completed the acquisition of DWNA.[3]

While Danone continues to sell bottled water in the United States with its Evian brand, the Dannon spring water brands that were sold under the joint venture are now in Coca-Cola's portfolio of brands.

Danone Waters became the biggest player in the home and office delivery business (HOD) by joining forces with Japanese-based HOD specialist Suntory to create DS Waters, LP. Through this joint venture, Danone secured a 40% share in the lucrative HOD market, where profit margins run as high as 60%.[4]

In November 2005, following Danone's decision to exit the home and office delivery water business in the United States, the company bought out Suntory's share of the joint venture and then sold DS Water, LP to the Kelso investment fund.

In 2006, Groupe Danone unloaded the remainder of its North American HOD operations when Birch Hill Equity Partners Inc. acquired Danone Waters of Canada (DWOC). DWOC was the leading distributor and manufacturer of large-format bottled water in Canada under the Canadian Springs and Labrador Source Brands. The company will now be called Aquaterra Corporation Ltd. and it will retain the Canadian Springs and Labrador Source Brands.[5]

In recent years, Coke's and Pepsi's aggressive marketing of their bottled water brands has had an impact on the sales of Danone's flagship product, Evian. In 2003, Evian's sales dropped $46 million (U.S.) over the previous year, while its share of the overall U.S. bottled water market fell from 2.5% in 2002 to 1.7% in 2003.[6] There are signs that Danone is placing less emphasis on the U.S. market, and instead is turning its attention to markets in Asia and Mexico.

In Asia, where the population density is high, bottled water consumption rates grew by 15% during the period between 1999 and 2001.[7] Here Danone targeted India, Indonesia, and China. In Indonesia Danone purchased a 40% stake in Indonesia's leading bottling company, Aqua, increasing its share to 74% in 2001. At the end of 2000, Danone also bought 50% of China's largest supplier of home and office delivery water, the Aquarius Water Co. As a result, Danone now controls 24% of the bottled water market in three Asian countries—10 times that of its nearest Asian competitor. In the words of one marketing agent: "If you win these three countries, you win Asia."[8]

In Mexico, per capita bottled water consumption is among the highest in the world (179 litres in 2005).[9] Mexico is a country that does not have a consistent supply of safe drinking water,[10] so bottled water has become the default choice for most Mexicans. In 1995, Danone made its first move into the Mexican market by purchasing a 50% share in Bonafont, Mexico's number-one bottled water company. Then, in 2001, Danone acquired 50% of Pureza Aga, Mexico's second-largest HOD company.

Compared to its Big-Four rivals, Groupe Danone has a relatively good social and environmental track record. Throughout France and much of Europe, the company is recognized as a pioneer in this field. According to its own social and environmental audits, Danone has reduced the amount of overall energy used to produce bottled water, biscuits, and dairy products. It has also introduced measures to reduce the amount of packaging weight versus content weight for its products. By the end of 2003, 64 of Danone's plants had also been audited and certified by ISO 14001,[11] thereby meeting a set of internationally recognized social and environmental standards.

But Danone's record is not completely rosy. In Quebec, where Danone owns 70% of the bottled water industry, the company came under fire between 1995 and 1998 for its water taking practices in the municipality of Franklin near the U.S. border, where a huge amount of water was being withdrawn from the local aquifer. Throughout the dispute, Danone deployed a range of tactics to quash public criticism of its water takings, which included conducting discrete negotiations with land owners occupying land above the aquifer; committing to create jobs that dropped from the promised 150 to 50 as the conflict wore on; and benefiting from accelerated public land use permits that were not typically granted by government departments. It is worth noting the Quebec government was supporting the amalgamation of small independent bottlers into a single entity that was sold to Danone.

In 1998, Danone abandoned the project on the Canadian side of the border, but continued concentrating on the U.S. portion of the aquifer in New York State.[12] Although the Franklin incident may be an isolated one for Groupe Danone, it raises an important question: Are these the tactics the company expects to employ when it faces opposition in the developing countries where it intends to concentrate more and more of its operations?

Now that we know something about the bottled water industry and its four major corporate players, we need to take a closer look at how these companies are expanding.

5) Global Reach

The bottled water industry is certainly not confined to the North American market. Nor are the Big-Four corporate players. As we have seen, Europe was the cradle of the bottled water industry. It is only recently that the major European bottled water companies, Nestlé and Danone, focused their attention on expanding into the North American market, while the U.S. soft drink giants, Coke and Pepsi, emerged as new players in the bottled water sweepstakes and developed their own flagship products to rival their European counterparts. Now, as Coca-Cola and PepsiCo expand their operations in Europe, all four of the big players are opening markets in Eastern Europe, Asia, the Middle East, Africa, and Latin America.

As was the case in much of Europe and North America before the Big-Four started buying up local independent bottled water companies, water is being packaged in containers and sold by small entrepreneurs all over the world today. As a result, worldwide production and sales of bottled water remain sketchy at best. In its 2006 report on bottled water, the Earth Policy Institute went so far as to say that annual sales of bottled water worldwide now amount to $100 billion dollars.[1] This indicates a

RANK	COUNTRIES	GALLONS/CAPITA 2000	GALLONS/CAPITA 2005
1	Italy	42.2	50.5
2	United Arab Emirates	30.1	47.7
3	Mexico	32.7	47.3
4	Belgium-Luxembourg	31.2	42.4
5	Spain	27.8	38.7
6	France	33.2	36.6
7	Germany	26.8	33.8
8	Lebanon	20.3	28.2
9	Switzerland	23.8	27.4
10	United States	16.2	26.1
11	Cyprus	19.1	26.0
12	Saudi Arabia	21.2	24.6
13	Czech Republic	18.0	23.8
14	Portugal	18.9	22.0
15	Slovenia	14.9	21.5
	GLOBAL AVERAGE	**4.7**	**6.7**

Source: Beverage Marketing Corporation, 2005

staggering increase over what has been reported by beverage industry surveys worldwide in previous years. While we question the accuracy of this figure, there is no doubt that annual bottled water sales are rising rapidly and that more accurate and comprehensive surveys are required to obtain a complete picture of the global market.

Around the world, reports indicate that bottled water consumption is on the rise. According to data compiled by the Beverage Marketing Corporation,[2] the United States still leads in daily bottled water consumption. In 2005, U.S. consumption of bottled water topped 28 billion litres. Mexico was second with 18 billion litres of bottled water consumed on a daily basis. China and Brazil were third and fourth, respectively, with daily consumption rates over 12 billion litres each. Italy and Germany followed in 5th and 6th place each, with around 10 billion litres. Yet this ranking changes when bottled water consumption is measured on a per capita basis. In 2005, Italians were the number-one bottled water drinkers at 191 litres per person annually. The United Arab Emirates and Mexico are next with 180 and 179 litres per person, followed by Belgium (160L), Spain (149L) and France (138L).

As the Earth Policy Institute points out, the largest increases in bottled water consumption appear to be taking place in developing countries of the global South. Countries like Lebanon, Mexico, and the United Arab Emirates increased their per capita consumption rates between 44% and 50% during the five-year period from 1999 to 2004. Indeed, these three countries had the highest rate of growth in consumption of the 15 top bottled water-consuming countries in the world. Although their per capita consumption rates were not as high, India managed to triple its overall bottled water consumption during the same five-year period, while China's rate more than doubled.

Of course, the Big-Four corporations in the bottled water industry are well aware of these current consumption rates and potential market trends for the future. Their long-term strategy has been to market their bottled water products on a global basis. Even though North America remains their primary market for bottled water sales, they are rapidly expanding their operations into eastern Europe while opening up new markets in Asia, Africa, Latin America, and the Middle East. Their production strategies may differ from country to country. Unlike Nestlé and Danone, for example, Coca-Cola and PepsiCo have their networks of bottling companies and the infrastructure for expansion. But the sources for their water takings are often different in developing counties than in North America. Instead of taking water from municipal water systems, as they do in the U.S. and Canada, the soft drink giants operating in developing countries frequently take their water now from rural springs in the countryside. What's more, both companies require huge volumes of water for all of their products.

The following is a snap shot of the global production and marketing strategies of the Big-Four on a region-by-region basis.

European Expansion
Since 2000, Nestlé Waters has made a series of moves to consolidate its toehold and leadership in Europe, particularly in Home Office Delivery

[HOD]. Thanks to several acquisitions, Nestlé Waters was able to secure a solid base in seven European countries by the end of 2002 [including the United Kingdom, Germany, the Netherlands, Portugal, Denmark, and Italy]. In February 2003, Nestlé made a couple of key acquisitions. First, the bottled water giant purchased Powwow, the number one HOD operator in western Europe with operations in seven countries, thereby establishing a pan-European presence in the HOD market. Then, two weeks later, Nestlé Waters announced its purchase of the Clear Water group, the leader of the bottled water HOD market in Russia. With annual growth rates averaging between 15% and 20% a year in Europe, Nestlé Waters has positioned itself to cash in on this expanding lucrative segment of the bottled water market. Moreover, Nestlé has come out with its own European brand for the HOD market, Nestlé Aquarel, which is designed to serve family household hydration needs.

At the same time, Coca-Cola has been rapidly expanding its operations in both western and eastern Europe. In 2002, for example, the Coca-Cola Hellenic Bottling Company bought a controlling stake in the Romanian mineral water company Dorna, thereby strengthening its presence in the emerging markets of eastern Europe such as Russia, Bulgaria, and Yugoslavia. Through its subsidiaries, Coca-Cola made other acquisitions in western Europe such as Chaudfontaine, the Belgian high-quality mineral water company in 2003; Roemerquelle, the Austrian mineral water company in 2003; and Portugal's mineral water company Refridge in 2004. In 2005, Coke's second largest bottler in the world, the Coca-Cola Hellenic Bottling Company, made additional acquisitions of mineral water companies in Bulgaria and Serbia. Then, in 2006, Coca-Cola took over Germany's mineral water company Apollinaris, and plans to purchase Italy's mineral water company Traficante. Furthermore, both Coca-Cola and Nestlé have developed a joint venture called Beverage Partners Worldwide, which is aimed at tapping the market growth potential for the beverage products of both companies.

Meanwhile, Groupe Danone, which is the world leader in the HOD market, has expanded its operations in Europe with the acquisition of a number of European bottled water companies since 2002. In 2006, Groupe Danone acquired 49% of the Danish bottled water company Aqua D'or. With the acquisition of the Sparkling Spring Water Holdings company in 2002, Danone also strengthened its position in the U.K. and Dutch water jug markets. And, in 2002, Danone also made its move to enter eastern Europe with its purchase of the leading bottled water company in Poland, Zywiec Zdroj.

Emerging Asian Markets

Nestlé has made a series of moves to open up new markets for its bottled water business in Asia, particularly China and Indonesia. In 1997, for example, Nestlé set up an HOD plant in China, followed by another plant in 2000. Unable to compete effectively with local businesses in the jug water market, Nestlé scrapped its original strategy in China in 2002 and began in 2004 to focus its attention on producing "functional waters" in curvy bottles and marketing them to high-end consumers as containing health benefits.[3] In July 2004, Nestlé and Coca-Cola together announced the creation of a 50/50 joint venture in Indonesia called Water Partners Bottling. This joint venture was based on the acquisition of the second largest bottled water company in Indonesia, PT AdeS Alfindo Putrasetia, Tbk [AAPS]. Indonesia is the second largest bottled water market in Asia, after China, and the seventh largest in the world.

Of the Big-Four, Coca-Cola is in the best position to cash in on the China's bourgeoning bottled water market in the long run. Coke's history in China dates back to aftermath of World War I when it built its first bottling plant in that country. It was also the first U.S. company to market its goods in China when the doors were opened to foreign investment in 1979. Today, with its ownership stake in 24 bottling plants, Coca-Cola is well positioned to produce and sell its bottled water products. Similarly, in India, Coke's longtime presence has given the company a toe-hold in a country that is currently ranked 10th in worldwide bottled water sales. Increasingly, Coca-Cola's bottled water product, Kinley, has been gaining ground to the point where it now has a market share of between 20% and 25%, second to local brand Parle Bisleri at 40%.[4] Coke's market growth might have been greater had there not been the 2003 government reports showing high levels of pesticide residue in Coca-Cola and PepsiCo products. In addition to the joint bottled water venture with Nestlé Waters in Indonesia, Coca-Cola acquired bottled water companies in Australia, including in 2004 Palm Springs Ltd., the country's second largest spring water company.

Groupe Danone, however, is still the largest player when it comes to Asia's HOD market. In both China and Indonesia, Danone is the market leader in jug water sales. In Japan, Danone's flagship bottled water products, Volvic and Evian, have been ranked numbers 1 and 2, respectively. In 2002, Danone consolidated its bottled water sales in Japan by signing a partnership agreement with Kirin Beverage Corp. and the Mitsubishi Corp. On the other hand, PepsiCo's involvement in the Asian bottled water market has been modest compared to the other major players. Despite the pesticide scandal in India, Pepsi's Aquafina sales have grown to the point where it now has 10% of the country's bottled water market.

Latin American Growth

Having the second highest consumption rate of bottled water in the world, Mexico has been a prime target for market growth among the Big-Four. While there are some 6,000 brands of bottled water sold in Mexico, over 50% of the market is controlled by the four majors. Between them, Coca-Cola and PepsiCo have a 30% share of the Mexican bottled water market. Coca-Cola's flagship brand is Ciel, while PepsiCo, which has been in Mexico for over 100 years, now owns Electropura, one of the oldest brands of bottled water in the country, which is sold in 19 states. More recently, Coca-Cola has developed a more aggressive strategy for securing control over water sources in Mexico; its prime target is the Mexican state of Chiapas, which is said to possess 40% of the country's freshwater sources and 50% of its total rainwater recharge.

At the same time, Danone has also developed a strong presence in Mexico. Its leading bottled water brands in Mexico are Bonafont, Evian, and Pureza Aga. Danone is also the leader in the HOD water business in Mexico, with Pureza Aga as its flagship product. Mexico is also the world's leading market for HOD sales. In 2004, Danone strengthened its position by purchasing Arco Iris, one of the major players in the Mexican HOD market. These moves were preceded in 2003 by Danone's takeover of Ultra Pura in Tijuana and AquaPura in Monterrey, both of which play a significant role in Mexico's HOD market.

Brazil has been another major market for bottled water in Latin America. Both Coca-Cola and PepsiCo have established roots in Brazil, which include a string of bottling companies that serve their soft drink production as well as their bottled water production. But Brazil is no stranger to producing bottled water itself. More than 70 brands of bottled water are produced and sold in Brazil, involving many independent Brazilian companies besides the Big-Four. Nestlé is also very active in Brazil with its Pure Life product, which has become the source of considerable conflict. In the mineral water park of Sao Lourenço, Nestlé has been challenged by citizen groups and municipal councillors for violating the laws regulating mineral waters. The charges include both the depletion of groundwater springs and the use of reverse osmosis methods of production, which change the natural composition of mineral and healing waters.[5]

Africa - Middle East

Nestlé and Danone have also been positioning themselves to take advantage of market opportunities for bottled water in North Africa and the Middle East. In 2005, Nestlé Waters announced it had signed a partnership with the Zahaf brothers, owners of one of the leading players in Algeria's beverage industry [Boissons Gazeuses des Freres Zahaf Group]. Algeria is expected to play a pivotal role for Nestlé Waters as a "growth booster" for its market strategy in North Africa and the Middle East. As the chairman of Nestlé Water, Carlo Donati, put it, "North Africa offers real development opportunities for our brands." In 2006, Danone signalled that it was also moving into the region with the purchase of an Algerian bottled water company, Tessala, from the Algad beverages group.

Meanwhile, Coca-cola has made moves to secure control of the bottled water market in South Africa at the other end of the continent. In 2003, the South African operations of Coca-Cola announced the company was buying out Valpre, the leading bottled water company in that country. Previously, Coca-Cola had about 5% of the market share of bottled water sales in South Africa with its brand name Bonaqua, but, with the acquisition of Valpre, Coca-Cola's share of the South African market was expected to climb to 45%. Moreover, the bottled water market in South Africa was projected to grow by more than 20% in the next five years [i.e. between 2003 and 2008]. Meanwhile, Nestlé Waters, which owns Valvita, the second largest selling brand of bottled water in the country, announced in 2003 that it would expand its portfolio by making additional acquisitions.

It is clear the Big-Four have every intention of producing and marketing their bottled water products on a global scale. What has been presented here is merely a snap-shot of the Big-Four expansion plans on a region-by-region basis. Much more information and intelligence on the global operations of the Big-Four companies is needed to come up with a complete picture. Nevertheless, this snap-shot is sufficient to provide an idea of the future trend lines emerging in the bottled water industry. We can begin to see from this picture how certain trends in production and marketing could lead to others.

Not all of this bottled water, for example, is being produced for domestic markets. Increasingly, bottled water is transported over long distances to reach its markets. It is estimated that one-fourth of the bottled water produced is transported across national borders by boat, train, airplane, and truck. In 2004, a Helsinki company shipped 1.4

million bottles of Finnish tap water 4,300 kilometers [2,700 miles] to Saudi Arabia.[6] Whereas tap water is delivered through a relatively energy-efficient energy system, this is not the case with bottled water. On the contrary, bottled water tends to be energy-inefficient, especially when additional fossil fuels are needed to transport it long distances to market.

Now that we know something about the bottled water industry and its four main corporate players, we are in a position to look more closely at some of the key questions and concerns about the production and sale of bottled water today. To do so, we have selected 10 issues covering the most frequently raised questions and concerns about bottled water. We examine each of these issues and illustrate how the Big-Four bottled water companies are involved. We have divided these 10 issues into two sections: [1] Environmental-Health Issues and [2] Social-Economic issues. In order to complete this assessment, we invite our readers to probe each of these 10 issue areas in terms of what is going on in their own local communities regarding the production and sale of bottled water.

2

ENVIRONMENTAL AND HEALTH ISSUES

THE FOLLOWING ARE FIVE ISSUES of environmental and health concerns associated with bottled water in North America today.

1. WATER TAKINGS

So you've just bought yourself a bottle of Aquafina or Dasani—or maybe it's Perrier, or Poland Spring, or Evian. The label on the bottle says the water is pure spring water from an unpolluted snow-capped glacier. But where does the water really come from in the first place? Who owns this water and how is it regulated?

Bottled water comes from two sources: Water from ground sources, springs, rivers, streams and glaciers in rural or outlying communities, and purified or processed water, which is taken directly from municipal tap water systems. Since companies are not required to provide specific information about their product, or identify the source, consumers can be misled about the water they are drinking.

companies to provide the same public information about water that municipalities are required to provide, is currently facing similar resistance from the IBWA.

The U.S. Food and Drug Administration, which is responsible for determining what information companies must provide on bottle labels, has been less than helpful in this matter. The FDA does not require that companies disclose the source and geographic location of the water takings. Instead, the FDA's labelling regulations require only three kinds of information: the type of water (whether it is mineral, purified, or spring), the volume of water, and the manufacturer. By contrast, Health Canada, which regulates the labelling of Canadian bottled water, requires information on several specified ingredients, plus the geographic location of the underground source of both "spring" and "mineral" water.[4]

In other words, in the United States, companies selling bottled water are not required to publicly disclose the source of their water. This means that people living in dozens of communities across the U.S. where Pepsi has its bottling plants—like, for instance, Cicero, New York; Ayer, Massachusetts; and Knoxville, Tennessee—do not know that the water being bottled for Aquafina in these plants actually comes from their municipal water utility. Similarly, people living in communities where Coke has bottling plants—like Washington, Pennsylvania; Stanton, Virginia; and Needham, Massachusetts—may have no idea that their municipal water supplies are being used to produce the Dasani brand.

The issue becomes more disturbing when we look at the question of how water takings are actually regulated. Who owns and who has rights to the water used for bottling? Who benefits? And who pays? In both the U.S. and Canada there are more laws governing surface waters than there are for groundwater. Where groundwater regulations do exist, they differ from state-to-state and province-to province. Moreover, as one "Save Our Springs" community leader in Florida put it: "[Our state] has severely outdated laws concerning the protection of their water and who has the right to take it, for what purpose, and how to withdraw it."[5]

In the U.S., the "riparian doctrine" has generally been used as the basis of laws governing water takings east of the Mississippi River. It allows landowners "the right to make reasonable use of water so long as it does not interfere with the reasonable use of water by other riparian users."[6] West of the Mississippi, the doctrine of "prior appropriation" is generally applied, and it operates quite differently.

Take, for example, Alaska Premium Glacier and Nestlé's Poland Spring brands. The label on the Alaska Premium Glacier bottle claims that it is "Pure Glacier Water from the Last Unpolluted Frontier." In fact, the water used for this brand is drawn from the municipal water system in Juneau, Alaska, specifically pipe #111241, which is not a glacier. Similarly, Nestlé's Poland Spring brand is not, as its label portrays, spring water drawn from a pristine and protected source, but is usually supplied by borehole wells located near Nestlé's bottling plants. Nestlé also sells reprocessed distilled tap water as Poland Springs.

As a result, Nestlé Waters has faced a series of class action suits alleging that the company's advertising and labelling of its water products are both misleading and fraudulent. In Illinois, for example, a class-action law suit was filed by the Sheriff of Kane County against Poland Spring in 2003. Sheriff Ken Ramsey and his lawyers "alleged that Poland Spring Water, a Nestlé subsidiary and the nation's third-largest bottled water company, advertised their water in a false, fraudulent, deceptive, and misleading manner."[1] The suit covered thousands of Poland Spring customers across the country. It claimed that, contrary to what it advertises, Poland Spring does not come from "deep in the woods of Maine"; is not naturally purified; is not "spring water"; and even that the water is not safe to drink.

Meanwhile, Nestlé Waters has faced class-action suits in several other states, such as Florida, California, Maine, Michigan, and Pennsylvania. In most of these cases, the company has been charged with the depletion of water sources as well as misleading advertising.

Nestlé Waters is certainly not the only major bottled water company that can be accused of misleading the public about the source of its bottled water. Many bottlers use terms like "pristine," "pure," or "natural" to "emphasize the alleged purity of bottled water over tap water."[2] Pepsi's Aquafina uses the images of snowy mountain tops and flowing rivers to sell its product, despite the fact the water comes from municipal water systems.

In the state of Maine, steps were taken to introduce legislation requiring bottled water companies to provide information on the location of their water takings. In response, the International Bottled Water Association (IBWA) and the Grocery Manufacturers Association (GMA), the former supported by the industry and the latter funded by PepsiCo and Coca-Cola, mounted a major lobbying campaign to have the bill defeated.[3] In California, a citizens' campaign promoting "right-to-know" legislation, which calls on bottled water

Often described as the "first in time, first in right" doctrine, it states that the first person to appropriate water by taking it from a stream or underground aquifer, and then using it for a specific purpose, has the first rights over that stream system. That person then becomes the "senior water rights holder" and "that water right must be satisfied before any other water rights are filled."[7] What's more, these water rights can be transferred or sold.

This is how bottled water companies like Nestlé Waters have been able to secure control over underground aquifers and streams. A farmer who has "senior water rights" over part of an underground aquifer for the purpose of irrigating a tract of farmland can sell or transfer these water rights to a company to use for bottling water. The bottled water company now has "senior water rights" over the common aquifer stream, while the other farmers in the area are relegated to the position of "junior water rights holders." If a drought occurs, the state water authority is obliged to ensure that the bottled water company, as senior rights holder, receives all the water it is entitled to, even if that means shutting down access to junior water rights holders, the local farmers and towns.

Elsewhere in the U.S., the "rule of capture" provides bottled water companies with the legal tools to gain control over water sources. According to this law, "groundwater is the private property of the owner of the overlying land," and they "have the right to capture the groundwater beneath their land."[8] In Texas, for example, this is the law that is used to regulate groundwater sources. It is often referred to as the "law of the biggest pump," because the landowner with the largest pumping capacity "can dry up an adjoining landowner's well."[9] Moreover, the landowners with the dry wells have no legal protection or rights to the groundwater.

Take, for example, a case in Henderson County, Texas, where Great Spring Waters of America, owned by Nestlé, began pumping large volumes of groundwater for its Ozarka bottling plant. Four days after the pumping began, the well of a local landowner, Bart Sipriano, went dry.[10] When a lawsuit was subsequently filed to protect Sipriano's water rights, the court upheld the "rule of capture," declaring that Nestlé was not liable. When the case was brought to the Texas

Great Lakes Loophole

The Great Lakes are the largest single body of freshwater on the planet. Yet the new Great Lakes Annex Agreement contains a striking loophole.

Under Article 207.9, water bottling companies will have free rein to extract water from any of the five Great Lakes and package it for human consumption, provided that the containers they use are 5.7 gallons [or 20 litres] or smaller in size.

This loophole amounts to nothing less than a bonanza for the bottled water industry. Granting this industry in essence unlimited access to the Great Lakes basins is a monumental gift.

Even more disturbing is that Article 207.9 provides yet another tool for corporations to open the floodgates for bulk water takings and exports. Under international trade treaties like the North American Free Trade Agreement [NAFTA], water is understood to be an economic good and, therefore, once it is extracted and sold for commercial purpose, no government or regulatory regime would be allowed to put a ban or even a quota on water taking.

In other words, since Article 207.9 permits companies to extract water from the Great Lakes basin for sale as bottled water, it triggers the provisions and rules of NAFTA. Once this happens, there is nothing to stop a bulk water export company [or consortium of companies] from using the rules of NAFTA to compel governments to lift their restrictions on bulk water takings from the Great Lakes.

Supreme Court in 1998, the "rule of capture" was unanimously reaffirmed, and calls to modify the law to protect rural homeowners and domestic users of water were flatly rejected.[11]

In California, companies can take advantage of the considerable confusion that exists in the area of water law and water management. There is no statewide management program or permit system to regulate the appropriation of groundwater. In theory, the riparian doctrine applies to groundwater in this state. Those who own land above an aquifer are entitled to make reasonable use of the groundwater, thereby preventing unlimited use by any one landowner. In practice, however, groundwater is left to the counties to regulate, each having its own set of regional rules.[12] This allows water bottling companies to play one county's regulations off against another's.

In Ontario, the regulations concerning water takings are similar except that there is a lower daily limit of 13,200 gallons.[13] In British

Community**PROBE**

What natural resource or environmental regulations apply to water takings in your community? What is the current position of your local state or provincial government on this issue?

If permits are required, can you find out how much the permits cost, and if the water takers have met the regulations fully? Is this information easily available to the public? What are the companies taking water obligated to disclose — and what can they withhold? How long are the permits valid, and how are they enforced?

In some communities, citizens' groups are battling water takings by using legal challenges, or petitioning environmental, land use, or planning boards that have authority or interest in the issue. Are there such boards and/or legal offices in your community that can be approached to challenge water takings?

Go to www.insidethebottle.org for a detailed map identifying more than 70 bottled water plants in Canada and the US that are operated by the Big-4.

Is your community on the map?

Our Inside the Bottle map project invites you to add local information you uncover about environmental regulations, permits, and disclosure rules.

Share your community-based inquiry on water takings via our web portal and help build a citizens' database that exposes how the industry operates at the local level.

Columbia, the restrictions are even less stringent. For water takings of less than 1,710,000 gallons per day, no permit is required unless the water comes from a spring source, where it falls under the province's surface water laws and regulations. If takings are over the specified amount, an environmental assessment is necessary and a license must be obtained through Land and Water British Columbia, Inc., a Crown corporation.[14]

Whichever way you look at it, this is the most unregulated resource industry in the U.S. and Canada. Where water laws do exist, they are easily exploited by the Big-Four and other bottled water companies. Even more shocking is the fact that these companies are extracting a resource while paying little or nothing in fees. At the same time, consumers are provided little or no information about where the water is coming from, how it is taken, or whether the process meets adequate environmental standards. When it comes to laws regulating the labelling of bottled water products in the U.S. and Canada, 'the truth is in the lie.'

2. Transforming Water

If bottled water is taken directly from either tap water or groundwater sources, then what do the companies do to turn real water into bottled water? Is bottled water composed of real water, or isn't it?

In March 2004, Coca-Cola officials were surprised when the British media mocked their Dasani product when it was launched in the U.K. The Independent claimed that Dasani water was nothing more than tap water from the Thames River, bottled at Coke's Sidcup Kent bottling facility. The British press was further amused when it became known that Dasani really was purified tap water.

Herein lies a dilemma for the Big-Four. Whether it's Coke or Pepsi who get water from the municipal

One of the dangerous by-products of these water treatment processes, particularly "ozonation," is bromate, which is a suspected carcinogen.

tap, or Nestlé and Danone who take water from groundwater sources — they all boast of elaborate filtering and purifying processes. But, unlike other resource production processes, where raw materials like timber, minerals, and oil are transformed into new products, bottled water is different. Bottled water is about "turning water into water." Herein lies the scam inherent in the bottled water industry.

PepsiCo and Coke use tap water as raw material for both soft drinks and bottled water. In the case of bottled water, both claim almost supernatural treatment of their water. In fact, the process used to treat water for bottling is basically the same process used for water in soft drinks, although each of the pop kings hails its own "proprietary" method.

For the production of Dasani, Coke maintains that "bottlers start with the local water supply [tap water], which is then filtered for purity using a state-of-the-art process called reverse osmosis."[1]

Afterwards, a special blend of minerals developed by Coke is added "for a pure, fresh taste." The treatment process for Coke's bottled tap water is as follows: water is filtered three times, treated through reverse osmosis, doctored with minerals, and then ozonized.[2]

To produce Aquafina, Pepsi makes use of what it calls the "HydRO-7 Purification" treatment. As Pepsi's own trademarked treatment process, 'Hyd' stands for water, RO for reverse osmosis, and 7 for the seven steps used to process tap water. The process starts with prefiltration, polishing filtration, and high-intensity light. The water is then treated through reverse osmosis, filtered again through charcoal filters, forced through another polishing filter, and then ozonized. Unlike Dasani, no minerals are added.[3]

Nestlé is less forthcoming when it comes to providing public information about their treatment processes, although they both claim special "proprietary" methods. Nestlé Waters North America says it uses what it calls a "multiple barrier approach" to water treatment. This involves controlled filtration and disinfection processes. Nestlé's own bestseller, Poland Spring, is filtered, UV light-processed, and filtered two more times. There is no mention of ozone treatment in the information provided by the company.[4] Most of the other non-tap water from Nestlé Waters is said to be treated along similar lines.[5]

These are the different treatment techniques used by, Coca-Cola, PepsiCo and Nestlé to "turn water into water" *(see below)*. It should be noted, however, that some of these techniques are essential for stabilizing the product itself — first by minimizing bacterial growth, and then by regulating other changes that may take place once bottled water leaves the plant and is transported to retail outlets. The accompanying table explains the basic treatment techniques and their applications.

Basic Treatment Techniques

Microfiltration is the initial treatment applied by most bottlers, a "process of separating solids from a liquid by means of a porous substance..."[6] Microfiltering treatments can be divided into three classes:[7]

1. those that remove unstable constituents, or non-dissolved matter;
2. those that influence the microbiological population; and
3. those that influence the chemical composition.

The last two techniques may be applied to spring and tap water, but the first one is used only for mineral waters. Successive filtering treatments, used by Dasani or Sparkletts, are for removing smaller particulates and to protect finer downstream filters.[8]

Reverse Omosis (RO) processes involve "forcing water through a semi-permeable membrane capable of blocking 90% of almost all constituents" and is recommended for water with high mineral content.[9] RO is one of the two most popular technologies in bottled water operations. Reverse osmosis, as the name implies, is "a reversal of the natural phenomenon of osmosis" capable of producing high-quality water at a low cost.[10]

RO is what Pepsi, Coke, and other bottlers claim as their "state-of-the-art" or "highly sophisticated" purification process. However, "reverse osmosis filters are more often seen in little boxes under some household sinks."[11] RO rement devices are sold for less than $200 by many suppliers throughout the U.S. and Canada, where sales have been escalating. So the process can hardly be termed "state-of-the-art." There are also concerns that an RO reservoir can be breeding grounds for pseudomonas bacteria, which is relatively harmless to healthy individuals, but can pose a threat to immuno-compromised individuals.[12]

Basic Treatment Techniques, cont'd

Distillation is the other popular treatment technique among water bottlers. Distillation is an age-old technique consisting of boiling water and collecting the condensed steam vapors. This technique removes all dissolved minerals, non-metallic inorganics, metals, microbiological contaminants, physical contaminants, synthetic organic compounds, and most pesticides and radiological contaminants.[13] Poland Springs uses distillation for non-spring bottled water.

Ultraviolet light (UV light) "works by passing the process water stream through the high intensity light contained within a reactor tube."[14] UV light is used to disinfect water (as opposed to RO, which clears water). UV light effectiveness depends on exposure time, light intensity, and the types of micro-organisms in the water.[15] The treatment disrupts "sensitive RNA and/or DNA of the bacteria, thus preventing the organism from reproducing. UV light essentially prevents any further [bacterial] activity."[16] Even though UV light effectively purges water of bacteria and viruses, "it does not kill Giardia and Chryptosporidia, nor does it remove chemicals, lead, or asbestos."[17]

It is important to note that "relying solely on UV [light] in a [bottling] plant increases the risk of having biological re-growth in the bottle while the product is on the shelf."[18] That's why many bottlers, including Coke and Pepsi, rely on ozone.

Ozone is a colourless gas consisting of molecules [O_3] containing three oxygen atoms, with strong oxidizing capabilities. "Most bottled water plants will utilize ozone to maintain the freshness of the bottled water and to ensure the water going into the bottle remains bacteria free."[19] Ozone is the last piece of the treatment puzzle in most bottling operations.

Ozone acts in two ways when it is injected into water. First, it works as a disinfectant by killing bacteria, viruses, and parasites such as Giardia and Chryptosporidia. Second, the oxidizing properties of ozone successfully combat taste and odour-causing organic materials and oxidizable inorganics.[20] But using ozone isn't risk-free. A leading expert in ozone treatment has stated that, "because of the relative and perceived ease of ozone treatment, many bottlers still don't use proven ozone process controls and monitoring technology."[21]

One of the dangerous byproducts of these water treatment processes, particularly "ozonation," is bromate, which is a suspected carcinogen. Bromate itself is a byproduct of ozone in waters containing organic bromide. Bromide is a naturally occurring salt found in spring and underground water sources. Ozone treatment facilitates the conversion of bromide into bromate, which. If swallowed in significant amounts, could have deadly consequences.

In response to these and related findings, the U.S. Food and Drug Administration issued a set of rulings in 2001 with regards to "Disinfection By-Products."[22] For bromate, the FDA set the maximum contaminant level (MCL) at 10 parts per billion.[23] In order not to exceed the MCL for bromate, the FDA warned that caution must be given to ozone dosage and/or contact time.[24] This prompted the national technical manager of Nestlé' Perrier Group of America to announce that ozone applications to water bottling "needs to be properly managed, properly controlled, and more technically understood from a vendor standpoint."[25]

As a result, Perrier decided "unofficially" to stop using ozonation for its bottled water products. Meanwhile, Danone continues to use the ozone process in the treatment of underground water, and Coke continues to use it for disinfecting and oxidizing tap water.

Yet, whatever dangerous side effects that may exist in these filtering and disinfecting processes, the issues raised here are much greater. Selling water itself, which is really water transformed into water, is not only misleading, but also raises questions about the possibility of fraud. Although the various filtering processes used by the Big-Four take impurities out of the water, studies have shown that neither spring nor purified bottled water is necessarily safer than water that comes out of the municipal taps in many North American communities. What's more, the regulation of safety conditions for municipal tap water is often much more strict than it is for bottled water in many jurisdictions of the U.S. and Canada.

Meanwhile, the bottled water giants, especially Pepsi and Coke, continue to peddle their products as essential for a "healthy lifestyle." The "Contaminating Water" section will tell us more about just how "healthy" these various bottled water products are. But the art of "turning water into water" and selling it is reminiscent of the tricks used by slick peddlers in the American West who, with sleight of hand and verbal talents, convinced people to buy their coloured-water nostrums to heal their ailments.

NOTE: Please help complete this picture of the "transforming water" process by making use of the following tool to investigate these issues in your own community.

Community**PROBE**

If there is a bottled water plant in your community, can you find out what treatment techniques it uses? Who are the suppliers of these treatment processes? Are they regulated by public authorities?

If reverse osmosis processes are used, ask how the bottler deals with this waste material. What disposal, environmental or health safety protocols are being followed? How often are public authorities able to monitor corporate practices?

For a comparison, contact your local water utility to find out what filtration processes are used for municipal water. Ask about the regulatory process that they must follow, and how many local people are involved in making sure the water is potable.

Go to www.insidethebottle.org for a detailed map identifying more than 70 bottled water plants in Canada and the US that are operated by the Big-4.

Is your community on the map?

Our Inside the Bottle map project invites you to add local information on treatment processes, suppliers, and environmental and public health protocols.

Share your community-based inquiry on transformation techniques via our web portal and help build a citizens' database that exposes how the industry operates at the local level.

3: Contaminating Water

The bottled water industry claims that bottled water is superior to tap water in terms of safety, purity, and health. Is this true? What evidence is there to support this claim? And is bottled water regulated like tap water?

The claim that bottled water is safer and more regulated than tap water has been a key part of the marketing strategy of the Big-Four and other bottlers to lure people away from their household taps. But studies conducted by microbiologists, food safety experts, and environmental specialists have shown that bottled water is not necessarily safer or purer than tap water, nor is it better regulated.

In the U.S., the International Bottled Water Association (IBWA) relentlessly advocates that the quality of bottled water is superior to tap water. As one IBWA "fact sheet" puts it: "Quality is in every container of bottled water. It's consistent and it is inspected and monitored by governmental and private laboratories. Unfortunately, tap water can be inconsistent—sometimes it might be okay while other times it is not."[1] The association claims that water bottlers must comply with three regulation levels: federal, state, and their own association's code of conduct.

However, the Natural Resource Defense Council presents quite a different picture. According to the NRDC, water-bottling plants in the U.S. are likely to be inspected once every five to six years. Furthermore, "according to FDA (Food and Drug Administration) staff estimates, the agency has dedicated just one-half of a staff person (full-time equivalent) to bottled water regulation, and less than one to ensuring bottled water compliance".[2] The NRDC study also shows that tap water regulations are almost always stricter than bottled water regulations.

In Canada, the Canadian Bottled Water Association (CBWA) makes similar claims. As the CBWA website describes it: "Bottled water is extensively and strictly regulated as a food product at the federal, provincial, and association levels. Tap water, by contrast, is only regulated as a utility at the provincial level".[3] Note the emphasis on the word "only," which suggests that provincial regulatory authorities are inferior to federal authorities, with the resulting implication that bottled water is safer than tap water.

According to a food specialist at the Canadian Food Inspection Agency (CFIA), 125 bottling plants were inspected each year between 2002 and 2003, representing two-thirds of all bottling plants across Canada. This means that all Canadian water bottling plants are inspect-

Dasani's Bromate Contamination

On March 19, 2004, shortly after Coca-Cola launched its Dasani product in the U.K., the company suddenly announced it was withdrawing nearly 500,000 bottles of Dasani due to bromate contamination.[4]

In a statement, the company said: "Calcium is a legal requirement in all bottled water products in the U.K., including Dasani. To deliver the required calcium, the company adds back Calcium Chloride into the product. Through detailed analysis, the company discovered that its product did not meet its quality standards. Because of the high level of bromide contained in the Calcium Chloride, a derivate of bromide, bromate was formed at a level that exceeded U.K. legal standards. This occurred during the ozonisation process the company employs in manufacturing." [5]

The sample tested contained between 10 parts per million (ppm) and 22 ppm of bromate, exceeding U.K.'s 10 ppm limit. This is not health-threatening, but for a water supposedly "as pure as water can get," processed with a "highly sophisticated purification process" and sold for hundreds of times the cost of its main raw material, this should raise a few eyebrows. It once again illustrates, in a more concrete way, the problems inherent in this industry.

Shortly after the recall, the Food and Safety Agency (FSA) launched an investigation of the Dasani labelling claim, since the product was described as "pure still water" when in fact it was drawn from the municipal supply system.[6]

ed, on average, only once every three years. But, since bottled water is considered a low-risk food product, the number of inspections is likely to decrease due to a lack of resources and increased concerns about other "higher-risk" food products. So, in Canada, bottled water has been put on the back burner as far as safety inspections are concerned.[7]

Arsenic and mercury have been found in bottled water samples...

Regulating the quality of bottled water is more complicated than regulating tap water. From its point of origin to its point of consumption, water contained in bottles undergoes a multi-step process. Many factors need to be considered when testing, including: the type of source (spring, well, municipal supply); the distance between the point of extraction and the bottling plants; the quality of the bottling and pumping equipment and the necessity of testing these devices for contamination; plus the treatment used, if any, to filter or disinfect the water. And, even after the water is bottled, contamination can occur by the "...growth of the previously stressed, dormant, or starved indigenous microorganisms owing to an altered environment."[8]

One of the more comprehensive studies on the quality of bottled water in the U.S. was conducted at the University of Tuskegee in Alabama. The study analyzed 25 brands of bottled water and evaluated how they measured up to the standards for drinking water set by both the U.S. Environment Protection Agency (EPA) and the European Union. Instead of living up to the purity claims made by the major bottled water companies and their associations, the study showed that some bottled water contains toxic chemicals.

Arsenic concentrations, for example, were found in one survey by the Tuskegee scientists. After examining samples from five bottled water brands — Aquafina, Crystal Springs, Dasani, Fountainhead, and Poland Spring — the study found 11 samples containing arsenic concentration exceeding the U.S. EPA limit of 10 micrograms per Litre (µg/L) for drinking water. The maximum arsenic concentration recorded was 29 µg/L."[9] It should be noted here that long-term exposure to arsenic in drinking water can "increase risks of skin, bladder, lung, liver, colon, and kidney cancer. Other health effects may include blood vessel damage, high blood pressure, nerve damage, anemia, upset stomach, diabetes, and changes in the skin."[10]

In addition, concentrations of mercury were prevalent. "Most of the brands analyzed," says the Tuskegee report, "had mercury levels above 1μg/L, and the potential health effect from ingestion of water with high mercury content may lead to kidney damage."[11] The study goes on to say that some of the samples analyzed might not have been suitable for human consumption. Furthermore, they contradict the claim of the absolute purity of bottled water, "since many toxic elements and organics may be present in mineral waters due to pollution effects on aquifers."[12] In particular, they recommended that there be a review of standards for drinking water contained in bottled water that was sourced from springs.

The Tuskegee study confirms the results of previous research conducted on bottled water in Canada by the Warburton team of microbiologists between 1986 and 1992. They concluded that, "On average, 40% of bottled water on the Canadian market between 1981 and 1989 had aerobic colony counts (ACC) that exceeded the standards set at the time."[13] In their subsequent study of the microbiological quality of bottled water sold in Canada between 1992 and 1997, they found that there had been only "marginal improvement in the reduction of ACC."[14] In both their studies, the Warburton team called for an improved surveillance system for the bottled water industry.

In 2002, University of Winnipeg Researcher Eva Pip tested 40 Canadian and international bottled water brands and discovered that seven brands had levels of total dissolved solids (TDS) that exceeded Canadian Water Quality Guidelines (CWQG), one brand exceeded CWQG for chloride, and three brands exceeded national standards for lead. While her tests concluded that carbonation, ozonation, and the type of packaging were not associated with differences in metal levels, the carbonated samples were consistently higher in TDS levels. In terms of labeling, Pip also noted that none of the brands listed radioactivity levels, thirteen brands had no expiry date, and two brands had already passed their expiry date. Pip's study concluded that there needed to be more quality control, labeling and monitoring of the bottled water industry along with further examination of the the effects of packaging materials and storage conditions on product quality.

In November of 2004, Dutch researchers reported to the American Society of Microbiology that bacterial contamination of bottled water is real and holds risks, especially for populations with a compromised immune system. Motivated by the increased use of bottled water in hospitals, Dr. Rocus Klont from the University Medical Center Nijmegen in the Netherlands looked for bacterial and fungal contamination in 68 commercial mineral waters, one tap water, and one

Bottled water Industry lobbied for the passage of dangerous food labeling legislation in the US.

When the U.S. House of Representatives passed a bill on March 8, to create uniform food labels nationwide, Coca-Cola, PepsiCo, Nestlé USA and the International Bottled Water Association were literally and figuratively behind the policy. All four are members of the National Uniformity for Food Coalition, a lobby group set up to put pressure on the United States government to pass the National Uniformity for Food Act, in what the lobbyists say is a move aimed at simplifying food labels. In reality, however, the act will eliminate over 200 state food safety laws and, in the words of a critic of the measure, "keep the public from knowing about the harm they may be exposed to in food". Under the bill, any state that wanted to keep tougher standards would have to ask permission from the Food and Drug Administration.

For the bottled water industry, companies would no longer have to warn consumers about arsenic, benzene, or other dangerous elements in their products. In California, for example, the state's Proposition 65, a law requiring labelling of substances that may cause cancer or birth defects, would be undone. In the past, Proposition 65 has forced bottled water companies to cut arsenic levels in their products.

In particular, the finding of benzene in soft drinks is raising alarm for certain Senators who will be tasked with debating and voting on the bill before it becomes law. One Democratic staffer commented, "Given these benzene findings, this is not a recipe for quick action. It's hard to see the Senate launching into action on this, given the concerns raised in the House and the push by the soft drink companies" to pass the bill.

However, the lobby machinery behind the bill is extremely powerful and could eventually succeed in pushing the law through. Along with its friends at the National Uniformity for Food Coalition, the bottled water industry used its incredible financial power and political influence to push this bill through. According to the Center for Responsive Politics, members of the Coalition have contributed more than $3 million to members of the House of Representatives in the 2005-2006 election cycle. This is a small price to pay in order to save millions on labelling, while the health of consumers will be put at considerable risk.

Source: Spring 2006 NewsBytes, Notes about the bottled water industry (www.polairisinstitute.org)

water sample from a natural well. The samples came from Norway, France, Italy, Germany, Greece, Austria, Spain, Hungary, and Turkey. They also tested water from India, Morocco, Australia, Canada, Tanzania, Mexico, and Cuba.

"We found high levels of bacterial contamination in commercially bottled mineral water," Klont told Reuters Health. Overall, 40% of all samples showed evidence of contamination with either bacteria or fungi. Their study warned that bacteria could be grown in lab cultures from 21 samples. "These findings indicate that the general perception that bottled water is safe and clean is not true," Klont noted. "The risk of disease to healthy individuals may be limited, but immuno-compromised patients are generally more susceptible to infection and therefore might be at higher risk of becoming infected," he added.[15]

It is clear from these studies and the industry's influence with food safety label legislation (see boxed story on the previous page) that the bottled water industry requires much more quality control. In the U.S., the IBWA claims that bottled water is subject to three levels of regulation. But, upon closer examination, much of this regulation rests on the role of the FDA. To be sure, the FDA is playing an active role in monitoring bottled water, but it seriously lacks the staff resources required to carry out these obligations. This is especially true because the water industry keeps growing by leaps and bounds. At the state level, more and more states are adopting regulations covering the quality control of the bottled water sold and produced in their territory. Many states adopt FDA regulations, although some states have no regulation standards or measures at all. It is worth noting that water sold and produced in the same state does not have to comply with FDA regulations, which represents a huge credibility gap for an industry that claims its standards are superior to those set for tap water.

It is worth noting the many health benefits that bottled water companies claim for their products are also being challenged by scientists studying water quality. Take, for example, the case of oxygenated water sold under brand names such as Clearly Canadian O2, flo2, OxEnergy, Aqua Rush, and AquOforce. The advertising for these bottled waters, which sell for $1.00 to $2.50 per half litre, (20 fl oz) maintains that "...the body absorbs the extra oxygen, resulting in improved stamina and athletic performance, reduced recovery time, and better mental clarity."[16] Companies cite a 1997 study conducted at Texas Women's University to back up these assertions.

"In March 2006, the Australian Dental Association said that its members were seeing the first real increase in cases of tooth decay since the introduction of fluoride to Western Australia's drinking water in 1968. Peter McKerracher, the WA branch chief executive officer, said it was clear that children needed to be drinking more freely available tap water because it guaranteed they obtained the fluoride their growing teeth needed. McKerracher said, "Bottled water and sports drinks do not contain the fluoride which has been so successful in reducing decay." [17]

The problem, according to a 1998 Penn State Sports Medicine Newsletter, is: "...[the] study on which the company's claims are based has not been subject to peer review or published in a scientific journal." [18] After all, oxygen absorption is a function of the respiratory system and not the digestive system, which should immediately call into question the health claims for oxygenated water. And, by opening one of these bottles or pouring its contents into a glass, all the added oxygen is lost. In a study conducted by John Pocari from Wisconsin University, college men and women were asked to drink tap water and oxygenated water and then carry out several physical activities. Oxygenated water had no measurable effect on "...the subjects' resting heart rate, blood pressure, or blood lactate value... Therefore, any potential benefits of super-oxygenated water would undoubtedly be attributed to the placebo effect." [19]

A kinesiologist at McMaster University in Hamilton, Ontario, suggests there is a more productive use for these kinds of high-oxygen waters. "Pour them in your fish bowl and your fish will be able to exercise a lot better because, of course, fish exchange oxygen directly from water, unlike humans." [20]

So, in summary, in order to grow the market for their products, the Big-Four and their competitors trumpet the superiority of bottled water over tap water in terms of safety, purity, and health. Yet, as we have seen, the opposite is more often the case. Across the board, studies conducted by microbiologists and food safety specialists have shown there is no evidence to suggest that bottled water is any safer, purer, or healthier than tap water, and in fact tap water often outshines bottled water in terms of quality and safety. Given that bottled water is subject to fewer regulations than tap water, this should come as no surprise.

NOTE: Please help complete this picture of "contaminating water" by making use of the following tool to investigate these issues in your own community.

Community**PROBE**

When was the last time the bottled water plant in your community was inspected by an independent public authority? How concerned is your local government about quality control?

What laboratory facilities does your local bottled water plant use to test its product for safety? Is it a private or public firm? What do you know about the laboratory's track record?

Compare the quality controls used to regulate the municipal water system in your community to those used in your local bottled water plant. Chart and compare the number of times they are each inspected. Identify and compare what types of tests are used.

Are there any local experts who could be consulted for your community probe? Consider approaching environmentalists, university scientists, or local unions and workers in bottled water and/or municipal water plants.

Go to www.insidethebottle.org for a detailed map identifying more than 70 bottled water plants in Canada and the U.S. that are operated by the Big-Four. Is your community on the map? Our Inside the Bottle map project invites you to add local information on water quality testing protocols and the role of local authorities.

Share your community-based inquiry on local testing and quality standards via our web portal and help build a citizens' database that exposes how the industry operates at the local level.

4: Eco-Threatening

Bottled water, with its many symbols of purity, has come to be associated with nature and good health. But what about all those plastic bottles that are tossed away every day? How are they affecting our health and the health of our environment?

The bottled water industry likes to portray itself as being part of a green generation. It does so by relentlessly presenting its products alongside symbols derived from the pristine landscapes of nature. What the industry does not talk about is the damage its plastic bottles are causing to those very same landscapes. Today, skyrocketing sales of bottled water have translated into a frightening number of discarded plastic bottles, an increasing demand for non-renewable resources, and a devastating release of toxic chemicals into the air and water — all major contributors to global warming and acid rain.

In the past decade, there has been a major shift towards plastic as a substitute for glass and paper in the manufacture of containers and other packaging. Between 1995 and 2001, there was a 56% increase in the production of plastic resins in the U.S. alone — from 32 million tons to over 50 million tons annually.[1] According to the U.S. Environmental Protection Agency, plastics are the fastest growing form of municipal solid waste in the country.[2]

This shift from glass to plastic containers occurred during the 1990s and was largely driven by packaging decisions made by Coca-Cola and Pepsi.[3] Carbonated soft drinks historically accounted for most of plastic bottle waste, but the discarded containers of the bottled water industry are rapidly taking over. The share occupied by the bottled water industry has grown rapidly to almost 25% of this form of plastic resin production.[4]

It's ironic that many people drink bottled water because they are afraid of tap water, but then the bottles they discard can result in more polluted water.

Indeed, two types of plastic resins account for nearly 99% of the food and beverage bottle market today. One is called HDPE, which stands for "high-density polyethylene," and it is used to make almost one-third of the total plastic bottles manufactured. The other is called PET, which stands for "polyethylene terephtalate," and is used to make the other two-thirds.[5] PET dominates the 20-ounce single-serve segment of the bottled water market because of its strength, clarity, light weight, shatter resistance, ease of handling, and flexibility of design. HDPE resin, which is stiffer, stronger, and more resistant to moisture, is primarily used for large water containers such as the one-gallon and 2.5-gallon size.[6]

Few people realize that plastic bottles are composed of fossil fuels and chemicals. Little wonder, since the plastics industry constantly downplays this fact. Plastics are made from natural gas and crude oil that are non-renewable resources. In the production of plastics, substantial amounts of toxic chemicals (e.g., ethylene oxide, benzene, and xylenes) are released into the air and the water supply. Studies show that "many of the toxic chemicals released in plastic production can cause cancer and birth defects and damage the nervous system, blood, kidneys, and immune systems. These chemicals can also cause serious damage to ecosystems."[7] The production of the plastic used for bottled water containers is what some commentators call a "dirty business." The process used for manufacturing this plastic resin involves the polymerization of purified terephthalic acid and ethylene glycol. The acid comes as white crystalline powder, which is considered to be a neurotoxicant that can have adverse effects on the structure or functioning of people's central and/or peripheral nervous system.[8] What's more, ethylene glycol itself is a suspected neurotoxicant, which can do serious damage to people's reproductive, respiratory, cardiovascular, and blood systems.[9]

New studies are raising questions about the health risks of chemical migration from plastic packaging into beverages — a process better known as "leaching." A number of serious peer-reviewed studies have clearly shown that chemicals can migrate from plastic containers into food and beverage products.[10]

In a study published by the *Royal Society of Chemistry Journal* in 2006, Dr. William Shotyk and his associates from the University of

Heidelberg's Institute of Environmental Chemistry show that chemicals with toxic traces like antimony do leach from plastic [PET] bottles into the water. After observing that concentrations of antimony were very low in pristine groundwater samples, in comparison with much higher concentrations in bottled water, the Heidelberg team went on to probe whether this difference was due to geographical variations of the natural waters or to the plastic containers in which the water is bottled and sold. Some 90% of the PET bottles sold worldwide use antimony trioxide, a suspected carcinogen, listed as a priority pollutant by the U.S. Environment Protection Agency and similar bodies in the European Union. According to the Heidelberg study, there is substantial leaching of antimony from the PET containers into the water that is bottled. In one set of tests, the water bottled in PET containers contained between 95 and 165 times more antimony than the original source of water.[11]

Antioxidants such as polyethylene and acetaldehyde, which are used in the production of plastic bottles, are known to have contaminated food in plastic containers. Similarly, chemicals like phthalates, which are used to soften the hard plastics in home and office delivery water jugs, are known to leach into the water over time, potentially contaminating the water in these jugs. The longer bottled water stays on the shelves, the more danger there is of chemical leaching and contamination.

Meanwhile, the two major companies involved in supplying the raw materials for the production of plastics in the U.S. — British Petroleum (now renamed Beyond Petroleum) and Dow Chemical — have track records as dirty industries, according to the Environmental Defense's Scorecard. The British Petroleum Cooper River plant in South Carolina ranks among the dirtiest facilities in the U.S. Its track record includes release of chemicals that have negative environmental and human health effects. And Dow Chemical, which now owns the largest ethylene-glycol producing plant in the U.S., purchased from Union Carbide in 2001, is ranked by the Environmental Defense's Scorecard in the lowest 10th percentile on counts of carbon monoxide, nitrogen oxides, and volatile organic compound emissions.[12]

But the dirty side of the plastics industry does not end with these companies. The plants producing these plastics are no cleaner than those supplying the raw materials. Carbon dioxide emissions from plastic bottle production, for example, are a major source of global warming, while sulfur dioxide and nitrogen oxides are both ingredients that contribute to the formation of acid rain.

So when we see mountains of discarded plastic bottles in our municipal solid waste dumps, we need to think seriously about the potential environmental consequences. In 1960, plastics made up less than 1% of total municipal solid waste. By 2001, this figure had risen to close to 15%. That year, nearly 24,000 thousand tons of plastics were discarded. Although some plastics are removed for recycling or composting, the proportion is very low in the U.S., barely 5.5%. The vast majority of discarded plastics are either buried in landfills or burned.[13]

What happens when plastics are buried or burned? Well, for one thing, plastic bottles buried in landfills remain there for a long time. Plastics are very stable and can withstand the elements. The situation is made worse if plastics are buried and shielded from sunlight.[14] Once buried, plastics take valuable space and can pollute groundwater through the release of phthalates and other toxic additives.[15] As the executive director of the Container Recycling Institute in the U.S. put it, "It's ironic that many people drink bottled water because they are afraid of tap water, but then the bottles they discard can result in more polluted water."[16]

If not buried, discards are burned. Burning plastic bottles releases toxic pollutants — nitrogen, sulphur, and carbon oxides — into the air. Heavy metals are also deposited, in the form of ashes, on the ground. These pollutants include carbon dioxide, one of the three major emissions linked to global warming and climate change, plus sulfur dioxide and nitrogen oxides, both known to be among the prime causes of acid rain.[17]

Here's the problem: bottled water sales are skyrocketing. It is now estimated that over 3/4 billion pounds (more than 12 billion units) of plastic bottles for water are produced and sold every year.[18] As we have seen, the vast majority of these are discarded rather than recycled. Even worse, bottled water sales are driving up the production of plastic bottles in the United States and Canada. According to the Freedonia Group, an Ohio-based market research firm, "...by 2007, water will overtake beer and fruit beverages, becoming the third most widely produced packaged beverage by volume, after soft drinks and milk."[19]

Yet the bottled water industry continues to work hand-in-hand with the plastics industry to promote a green image of their products. Despite all evidence to the contrary, the plastics industry continues to argue that plastics are green and that the environmental dangers are minimal, or non-existent. To offset public criticism, the industry has hired private consultants to do comparative analyses of plastics, glass, and other container material, drawing the remarkable conclusion that plastics are "greener" and more "environmentally friendly" than the other options.

Meanwhile, the Big-Four, especially the pop kings Coca-Cola and Pepsi, continue to defend their growing use of plastic bottles. They refuse to acknowledge the environmental damage caused by the widespread use and discard of plastic bottles. In keeping with their promise of a pure, safe, and healthy lifestyle through bottled water, the Big-Four maintain that plastic bottles can easily be recycled.

So the bottled water industry portrays an environmentally-friendly image in order to rebut any public criticism that might jeopardize the expanding market and the creation of a bottled water consumer culture. What is somewhat different here is that the bottled water industry is working in collusion with the plastics industry to promote this perception. In addressing this matter, not only does one have to deal with bottled water companies like Coca-Cola and Pepsi that have been spearheading the use of plastic bottles, but also with the plastic resource companies like Dow Chemical and British Petroleum, which are fuelling plastic bottle production by supplying the raw materials.

Community**PROBE**

What kind of bottled water packaging is done in your local plant? Calculate the energy and environmental costs. For example, how many plastic bottles, or cases, does the plant produce in a day, week, or month? Calculate how many football fields, swimming pools, or parking lots those cases represent.

If your local plant is Pepsi or Coca-Cola, compare the environmental impact of taking water from the municipal water system, then packaging it in plastic bottles vs. using the municipal system, which uses underground pipes to transport water. Consider the trucking impacts, fuel costs, plastics use, and waste disposal costs compared to your community's network of pipes and filtration systems.

Contact your local health authorities to find out what rates of cancer and respiratory diseases exist in your community. What correlations can be drawn to the use and disposal of plastic resins?

Go to www.insidethebottle.org for a detailed map identifying more than 70 bottled water plants in Canada and the US that are operated by the Big-4.

Is your community on the map?

Our Inside the Bottle project invites you to add local assessments of the environmental impacts bottling plants have on your community.

Share your community-based inquiry via our web portal and help build a citizens' database that exposes how the industry operates at the local level.

5: Recycling Record

The bottled water companies claim that bottled water is environmentally-friendly because plastic bottles can be recycled. But only a small percentage of the plastic bottles used to contain water products are actually recycled.

In September 2003, journalist Brian Howard reported in E-Magazine: "The push to recycle plastic bottles has not been as successful as many consumers might like to think as they faithfully toss their used containers into those blue bins."[1] According to the Container Recycling Institute, (CRI), a non-profit environmental group that studies container sales and recycling trends, plastic-bottle waste has tripled since 1995. CRI executive-director Pat Franklin pointed out: "For every ton of plastic bottles recycled, another four tons are being wasted."[2]

The CRI also reports that "this [2002] recycling rate is exactly half the rate achieved in 1995."[3] In turn, this represents the seventh consecutive year of decline in the recycling rate of plastic bottles. Between 2001 and 2002 alone, says the CRI, "plastic bottle recycling in the U.S. dropped from 834 million pounds to 797 million pounds."[4]

Neither Pepsi nor Coke has done much to facilitate this kind of recycling. The two pop kings had promised to protect the environment by reducing their use of virgin plastic resin. Douglas Ivester, Coke's CEO in the early 1990s, said that "producing new plastic beverage bottles with a blend of recycled plastic is a significant step ahead in plastics recycling. The technology will allow the 'closed loop' recycling of our plastic bottles, just as our other suppliers use recycled aluminum and steel for cans and recycled glass for glass bottles."[5]

Back in 1990, both Pepsi and Coca-Cola pledged to use 25% recycled material in their products. Both companies failed to achieve this goal.[6] Ten years later, Coke pledged to use more post-consumer plastics, announcing it would use 10% recycled content in 25% of their plastic soda bottles. "That amounts to 2.5%, or a fraction of the 25% they used in 1993," reports the CRI.[7]

In the meantime, the plastics industry, which operates in collusion with the bottled water industry, devised two strategies to oppose the recycling of plastics. One involved the creation of a marketing plan that promotes plastics as "environmentally friendly." The second strategy was to mount organized resistance to bottle bills and other recycled-content legislation.

Recyclable Logo

The plastics industry has been very successful in misleading the public by stamping a logo on their products that is similar to the classic logo used for recycling. The triangular logo, provided by the Society of the Plastics Industry (SPI), features three chasing arrows in a triangle formation with a single digit in the centre. Although the SPI logo is intended to serve as a sorting symbol, and has nothing to do with recycling, it is remarkably similar to the traditional recycling symbol and is therefore confusing and deceptive. As the Berkeley Plastics Task Force argues, the SPI logo is both "unclear and misleading."[8]

This tactical move on the part of the plastics industry has proven to be both costly and inconvenient for companies that collect and process products for recyling. When people see the chasing arrows, they naturally assume these products can be recycled, and that local collectors and processors can handle them.[9]

Instead, local recycling firms end up with plastic materials for which they have no infrastructure to handle the reprocessing. Moreover, they may also be threatened with contamination of their supplies because plastic resin products can contain different properties which could have contaminating effects if mixed in together.

Coke's Dasani blue bottle, for example, threatens to become a future source of contamination for local recycling firms. Coca-Cola states that "major recyclers confirmed no problem with Dasani blue."

SPI Guidelines for Manufacturers

[including bottled water companies]

"All users of the code are encouraged to adhere diligently to the following guidelines:

- Use the SPI code solely to identify resin content.
- Make the code inconspicuous at the point of purchase so it does not influence the consumer's buying decision.
- Do not make recycling claims in close proximity to the code, even if such claims are properly qualified.
- Do not use the term "recyclable" in proximity to the code.

The SPI adds that "the code was not intended to be—nor was it ever promoted as—a guarantee to consumers that a given item bearing the code will be accepted for recycling in their community."[10]

But the Container Recycling Institute says that's true only as long as Dasani blue products remain a small percentage of the total number of plastic bottles collected. But if large quantities of Dasani blue are collected by local recyclers, they could become a real contamination threat.[11] Since Dasani is already number-two in U.S. sales, and getting more popular each year, it makes sense to give serious consideration to this potential problem.[12]

Meanwhile, the plastics industry continues to imply that plastics are recyclable by carrying on with the widespread use of its misleading SPI logo. However, in the corporate guidelines, the industry goes to some length to explain that the SPI logo has nothing to do with recycling. These guidelines are spelled out on the website of the Society of the Plastics Industry (see box above). Yet, despite the risk of confusion, the industry steadfastly refuses to withdraw or change its logo.

In effect, the plastics industry remains firm in its intent to send a double message: one to consumers in order to promote sales of plastic products (including bottled water); the other to its manufacturing clients (including the bottled water companies) in order to protect them against any reprisals. As the Berkeley Plastics Task Force put it: "The industry's continuing resistance to change the code suggest that the symbol's lack of clarity benefits plastics sales."[13]

Recycling Laws

In addition, both the bottled water industry and the plastics industry have been active in mounting opposition to legislation promoting beverage container deposits — better known as "bottle bills" — and recycle-content rules. In some U.S. states, for example, bottle bills have been passed requiring a minimum-refundable deposit on beverage containers. The Container Recycling Institute reports, "The financial incentive provided by the refundable deposit ensures high beverage container recycling rates, and dramatically reduces beverage container litter."[14]

Bottled water companies and the plastic resource companies have spent millions of dollars to weaken and/or defeat bottle bills and recycle-content legislation, often outspending their opponents as much as 30 to 1.

In the United States, according to the Container Recycling Institute in 2006, there are 11 states with bottle bills (*California, Connecticut, Delaware, Hawaii, Iowa, Maine, Massachusetts, Michigan, New York, Oregon, Vermont*) and they comprise more than 50% of total annual recovery for beverage containers. That means the remaining states recover fewer beverage containers than do the 11 states with bottle bills. On a per capita basis, the 11 states with bottle bills recover 2.5 times more beverage container units than the rest.[15] In Canada, bottle bills or deposit systems have also been a success. Recovery rates for non-refillable beverage containers by provinces range from a low 67% in Newfoundland to 83 per cent in Nova Scotia.[16]

Most bottle bills or deposit systems, however, only cover beer and carbonated soft drinks. Non-carbonated drinks such as bottled water are generally not included. Given the skyrocketing sales of bottled water, bottle bills advocates are now pushing for new laws that would include non-carbonated drinks. Bottle bills are effective and popular, with public support exceeding 70% in most U.S. states. But the industry is doing whatever it can to defeat such legislation.

Besides their own specific trade associations like the Society of the Plastics Industry and the International Bottled Water Association, the key corporate players in both the plastics industry and the bottled water industry have coalesced together through alliances like NAPCOR — the National Association for PET Container Resources. Through the lobbying campaigns of NAPCOR and related industry associations, the bottled water companies and the plastic resource companies have spent millions of dollars to weaken and/or defeat bottle bills and recycle-content legislation, often outspending their opponents by as much as 30 to 1.[17]

What unites the plastic resin and bottled water companies, of course, is their common interest in slowing or stopping the recycling of plastic bottles. By working together through NAPCOR and related initiatives, they have been effective in controlling the recycling of plastic bottles in North America. In addition to eliminating or weakening bottle bills, they have also made it difficult for manufacturers of recycled plastic to compete with the producers of virgin plastic products. According to the U.S. Energy Information Administration, "In recent years, several plastics recycling companies have closed their doors. They claimed they could not sell their products at a price that would allow them to stay in business. Thanks to the relatively low cost of petroleum today, the price of virgin plastic is so inexpensive that recycled plastic cannot compete. The price of virgin resin is about 40% lower than that of recycled resin."[18]

One of the recycling programs they do promote, however, is the "All Plastic Bottles" program. These are the curbside programs and drop-off centres where the cost of recycling plastic containers has been neatly transferred to the public. By shifting the responsibility and costs of recycling onto the shoulders of state and local governments, these programs subsidize the beverage corporations. In effect, the "All Plastic Bottles" programs, designed to operate in place of refundable deposit programs, ensures that governments and taxpayers, rather than the producers and consumers of plastic bottle beverage products, pay for the costs of recycling.[19]

All of this suggests one more effort on the part of the bottled water industry to mislead the public, this time in collusion with the plastic resins industry. Both industries insist the products they resource, produce, and sell are recyclable. Then they work hand-in-hand to prevent or weaken comprehensive laws and programs for the recycling of plastic bottles.

NOTE: Please help complete this picture of the "recycle record" by making use of the following tool to investigate these matters in your own community.

Community**PROBE**

Contact your local recycling station to find out what percentage of collected material is from bottled water plastics. Find out if they are able to handle these plastics or not. Ask if there has been an increase or decrease in volume in recent years, and what happens to the waste if they can't recycle it.

Contact local environmental groups, city councillors and recycling centre staff to find out what is being done to promote public awareness of the impact of plastics from bottled water products in your community.

Find out more about better "bottle bills" and what can be done to promote this kind of legislation in your province or state.

Go to www.insidethebottle.org for a detailed map identifying more than 70 bottled water plants in Canada and the U.S. that are operated by the Big-Four.

Is your community on the map? Our Inside the Bottle project invites you to contribute data on plastic recycling, awareness programs and bottle bills that your community may be sponsoring.

Share your community-based inquiry via our web portal and help build a citizens' database that exposes how the industry operates at the local level.

3

SOCIAL-ECONOMIC ISSUES

HAVING TAKEN A LOOK at five major environmental and health issues, here are five more social and economic concerns about bottled water.

1: Price Gouging:

Did you ever stop to think that your bottled water costs hundreds, if not thousands, of times more than the same amount of water taken directly from the tap?

When it comes to price mark-ups, the bottled water industry is in a class of its own. In its 1999 study, Bottled Water: Pure Drink or Pure Hype?, the U.S. Natural Resources Defense Council estimated that bottled water is between 240 and 10,000 times more expensive than tap water.[1] This, despite the fact that tap water, with very few exceptions, is a safe form of drinking water in Canada and the U.S. At first glance, the wide differences between these figures may make them seem a bit questionable.

But in carrying out its four-year study, the NRDC employed a very specific methodology. They purchased bottled water with prices ranging from $0.70 per gallon to more than $5.00 per gallon (e.g., imports in small bottles) and then compared the cost of these bottles with the cost of tap water throughout the U.S. When the cheapest bottled water was compared with the highest-priced tap water, the price differential came down to a low of 240 times. But, when the highest-priced bottled water was measured against the least-expensive tap water, the difference in price escalated to more than 10,000 times.

On average, a 1.5 litre, or a 50-ounce bottle of Aquafina costs around $2.70 U.S. ($3.10 Cdn), while the same sized bottle of Dasani sells for around $2.95 U.S. ($3.40 Cdn). A bottle of Evian sells for around $3.00 U.S. ($3.45 Cdn). Yet, by contrast, the corresponding amount of tap water costs a fraction of this price, depending on the rates charged by different municipalities. In New York City, for example, the same amount of tap water costs less than 1/100th of a cent, while in Montreal the price drops to 1/5th of the cost in New York City, or 1/500th of a cent. In Knoxville, Tennessee, the price drops even further still, to 1/800th of a penny.[2]

The difficulty here is in finding a uniform set of comparisons between the average retail price for bottled water and the average cost of tap water. While it is possible to determine the average retail price of bottled water, there is no such thing as an average set of costs for tap water because of the great variation in pricing between municipalities. But there is no escaping the clear signs of price gouging. The chart below illustrates the huge disparities between the retail price for brand-name bottled water and the cost of municipal tap water in sample jurisdictions.

BRAND/ BOTTLERS	RETAIL PRICES 50 FLUID OZ OR 1.5 LITRES	CITIES [SAMPLE]	TAP WATER PRICES [FOR 1.5 LITRES OR 50 FLUID OZ]
Aquafina [PepsiCo]	$2.70 US or $3.10 Cdn	New York, NY	$0.00110 US
Dasani [Coca-Cola]	$2.95 US or $3.40Cdn	Montreal, QC	$0.00022 US
Evian [Danone]	$3.00 US or $3.45 Cdn	Knoxville, TN	$0.00013 US

This price gouging becomes more apparent when we focus on those brands and bottlers that specialize in reprocessed tap water. In the U.S. today, between 25% and 40% of bottled water sold is purified water,[3] in other words, reprocessed tap water. In Canada, 25% of bottled water sold is reprocessed.[4] Most of this reprocessed water is bottled and sold by PepsiCo, through its Aquafina brand, and Coca-Cola, through its Dasani brand. In essence, people are being sold something they have already paid for through their own municipal taxes: quality tap water. It has simply been filtered, mineralized (in Coke's case), bottled, and neatly packaged for sale.

In addition, Pepsi and Coke pay a great deal less for the water they take from the municipal tap system than what they charge, as this chart shows. The first column indicates how much customers pay on average for a gallon of bottled water. The other columns show what Pepsi and Coke pay for a gallon of water in three municipalities: Twinsburg, Ohio;[5] Marietta, Georgia;[6] and Knoxville, Tennessee.[7]

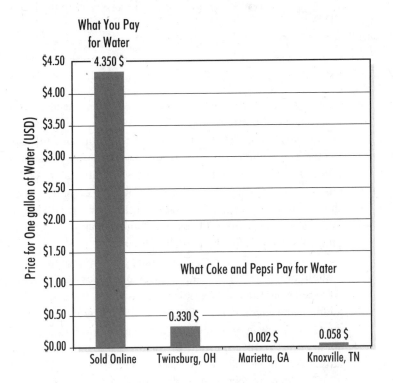

Even more astonishing is the fact that Nestlé and Danone pay little or no fees for the water they take out of groundwater streams and aquifers. Unlike other industries, such as forestry, mining, oil, and gas, in most jurisdictions bottled water companies are not obligated to pay a fee or tax on the extraction of the resource. The bottled water companies have been strongly opposed to being taxed at the source, or having to pay royalty fees on the water they extract, arguing that they are adding value to water in the way that farmers or golf course owners do.

BOTTLER	PEPSI		COKE		NESTLÉ		DANONE	
Product	Aquafina		Dasani		Arrowhead		Natural Spring	
Size	20 oz. (.6 litres)	33 oz. (1 litre)	20 oz. (.6 litres)	33 oz. (1 litre)	24 oz. (.7 litres)	33 oz. (1 litre)	33 oz. (1 litre)	101 oz. (3 litres)
Price	$0.95	$0.99	$0.89	$1.19	$0.60	$0.69	$0.59	$1.19
Price for 1 litre	$1.60	$0.99	$1.50	$1.19	$0.85	$0.69	$0.59	$0.39
Price hike due to smaller size	62%		26%		23%		51%	

The industry itself seems aware of these issues. According to a 2000 survey of bottled water prices in Ventura, California — conducted by Bottled Water Web, the industry's own "independent" association — the Big-Four charge substantially more on a volume basis for their smaller-sized products than for their larger-sized products. As the following chart reveals, Coke and Nestlé charge at least 20% more per volume for their 20-fluid-ounce (.6 litre) water bottles than they do for the 33-fluid-ounce size (one litre), and Pepsi and Danone charge more than 50% more on a volume basis for their small bottles.[8]

The situation appears even more alarming when you consider the amount of money these companies spend on advertising and marketing. After all, what the Big-Four are selling is water. For consumers, the value added comes mainly in the form of marketing and labelling, or beverage container packaging. Coke's 2005 annual report indicates $2.47 billion spent on the production of print, radio, television, and other advertisements, while PepsiCo spent $1.8 billion on advertising. Nestlé's 2005 annual report states the company spent $26.73 billion on "marketing and administrative" expenses. Group Danone's annual report cites 3.33 billion Euro spent on what it calls "selling expenses," which includes advertising and promotional expenses, distribution costs, and costs related to the sales force. Coke's *Beverage Digest* estimates that the bottled water industry spent $93.8 million (U.S.) on advertising alone in 2002.[9] Most of this money is not used to sell the water itself, but rather to create the emotional connections to the product that will ensure consumer loyalty.[10]

Not surprisingly, bottled water has become a leading profit-maker for each of the Big-Four. According to industry analysts, profit margins are as high as 35% on premium-priced bottled water[11] and nearly 60% on home and office delivery.[12] Industry analysts point out that, for soft drink giants PepsiCo and Coca-Cola, revenues from bottled water per unit already outstrip those of carbonated soft drinks. As one *Beverage World* analyst put it, "average revenues per case for carbonated soft drinks are in the $5-6 range while water falls in at $13-15."[13] What these figures show is that prices charged for bottled water generate over twice the revenues per unit that soft drinks do. And, while market growth projections in carbonated soft drinks remain slim, bottled water is expected to contribute 45% of volume growth in the non-alcoholic beverage sector.[14]

There are three price tiers in the bottled water market: upscale, mid-priced, and low-end. With its unique blend of national and regional brands, Nestlé's Perrier has been able to establish itself as number-one in all three categories in North America. Nestlé's nationally distributed Perrier is the bestselling brand of sparkling mineral water in the premier tier. Nestlé also has a multitude of regionally distributed brands in the mid-range and low-end tier, such as Poland Spring, Arrowhead, Deer Park, Ozarka, and Zephyrhills, all of which are bestsellers in the region where they are sold. Meanwhile, Coke's Dasani has positioned itself in the upper part of the mid-priced tier, where it generates tremendous revenues. Given that it is really reprocessed tap water, it is amazing to see that Dasani's retail price, on average, is just 20% lower than that of Evian, which is shipped across the Atlantic from Europe.

High brand-name recognition ensures that market sales will continue to grow, despite inflated price levels. According to data from NFO World Group, a market research organization, consumer loyalty to Dasani has reached 62%, which means that Dasani drinkers use Dasani for 62% of their total bottled water consumption.[15] Given Dasani's recent entry into the bottled water market, this is impressive, and shows that its relatively high retail price can be sustained. By comparison, Nestlé's products, which have had a long-standing place in the bottled water market, have a brand loyalty mark of 77%.[16] The same holds true for Pepsi's Aquafina. What these high levels of brand loyalty imply is that not only are consumers hooked on these products, but also they have been conditioned to accept the high prices.

Consumer acceptance of the high prices of bottled water becomes even more obvious when compared to public reaction to rising gasoline prices. Although gas prices have been "going through the roof," the price of a gallon [litre] of gas is often just one-third that of the retail price charged for a gallon [litre] of bottled water.[17] Consumers are far more ready to accept price gouging when it comes to bottled water than they are to any variation in the cost of gasoline. Unlike bottled water, however, gasoline is taxed, creating revenues that can be used to finance social needs such as health care, education, and the public infrastructure. With bottled water sales, there is no added social value. Revenues go directly back to the company to be used for more advertising, bottling, labelling, and packaging.

The price of a gallon [litre] of gas is often just one-third that of the retail price charged for a gallon [litre] of bottled water.

The price gouging is likely to continue as the industry sells its "enhanced bottled water" line, which includes flavored water, and water with added vitamins, minerals, aspirin, nicotine, herbs, caffeine, and oxygen. In 2002, Pepsi entered the "enhanced waters" market by launching Aquafina Essentials and Propel Fitness. While the health-enhancing quality of these new product lines needs to be seriously questioned (see *Contaminating Water*), so too does the "enhanced price" that accompanies these products. One company is marketing its health-enhancing water by recommending people consume three 500-ml bottles per day at a price that is more than twice the retail price of the most expensive bottled water currently on the market.

NOTE: Please help complete this picture of "price gouging" by making use of the following tool to investigate these issues in your own community.

Community**PROBE**

How much does your local utility charge for water? Are there different rate structures for residential compared to commercial users? It's easy to find out – just call your local water utility office.

How does your community rate structure compare with others? A comparative survey of water and waste water services for nearly 200 U.S. locations, some Canadian cities and international cities is available at http://www.raftelis.com. Are there are any bottled water plants in or near your community? If they are taking their water from a municipal system or from a ground source, what is the rate they are charged?

Did these companies receive any incentives or tax breaks to locate their plant in your community?

Go to www.insidethebottle.org for a detailed map identifying more than 70 bottled water plants in Canada and the U.S. that are operated by the Big-Four.

Is your community on the map?

Our Inside the Bottle map project invites you to add local information you uncover about rate structures, tax incentives and subsidies that have been granted to the bottled water industry.

Share your community-based inquiry on pricing issues via our web portal and help build a citizens' database that exposes how the industry operates at the local level.

2: Marketing Schemes

So what is the real value of bottled water, anyway? What kinds of marketing and advertising techniques are used by the major bottled water companies to sell their product? What kinds of images and perceptions are created to attract consumers? How real are they?

PRISTINE

Perhaps the tagline of Pepsi's 2003 campaign for Aquafina says it all: "So pure we promise nothing." In other words, consumers should expect nothing more from bottled water than an image. The Big-Four have been remarkably successful in selling the perception that bottled water is better than the alternative. After all, "we sell water... so we have to be clever," says Nestlé Waters' senior vice-president of global marketing.

As we have tried to demonstrate, there is nothing particularly special about bottled water. Although the bottled water companies highlight the "purity" of their product, there is really no such thing as pure water, except perhaps certain distilled waters used for pharmaceutical purposes, or in the semi-conductor industry. Water, whether it is bottled or comes from the tap, retains different characteristics in terms of its mineral and bacterial content, depending on its geographical source and location. Nor can the Big-Four make a legitimate claim about the "freshness" of their product in comparison to tap water. If by "freshness" they mean the time that water takes to move from its source to consumption, then tap water is "fresher" than bottled water because, on average, tap water remains in the pipe system for only one to three days. Who knows how long water has been in the bottle?[1]

So the real market value of bottled water is not found in the product itself. Instead it lies in the perceived social value, a perception companies have worked hard to create. Today, it is much more fashionable to serve bottled water than tap water. It has become a symbol of social etiquette to the point where, as one Canadian marketing

"We sell water, so we have to be clever."

—Nestlé executive

teacher put it: "It has now become a shame to offer a glass of tap water to your guests."[2] What's more, the industry has been successful in associating bottled water with an "active" and "healthy" lifestyle. Buying bottled water, says marketing consultant Laurie Ries, is buying "America's most affordable status symbol."[3]

Marketing and advertising, of course, are what makes the difference when it comes to selling various brands of a similar product like bottled water. This is even more necessary when the product is colourless, nearly tasteless, and odorless. Between 10% and 15% of the price paid for each bottle of water goes to cover advertising costs.[4] Through

'Pure Packaged Product' "...In an editorial published in Beverage World, Kent Phillips tells the story how his wife thought that tap water was not as pure as bottled water. She preferred the "pure packaged product" promoted by the water bottlers. To prove a point, Phillips repeatedly refilled empty water bottles in their house with tap water — and noted how the deception was never detected. He concludes with several observations about how the bottled water industry works: "Number one, we have a consumer generation who perceives that bottled water is better for them. Number two, if you have bottled water on your trucks you had better make sure you are leading the market to capitalize on the growth. Number three, this is the first category I can remember that is not price sensitive, but it's extremely execution-placement and display-sensitive."[5]

advertising, says Catherine Ferrier of the University of Geneva, emphasis is put on the supposed purity of bottled water, in many cases contrasting "pure" and "protected" bottled water with "inconsistent" or unpredictable tap water quality."[6] In the words of a leading industry consultant: "Water bottlers are selling a market perception that water is 'pure and good for you'..."[7]

This marketing scheme started with Perrier in the 1980s when it first came to the U.S. Having established its brand name in the more mature markets of Europe, Perrier was introduced as the choice drink of a new generation. Perrier became a perfect product for "yuppies," meeting their need to distinguish themselves, consume a healthy beverage, and display their wealth.

The marketing of bottled water in North America did not really take off until the 1990s when social hygiene became a big issue. This was the period when cigarette smoking was being banned and concerns and about obesity were on the rise. It was during the 1990s that the fast food industry, along with its counterpart the soft drink industry, was targeted for promoting an unhealthy lifestyle. The industry's solution was the widespread marketing of bottled water — linking the product to purity, healthy living, the need to exercise, and, of course, concerns about the environment itself.

The following chart portrays the various themes, symbols, and slogans used by Nestlé, Pepsi, Coke, and Danone to peddle their bottled water in the era of social hygiene.

BRANDS	REMOTE AND PROTECTED SOURCES	PURITY	FRESHNESS	HYDRATION EMPHASIS	HEALTH/ ACTIVE LIFE	TASTE	TAGLINE
Aquafina (Pepsi)		●		●	●	●	Aquafina 2006 tv ads — 'Make your body happy, drink more water, aquafina'
Dasani (Coke)		●	●	●		●	Dasani 2006 TV ads — 'Dasani, the water that makes your mouth water'; 'When it comes to water, it's quality not quantity.'
Poland Spring (Nestlé)	●	●	●	●	●	●	'What it means to be from Maine' (current)
Arrowhead (Nestlé)	●	●		●	●	●	'It's better up here' (current)
Evian (Danone)	●	●		●	●	●	'Your natural source of youth'; and 'Live young'

Note how all these brands insist on the purity of their product. For spring water and mineral water, this emphasis on purity is linked directly to nature itself. Both of Nestlé Waters' brands, Arrowhead and Poland Spring, capitalize on this. Arrowhead's tagline is "It's better up here" — that is to say, in the mountain where our water comes from, and where the air is pure and the pollution non-existent. For Poland Spring it's a little different. The brand tagline — "What it means to be from Maine" — is an extension of Nestlé's strategy to buy local bottlers already well established in their region.

In the case of Evian, Danone has developed a slightly different marketing strategy built around the European spa tradition. Its tagline, "Your natural source of youth," comes as no surprise since spas are said to provide health benefits. But, as Stephen Kay of the IBWA points out: "There's not enough (minerals) in there to make a difference."[8] Evian is clearly trying to capitalize on the "be active/be healthy" trend, and on consumer demands for healthier food products.

As noted in the *Introduction*, one of the industry's main marketing tools has been its "Get-Hydrated or Die" message. Here bottled water companies use the "eight-by-eight" formula — that eight eight-ounce glasses of water a day are needed for a healthy diet — and happen to boost sales. But the origins of this formula and the scientific evidence to support it have been called into question by a growing number of health and medical experts. Moreover, for the two soft drink giants in particular, the "Get-Hydrated or Die" marketing message poses a real contradiction. On the one hand, both Coca-Cola and Pepsi see themselves as being in the hydration business and are quick to highlight the hydrating qualities of Dasani and Aquafina. Coke has boasted that it is responsible for 10% of the world's TLI (total liquid intake) and its corporate goal is to double that number.[9] On the other hand, Coke and Pepsi are the number-one and number-two soft drink sellers in the world, and carbonated drinks cause dehydration.

Nevertheless, to get more people hooked on bottled water, Coke's 2003 Dasani campaign was organized around the slogan "Can't live without it." A key component of this campaign was a seven-day trial offer: "Try it for seven days and see how you feel." The promotion encouraged people to download a small program designed to help them keep track of their own daily water consumption. Meanwhile, Pepsi's advertising campaigns point out that since the human body is up to 70% water, "every part of your body needs pure water," and people can replenish this vital liquid by drinking Aquafina.

Even the brand names for these products are designed to evoke "feelings" about water. Take the name Dasani for instance. On its website *(www.dasani.com)*, viewers are asked about the meaning of the name Dasani. In creating the name, Coke says it wanted the word on the outside of the bottle to reflect the essence of the water inside. After focus group testing, the company settled on Dasani — which suggests "relaxation," "pureness" and "replenishment."

For Pepsi, the name Aquafina says it all. According to the publication *Packaged Facts*, the marketing strategy for this product was carefully designed with "graphic labels depicting abstract snow-capped mountain peaks against a water-blue background."[10] Since Aquafina is not bottled at source, it could not be identified with a particular spring or geographic location. So Pepsi chose to package and sell Aquafina as bottled water with broad-based national appeal, thereby bypassing the need to tie it to any particular natural setting.

Coca-Cola's advertising strategies demonstrate how far this marketing scheme can be taken. Through its "Life Simplified" campaign, Coke promoted Dasani as replenishing the body's water, thereby restoring relaxation, health, and wellness to a busy and stress-filled life. This was followed by the Dasani "Treat Yourself Well. Every Day" campaign, aimed at women between the ages of 25 and 49. In May 2001, Coke announced a partnership with *Village*, an online website whose core audience is women, to promote tips on cooking, nutrition, fitness, and stress management from Dasani's "Wellness Team." A key part of this promotion was "The Healing Garden," a gift box of lavender lotions, bath crystals, and incense sticks, along with a "Personal Balance Index."

Coca-Cola's partnership with the Olive Garden restaurant chain on the H2NO project provides yet another illustration of this kind of marketing. In 2001, the *New York Times* published an article describing how the H2NO project was designed to get restaurant customers to stop ordering tap water with their meals in favour of Coke's products, notably Dasani.[11] A staff education kit was prepared, containing suggestive selling techniques to be used during the ordering process. "Just say No to H2O" was a key slogan. The H2NO project was incorporated into the Olive Garden's monthly skill sessions, where sales managers conducted training exercises, and an employee incentive contest was promoted whereby increased sales of Coke products could result in more cash in servers' pockets.[12]

Coke, of course, is by no means the only company resorting to these strategies. All of the Big-Four, in varying ways, are making use of these marketing techniques to lure people away from their reliance on low-cost, publicly-provided tap water, and to cultivate instead a taste for and dependence on much more expensive bottled water products.

For example, Nestlé Waters' new water product for kids called Aquapod involves rocketship-shaped 11-ounce bottles of spring water. In the U.S., Nestlé is promoting animated ads proclaiming "Aquapod spring water. A blast of fun" on Nickelodeon and other popular kids' channels, along with DC Comic books [Archie, Teen Titans] and a mobile marketing tour [two giant Aquapods on wheels].[13]

So far, the Big-Four have been successful in creating a mass market for bottled water — not because of the intrinsic value of the product itself, but by turning bottled water into a status symbol and by creating the image that it is essential for a healthy life.

NOTE: Please help complete this picture of "marketing schemes" by making use of the following tool to investigate these issues in your own community.

Community**PROBE**

Check out the advertising slogans used by bottled water companies in your community. What images are used? How many references to "purity," "health," or "natural settings" can you count?

Notice the people these companies have chosen for their TV and print ads. Do you think that they are targeting any particular type or group of people?

Do chain restaurants in your community have a program that encourages the use of bottled water over tap water? If so, which ones? By comparison, does your local utility have any advertising program for its water? Should it?

What other marketing techniques are used by the Big-Four in your community?

Go to www.insidethebottle.org for a detailed map identifying more than 70 bottled water plants in Canada and the US that are operated by the Big-Four.

Is your community on the map?

Our Inside the Bottle project invites you to add local insights on promotional schemes and target market groups.

Share your community-based inquiry on these schemes via our web portal and help build a citizens' database that exposes how the industry operates at the local level.

3: Manipulating Consumers

Skyrocketing sales in bottled water indicate a profound shift in attitude has taken place. Why are people turning from tap water to bottled water? What's really fuelling this new bottled-water culture?

Given the explosion in bottled water sales taking place in North America today, it is clear that the Big-Four bottled water corporations have experienced considerable success in luring people away from tap water. In creating a new consumer culture for bottled water, the industry appears to have focused its strategy in two ways. First, they have capitalized on fear, by taking advantage of every opportunity to raise doubts about the safety and reliability of tap water. Then they have offered a reassuring solution: their product, a "pure," "safe," "healthy" and *necessary* alternative. This strategy, so vigorously pursued by the industry, points to an underlying manipulation of consumers.

Ten years ago, most people drank water from the tap or the water cooler at their workplace or in other public institutions. Today, according to recent surveys, 20% of the U.S. population and 17.2% of Canadians drink bottled water exclusively. In Canada, 67.8% of the population say they still feel safe about tap water quality. Although 82% of people in the U.S. admit to drinking tap water, only 56% drink it straight from the tap; 37% say they use a filtering device.[1]

With close to one-fifth of the population in both countries depending exclusively on bottled water, the industry has convinced a significant number of people — over 62 million — that bottled water is "superior" to tap water. This despite a complete absence of evidence! Who are the consumers these companies have been able to reach with their marketing message?

According to a study on the bottled water industry published by Packaged Facts in March 2004, the profile of the typical bottled water drinker could be described as:

> "... adults who are on the young side, at 18 to 44 years of age. These young adults tend to fall into two (non-exclusive) groups: students and/or young adults with younger (pre-teen) children. Consistent with this profile, bottled water consumers overwhelmingly tend to be single (or divorced), and to be well educated. Standing alone as an independent factor, bottled water users tend to live in affluent households."[2]

The target audience is relatively young, upwardly mobile, mainly affluent, and well educated. The industry has chosen to zero-in on the more youthful half of the population — those between the ages of 18 and 44 — in order to create a new generation of consumers weaned on bottled water.

With these demographics in mind, marketing that has focused on fostering mistrust in municipal water supplies has been money well spent. According to the latest surveys, 12% of Canadians say tap water poses a high health risk, while 38% perceive tap water as presenting a moderate health risk.[3] In the U.S., recent surveys indicate that 50% of Americans are concerned about possible health contaminants in their water supply.[4] And when Americans were asked why they boil, filter, or buy water, health concerns ranked higher than taste (33.3% vs 27.7%).[5]

Capitalizing on fear has been a strategic priority for the bottled water industry. Wherever there are incidents of contamination or disruption in municipal water systems, companies have been quick to pounce, hammering home their message that bottled water is safer and cleaner than tap water. In so doing, they have skillfully played on a wide range of feelings that permeate modern North American society: fears about the spread of bio-terrorism, bacteria, germs and toxins, along with a growing lack of faith in governments' ability to provide security through reliable public services.[6]

"It's expensive, it's trendy, but the bottom line is it's no better for you than tap water."

This promise of security is then reinforced through marketing. Bottlers of spring water, like Nestlé and Danone, emphasize the remote rural locations of their water sources, far from the pollution and congestion of big

"A lot of bottled water is no better than tap water, and the people bottling it know it... If you can sell somebody something without spending money, and they'll buy it, you sell it to them. I'm just being honest."
—Jerry Smith, Chief Executive Officer of LeBleu, a North Carolina based bottled water company[7]

cities and urban centres. For bottlers of tap water like Pepsi and Coca-Cola, advertising tends to focus on the pure water that comes from a multi-step filtration process, thereby creating the assurance of a near-perfect product. On both fronts, priority is placed on "securing" purity, safety, and health for the otherwise-threatened individual.

The Big-Four are well-equipped to play on people's strong desire for "security" in an unsafe world. In a consumer- and market-oriented culture, the industry knows that, if people want it, they'll pay for it. So buying bottled water is linked to buying safety, or some sort of insurance against possible breakdowns in municipal water systems. Or buying bottled water is linked to restoring balance in a stress-filled life.

Either way, as Judy Harrison, a food safety specialist at Georgia University, points out: "It's expensive, it's trendy, but the bottom line is it's no better for you than tap water."[8]

This is the key difference between the new bottled-water culture in North America and its European counterpart. In Europe, the culture of bottled water is rooted in the spa tradition. It is associated with the wine culture, and a certain "art de vivre." There, taste is a major reason why people buy bottled water. The chart on page 97, which is based on a 2001 study conducted by the World Wildlife Fund, highlights these differences.

In the U.S., for example, 35% of the people surveyed drink bottled water because they believe it is a safe alternative to tap water. In France, only 23% share this belief. In France, 45% of the population considers taste the main reason to buy bottled water, compared with only 7% in the U.S. Actually, Americans love their water to have no taste at all. As Stephen Kay of the International Bottled Water Association put it: "Americans tend to drink bottled water for what's not in it as opposed to Europeans who drink it for what's in it."[9]

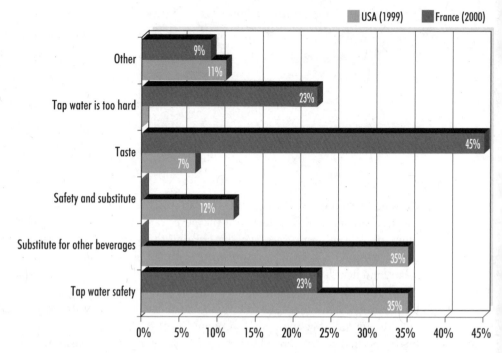

Attitudes toward Bottled Water, France and USA comparison
Source: Adapted from Catherine Ferrier

These comparisons, however, do not tell the whole story. There are deeper dimensions to this bottled water culture that are rooted in the broader market and consumer-oriented values that prevail in the U.S. and, increasingly, in Canada. The bottled water industry, particularly the Big-Four, not only know how to develop marketing strategies that play on these values, but they also recognize the importance of gearing their message to the individualism that lies at the centre of American culture. The industry understands how to pitch its message in such a way that people are made to feel they have the "power" to "buy" the "safety," the "purity," and the "health" they have been conditioned to crave.

In the end, it's all about perception. When the marketing message is taken out of the equation, there is nothing about bottled water that is qualitatively different from tap water, except it is more expensive. This is an industry that promises safety, security, and purity; it delivers price-gouging, resource exploitation, and threats to the environment and to communities. And the water produced from all of this isn't even as safe as the public alternative.

NOTE: Please help complete this picture of "consumer manipulation" by making use of the following tool to investigate these issues in your community.

Community**PROBE**

Conduct a survey in your school, workplace, or neighbourhood: find out how many people are regular users of bottled water. Inquire why they opt for bottled water. Take note of the age, gender, and race of those who are regular users. Are there signs of a "new generation" of bottled water drinkers emerging in your community?

If you have a local bottling plant in your community, ask area health boards, environmental agencies, and organized labour if they have a record of any health, environmental, or workplace safety violations for the bottling plant. Compare this data with the track record of your local water utility.

Check with the local water utility boards to find out when the last warning was issued about unsafe tap water. Compare this with the track record of the bottling plants operations. Think of creative ways to share this information with your community.

Go to www.insidethebottle.org for a detailed map identifying more than 70 bottled water plants in Canada and the U.S. that are operated by the Big-Four.

Is your community on the map?

Our Inside the Bottle project invites you to contribute your insights into local consumption patterns, and the track record of local bottling plants and public water systems.

Share your community-based inquiry via our web portal and help build a citizens' database that exposes how the industry operates at the local level.

4: School Contracting

What kinds of marketing techniques are being used to gain control over children and young people?

The marketing gurus at Pepsi and Coca-Cola know that capturing the youth market for bottled water, as they had already achieved with their soft drinks, is bound to have long-term payoffs. Coca-Cola's youth market representative summed it up, when he said, "We know high school students will continue to drink Coca-Cola products for 50-60 years... We're trying to gain their business for the future."[1]

The name of the game is to create a Coke or Pepsi drinker in the 6-to-24-age group. If the pop kings can create brand loyalty at that stage of life, chances are they will have nurtured a whole new crop of lifetime consumers of their products. For both Pepsi and Coke, the place to start was in schools, and college and university campuses. Their strategy: an ingenious marketing tool called the "exclusive beverage agreement."

Prior to the 1990s, corporations like Coca-Cola and Pepsi used to contribute cash to schools with no strings attached, "expecting nothing more than a mention in the school newsletter."[2] Then, when Channel One offered increasingly cash-starved schools a prepackaged form of educational programming in the U.S., the opportunity opened up for major corporations to market their products directly to school children.

This was achieved by establishing "exclusive beverage agreements" with schools and school districts. These marketing agreements give companies "exclusive rights to sell a product or a service on school or district grounds and to exclude competitors."[3] In other words, these deals provide companies like Pepsi or Coke with monopoly rights in a given school or school district.

When a school or school board enters into an "exclusive beverage agreement," the company's vending machines are installed, up-front

> *"We know high school students will continue to drink Coca-Cola products for 50-60 years... We're trying to gain their business for the future."*

payments are made, school scholarships are created in the company's name, and incentives are provided for selling more of the company's products.[4] In effect, these exclusive beverage agreements guarantee companies like Coke and Pepsi a captive audience of children whom they can cultivate as life-long consumers of all their beverages.

In the U.S., the National Association of Partners in Education — whose membership includes the Exxon-Mobil Foundation, Shell Oil Foundation, and Chevron Corp (all companies with direct interests in the plastic bottle and packaging industries) — report that partnerships between schools and businesses "grew considerably since 1990" — from less than $1 billion in 1990 to over $2.5 billion (U.S.) by 2001.[5]

Indeed, the Coca-Cola Company has set-up and funded its own organization to promote school partnerships. Known as the Council for Corporate and School Partnerships (CCSP),[6] its mission is to encourage the formation of exclusive beverage agreements and other kinds of corporate-school partnerships. The CCSP is chaired by none other than the former U.S. Secretary of Education, Richard W. Riley. Two Coke executives also serve as members of the CCSP Board: John H. Downs Jr., Senior Vice-President for Public Affairs for Coca-Cola Enterprises, and Carlton L. Curtis, Vice-President for Industry Affairs for the Coca-Cola Company.[7]

The Pepsi deal with Hillsborough Public Schools in Florida on page 101 provides a glimpse of what's involved in negotiating these "exclusive beverage agreements." Taking advantage of the vulnerable financial position that many schools and school boards are in, companies like Pepsi can provide cash in exchange for the chance to market their products directly to young consumers. Commenting on exclusive beverage deals, one critic noted: "Advertisers know that their presence in the schools can pay for years, if not decades, if they hook kids for life on their products."[8] The youth market has been estimated as a $20 billion (U.S.) business.[9]

In Canada, the Youth Network News (YNN) is the equivalent network to Channel One in the U.S. YNN tried three times to get its corporate-backed commercial package into the public school system, failing twice in 1992 and 1995, and gaining only limited access in 1999.[10] It was opposed by a grassroots coalition of parents, teachers, community organizations, and concerned individuals across the country, who used

Pepsi's Exclusive Contract with Hillsborough County

In late May 2003, the 11th largest school district in the U.S., Hillsborough County Public Schools, signed an exclusive beverage agreement with The Pepsi Bottling Group Inc. — a subsidiary of PepsiCo.[11] Hillsborough's 150 schools and its more than 183,000 students have Pepsi-only products in their vending machines. In exchange, Pepsi will contribute about $4 million worth of commission, equipment, and marketing perks every year for the next 12 years.[12]

The deal took over a year to negotiate and sign. During this period, three major issues surfaced[13]:

1) Pepsi wanted to make sure it would receive compensation if there was an "involuntary breach of contract" on the part of the State government (i.e., Florida), such as a ban on the sale of carbonated beverages in public schools;

2) Pepsi wanted flexible hours maintained for student access to the vending machines, while Hillsborough County requested that "no vending sales take place until an hour after the last lunch period;"

3) Pepsi wanted to ensure that its right to raise prices on beverage products like its Aquafina bottled water were protected under the contracts.

The deal expels competition and instates a Pepsi monopoly. This results in the weakening of local and regional economic diversity. Prior to the deal, agreements regarding beverage-vending machines were done on a school-by-school basis, thus offering opportunities to different suppliers. One local supplier declared: It's pretty scary for a small businessperson... It's a little scary what these people are trying to make happen, not Hillsborough County but the Pepsi World."[14] What's more, the revenues from the sales will be taken out of the local economy, going instead straight to Pepsi.

the Internet to build a groundswell of opposition to the spread of YNN. This eventually led to the condemnation of YNN by all teacher federations and most provincial Ministries of Education. Widespread resistance along with a series of corporate mishaps led to the eventual downfall of YNN in the early 2000s.[15]

Pepsi and Coca-Cola, however, have been very successful in obtaining exclusive beverage agreements with many school boards in Canada. According to a survey conducted by the Ontario Secondary School Teachers' Federation, nearly half of the schools that responded to the survey (205 out of 425) had exclusive soft-drink agreements.[16] Of those 205 schools, 115 had deals with Coca-Cola and 65 with Pepsi.

Canada's largest school board, the Toronto District School Board (TDSB), has negotiated agreements with both Pepsi and Coke, alternatively. Prior to January 2000, the school board had an eight-year contract with Pepsi. Then the board switched from Pepsi to Coke, signing a three-year deal which offered an estimated $6 million Canadian ($4.5 million U.S.).[17] In July 2004, the board switched back to Pepsi, signing a $6 million five-year deal. Interestingly, this amounts to only one-50th of one-percent of the TDSB's annual budget, suggesting that Coke and Pepsi have a better understanding of the value of what they are buying than the school board has of what they are selling.[18]

In order to catch the kids they may have missed in their public school marketing efforts, Pepsi and Coca-Cola have also turned their attention to colleges and universities. This trend began in 1992 with Penn State's agreement with Pepsi-Cola. Over the next five years, numerous contracts were signed so that: "... [by] December 1997, about 100 campuses and state higher education systems nationwide had inked deals with one of the two soft drink companies." [19]

Similar to the deals with K-12 schools, exclusive agreements between universities and beverage companies include up-front cash, marketing materials, and commission on sales (40% or more). University deals also embrace a number of clauses, such as "teacher of the year" awards, student scholarships, student internships, kiosks displaying back-to-school and drug awareness programs, and fund-raising opportunities.[20] The clauses are specious in nature, because they function as nothing more than sales mechanisms. Contracts obligate schools to sell a set amount of products over the course of the agreement in order to receive financial incentives. Some deals even include leadership retreats for members of the administration and board of education, as well as computer software and hardware.[21]

Campus activists have found that, once a contract is signed with beverage giants like Coke or Pepsi, vending machines are often positioned in strategic places throughout their schools. At Queen's University in Kingston, Ontario, students documented the placement of machines that obstructed access to water fountains. At the University of British Columbia (UBC), home of the first Canadian university exclusivity contract, maintenance staff (CUPE workers) found that 44% of water fountains were removed or disabled on the UBC campus in the first three years of the beverage contract.[22]

Like many public school boards, colleges and universities are also cash-starved, and these multi-year agreements appear to offer some relief. However, exclusivity contracts can have unforeseen costs. Queen's University professor Darko Matovic developed a utitlity calculator that shows how much energy vending machines on campus use. In the case of Queen's, he has shown that Coke's 150 vending machines' electrical usage can cost the university between $75,000 and $175,000 per year, which sizeably reduces the value of the "cash for access" deal valued at $500,000 per year.[23]

Ironically, it has been tax breaks for large corporations that have led to strained state and local budgets, which result in cutbacks to education. "We're all looking for ways of getting funds we're not getting from the state any more," asserts one campus administrator from the University of Missouri-Columbia. "Colleges and universities need those revenues to support our academic programs."[24]

Or in the words of another observer:

> *"An equitable and adequate funding system for public education can hardly flourish when state and local tax structures become more regressive and fall into serious deficit; school systems cannot function effectively when revenues earmarked for modernizing school buildings are instead diverted to corporate property tax abatements and other subsidies."* [25]

In Canada, exclusive beverage agreements with universities started a few years after it kicked-off in the U.S. The University of British Columbia was the first post-secondary institution to cave when it signed a deal with Coca-Cola in 1995.[26] Since then, virtually all universities in Canada have signed with either Coke or Pepsi. The confidentiality of the UBC-

Coca-Cola deal was challenged in court after a reporter from the UBC student newspaper was denied access to the contract by both the university and British Columbia's privacy commissioner. After five long years, the details of the agreement were finally released.[27]

But secrecy is not the only characteristic of such agreements. So is breach of contract. In 1998, the Université de Montréal signed a 10-year $10 million (Cdn) deal with Pepsi that was to start in 1999. In 2002, the university had to take Pepsi to court in order to get its annual $500,000 payment.[28] Pepsi claimed it had not provided the payment because it wanted to renegotiate the deal.[29]

And now cash-starved cities and towns are also getting into the act. In exchange for a cut on the revenues collected on the sales of soft drinks and bottled water, municipal governments are prepared to give companies like Coca-Cola and Pepsi exclusive rights to place their vending machines in public buildings and on city property, as well as in schools, colleges, and universities in their jurisdiction. In many ways, deals with municipalities are an even more comprehensive means for corporations to secure and maintain their access to young people.

Exclusive beverage contracts and naming rights are now a growing trend among municipal governments, big and small. So, too, is the competition for the soft drink giants. In September 2003, New York City's Chief Marketing Officer (sic) announced that Snapple — a subsidiary of Cadbury-Schweppes — "will become the [city's] official iced tea and water."[30] Too late for Pepsi and Coke, the five-year $166 million deal gives Snapple "exclusive rights to place vending machines in the city's 1,200 public schools [and] other city properties, including office buildings, police stations, and even sanitation depots."[31] New York City is not alone. San Diego, Oakland, and smaller cities like Amherst, NY, Lynn, Mass., and East Lansing, Michigan, have also signed similar contracts.

NOTE: Please help complete this picture of "school contracting" by making use of the following tool to investigate these issues in your own community.

Community**PROBE**

Check out what policies and exclusivity contracts may exist in your area school board. Ask your school trustee or school officials for information about these contracts. In most cases, contract details are confidential, but it can't hurt to file a freedom of information request.

Conduct a survey of the number of water fountains that exist (or existed) in your school or campus. If an exclusivity contract was signed, is there a connection between the presences of beverage vending machines and maintenance/existence of water fountains?

Does your school have obligations it must meet if exclusivity contracts have been signed, for example, minimum sales of the companies product lines, or granting of advertising rights to the company? Are there penalties or incentives linked to sales targets?

Working with a group of interested students, staff, and faculty, develop a pro and con list about exclusivity contracts with Pepsi or Coca-Cola in your local schools. Share your list with the student body, school administration, and staff, as well as school board officials.

Ask your city council representative if your local government has been approached to sign an exclusivity contract with any of the Big-Four bottled water companies in exchange for cash and exclusive rights as the city's official beverage supplier.

Go to www.insidethebottle.org for a detailed map identifying more than 70 bottled water plants in Canada and the U.S. that are operated by the Big-Four.

Is your community on the map?

Our Inside the Bottle project invites you to contribute your findings of the industry's presence as exclusive beverage suppliers in area schools or to local governments.

Share your community-based inquiry via our web portal and help build a citizens' database that exposes how the industry operates at the local level.

5. Water Privatizing

How does bottled water put low-cost free water at risk?

Despite the explosion in bottled water sales, the majority of Canadians and Americans still get their drinking water from the tap. In the U.S., close to 85% of the water utilities are publicly run, while in Canada over 95% are owned by the public. So everyone in both countries still has inexpensive access to one of the essential ingredients of life. So far, efforts by for-profit water companies to privatize the delivery of water services have met with only limited success. But this could change.

The world's largest for-profit water service corporations have set their sights on North America: Suez[1] and Veolia Environment from France and RWE from Germany. All three have major subsidiaries in North America: United Water, U.S. Filter, and American Water[2]. These corporations specialize in taking over public water services from cash-strapped governments and running them on a for-profit basis. Contracts often cover a 25-30 year term. In return, these corporations pledge to expand the service and improve the infrastructure. Invariably, water prices are jacked up to cover costs and water metres installed to control water use. As a result, millions of people in urban centres have found themselves faced with water cut-offs because they cannot afford the escalating water prices.

In January 2003, Suez, closely followed by Veolia (formerly known as Vivendi) and RWE, announced that they were going to target cities in the United States and Canada for their expansion. Their stated goal was to transfer 70% of the water services in both countries from public to private hands over the following 10 years.

The Big-Three water service corporations are getting a helping hand from the bottled water industry in their quest to privatize water services in North America. After all, the industries' main competitors continue to be municipal water utilities – and much of the marketing

*Cultivating consumers'
willingness to pay more
for a litre of bottled
water than they pay for a
litre of gas helps set the
stage for public
acceptance of the
privatization of water
services*

and advertising for bottled water is designed to wean people off tap water by undermining their confidence in public utilities.

As we have just seen, the big-four bottled water companies have been highly successful in pitching their message to consumers. Playing on fears of safety and insecurity of water supply, they have been effective in cultivating a consumer culture whereby people become increasingly dependent on buying bottled water to serve their daily hydration needs. In so doing, they have managed to undermine confidence in the public tap water system.

The numbers tell the story. In 1999, the National Environment Education and Training Foundation in the U.S. found that nearly 40% of all Americans are "very concerned" about their tap water, while another 40% are "moderately concerned."[3] During roughly the same period, other surveys reveal that 50% of the population in both Canada (1995-2000) and the U.S. (1999-2001) are concerned that their tap water contains contaminants. Drawing upon such surveys, the bottled water industry has been able to create the perception that tap water — and, by implication, public water utilities — are unreliable and hazardous.

A Culligan International (HOD division of Culligan) franchisee, for example, states in its promotional materials:

> "... the decision between tap water and bottled water simply comes down to personal preference and the degree to which you want to protect the health of you and your family."[4]

Another industry website, *bottledwaterweb.com*, talks about the "learning" process that takes place when one is being weaned off of tap water:

> "An unfortunate consequence of learning about the many drawbacks and dangers of tap water is that, now, when we turn our taste buds to bottled water, we have a long list of 'don't wants,' but a hazy idea of what we do want in our water. We're just learning. Understanding all the bottled water options is the first step to take as we begin to wean ourselves off of tap water."[5]

Cultivating consumers' willingness to pay more for a litre of bottled water than they pay for a litre of gas helps set the stage for public acceptance of the privatization of water services.

Consider that water service corporations advocate the establishment of cost-recovery rates for water utility operations because it has the benefit of regulating the use of water and generates revenues for improving water infrastructure. At the same time, many politicians maintain that the only way for cash-starved governments to improve their aging water infrastructure in their cities is by charging higher prices for water services. This position is often supported by academics and environmentalists, who argue that higher prices are an effective means of stemming the tide of water depletion.[6]

Establishing 'cost-recovery' pricing for water services almost always involves moving to a market model for running water utilities. More often than not, re-organization of a water utility will involve some form of arrangement with the private sector, typically handing over some aspect of the public water systems to the private sector to build, operate, and/or manage the water system.

Thus the stage is set for privatization. The advocates of water service corporations are now able to point to studies showing an increased "willingness-to-pay" for clean and safe water that is demonstrated by the high consumption of expensive bottled water. In other words, if people are willing to pay for bottled water because they believe it is safe and healthy, they'll also be willing to pay for privatized water services.

In response, public water utilities are beginning to fight back. Riverside Public Utilities in Southern California, for example, is bottling its own tap water for educational and public relation purposes. According to its director: "We want to make people aware of the [advantages of supporting] a municipal utility; what they are paying for — the revenues are funneled back to the city; they are not paying shareholders."[7]

In Canada, water utilities in the Greater Toronto Area are pooling more than $200,000 to buy bottling equipment in order to bottle municipal tap water for "promotional purposes."[8]

Meanwhile, the money spent on bottled water could be used to make public water utilities more reliable, secure, and sustainable. Based on research commissioned by the World Wildlife Fund in 2001, "The amount of money spent on bottled water per year ($22 billion) would enable enough water to be supplied through municipal systems to 2,000 cities, each with a population of 4 million."[9] In the U.S., the American Water Works Association (AWWA) estimates that between $250 and $300 billion (U.S.) will be needed over the next 30 years to maintain and improve the country's drinking water system.[10] In a single year, bottled water sales could finance more than 60% of AWWA's stated required investments.

Although bottled water could be regarded as a luxury good worth taxing, this is clearly not what the Big-Four have in mind. For years, water bottlers and their associations — both the International Bottled Water Association and the Canadian Bottled Water Association — have been opposed to any form of tax, fees, or royalties on their use of the resource. In its 2001 annual report, the IBWA claimed (as a way of promoting its track record in defending the interests of the bottled water industry), that it blocked two tax projects on bottled water in Tennessee and Texas. "Tennessee wanted to codify a 1.9% gross receipts tax on bottled water, and Texas tried to impose a 5-cents-per-container tax on bottled water to fund drinking water infrastructure."[11] (*see box, page 110*).

"These proposals, if left unchallenged, would have serious cost implications for your businesses, without any increase in public safety,"[12] declared the IBWA.

As we saw earlier, the Big-Four already pay next-to-nothing for the water they use in their bottles. No wonder they steadfastly resist taxes, fees, or royalties on their water takings. Indeed, two of the four draw their water from the same public water utilities that they are effectively undermining by their constant manipulation of public perception. In effect, the public system that provides Coke and Pepsi with their water resources has already been largely paid for by residents and taxpayers. By bombarding consumers with a barrage of charges — mostly unfounded — that water utilities are not up to the job, these companies not only persuade consumers to buy bottled water, but they also condition them to pay for it. The bottled water industry thereby sets the stage and creates a culture for the privatization of public water services.

Bottled Water Lobby Fights Tax Bill to Improve Water Services in Texas

When the Senate in Texas proposed a 5-cent tax on every bottle of water sold in the state, in order to finance up to $17 billion in improvements of local infrastructure for water services in 16 regional districts in 2001,[13] the bottled water industry began to organize a counteroffensive.

A coalition was formed, called "Texans for Prop 19," that included the Big-Four bottled water companies. Instead of mounting a direct campaign against the 5-cent tax, the bottler's coalition decided to block the tax bill by pushing for something called Proposition 19.

Proposition 19 would have authorized the Texas Water Development Board to issue up to $2 billion in additional public bonds that would then be used to make low-interest loans to municipalities in Texas for projects to improve water infrastructures.

The proposed tax bill on bottled water, of course, would have raised far more revenue for needed water service improvements than Proposition 19. But, as a citizens' watchdog group called "Texans for Public Justice" reported: "The industry balked at this tax [i.e., the 5-cent tax on bottled water], which would have increased public appreciation of tap water."[14]

As a result, the 5-cent tax bill on bottled water "never survived the trip across the lobby from the Senate to the House." When the tax bill died, other funding mechanisms were proposed, like Proposition 19.

In effect, the bottled water industry was able to prevent a tax being imposed on its own product sales by supporting another weaker funding mechanism for improving public water utilities, paid for by individual taxpayers.

NOTE: Please help complete this picture of "water privatizing" trends by making use of the following tool to investigate these concerns in your own community.

Community**PROBE**

Are there any indicators in your community that growth in bottled water consumption is undermining public confidence in your municipal water system? Are there any corresponding pressures to privatize your municipal water services?

Conduct interviews with workers and officials in your local public water utility. Ask them what needs to be done to maintain and improve the delivery of tap water in your community. What costs are involved for maintenance and improvements?

Consider the various proposals that have been made for taxing bottled water as a means of raising revenues to cover the costs of maintenance and improvements in public water systems. Could bottled water be taxed in your province or state for these purposes?

Go to www.insidethebottle.org for a detailed map identifying more than 70 bottled water plants in Canada and the U.S. that are operated by the Big-Four. Is your community on the map? Share your community-based inquiry via our web portal and help build a citizens' database that exposes how the industry operates at the local level.

4

RESPONSE AND RESISTANCE

Summing up and Moving on

IN THE FALL OF 2004, the bottled water industry held two industry conventions: one in Tampa, Florida, organized by the International Bottled Water Association (IBWA), and the other in Evian les Bains, France, which was dubbed the first "Global Water Congress."

The IBWA event in Florida included sessions that highlighted:

- consumer purchasing habits based on race;
- how to take advantage of school markets;
- how the industry has been affected by the new politics of bio-terrorism; and
- in a session entitled "All politics is local [sic], the importance of local communities to the industry.[1]

The Global Water Congress in France promised the high-profile presence of representatives from the Big-Four—Coca-Cola, PepsiCo, Nestlé, and Danone. The real priorities of the industry were exposed in ominous-sounding workshop titles such as *World Market Growth and Who Will Capture It* and *Marketing: What Matters Most to Consumers.* These sessions were accorded two hours on the schedule, while the topic of *Social Responsibility and the Environment* was given a mere 20 minutes.[2]

The promotional material for both events could barely contain the feverish excitement the industry sees ahead for itself in terms of growth and profits. Bottled water is now dubbed the industry's "growth superstar."[3] The theme slogans at both conventions are also revealing: the IBWA promoted its convention with the line *Uncap the Future*, and the Global Congress boasted, *Bottled Water: Source of Well-Being*.[4] Behind both tag lines you can imagine corporate executives anticipating their own "well-being," and not the well-being of communities, consumers, or the environment.

Clearly, the bottled water giants are on the move. Before they are allowed to continue with their aggressive plans to expand, we believe they must face up to a series of charges. Our book has demonstrated that the bottled water industry in general, and the Big-Four in particular, can be charged on five counts of environmental-health fraud:

1. misleading the public about the actual source of their water takings while paying little or nothing for extraction of the resource;
2. transforming water into water, then claiming elaborate treatment processes for their products to justify high prices, while in fact selling only plain water;
3. insisting that bottled water is safer than tap water when, in fact, bacterial contaminants such as arsenic, mercury, and bromate have been found in bottled water, which is not as regulated as tap water;
4. contributing to global warming and acid rain by using plastic bottles manufactured with resins containing toxic chemicals, which are then released into the environment when the bottles are discarded;
5. breaking their promises about the use of recycled materials while vigorously opposing comprehensive recycling laws, and masking the packaging of their products behind a misleading logo.

At the same time, our book shows The Big Four and the industry in general could be potentially charged on five more counts of social and economic forms of potential fraud:

1. price gouging by selling their products at prices that are hundreds, thousands, and even tens of thousands times greater than the cost of water from its original source;
2. mounting manipulative marketing campaigns that insinuate a healthier lifestyle and youthful look can be found inside their bottles;
3. luring people away from low-cost tap water by exploiting fears about

the safety risks of tap water while making false promises about the health benefits of their water;

4. infiltrating schools, colleges, and other public institutions by securing monopoly rights to sell their products exclusively to targeted groups using secret beverage contracts; and

5. paving the way for the takeover of public water services by for-profit water service corporations through fostering distrust in municipal water systems, and by conditioning people to pay high prices for their drinking water.

When all is said and done, these 10 counts illustrate the extent to which bottled water has become a "scam" in our society.

Reminiscent of the frontier days in the American West, today's bottled water peddlers are the contemporary con artists, deftly trying to snooker an unsuspecting public. The Big-Four will undoubtedly refute this assessment, declaring that their practices fall within the legal rules. However, the issues and concerns raised here go far beyond a lax regulatory environment or legal definitions. Ultimately, it is people and communities who will have to decide for themselves whether or not the marketing of bottled water today amounts to a "scam," and whether they are being set up for a "sting."

Although the bottled water industry has been highly successful to date in promoting and selling its products, several communities in the U.S. and Canada have mounted successful campaigns to force bottled water companies to curtail their operations, or to leave their communities altogether.

Whether it is a high school student challenging the secrecy of an exclusive beverage contract, or a long-time resident of a rural town using her expertise to change local planning laws to curb a company's water takings; whether it's a group of citizens who have mortgaged their homes to finance a legal challenge against a bottled water company, or local activists who have put their bodies in front of trucks pumping water out of an underground spring: communities are now taking a firm stand against the rapacious practices of the bottled water industry. The next chapter highlights some examples of this community-based resistance.

This does not mean that there is no role for bottled water in the future. As noted in the *Introduction*, it is generally accepted that bottled water has a role to play in emergency situations. Nor are community activists dismissing out-of-hand the economic benefits that may be associated with bottled water production. For many small towns located near groundwater springs or underground aquifers, bottled water production can be an important source of jobs and income. Shutting down plants could have serious social and economic consequences for these communities. But, as activists and this report have pointed out, the converse is also true. Allowed to continue, unlimited extraction of local water and production of bottled water could have serious ecological consequences, and provide no real long-term solution for communities seeking sustainable economic development.

Economic assessments must also consider the employment gains against the subsidies the Big-Four often negotiate to establish a plant. For example, in Madison County, Florida, Nestlé received a $1.3 million grant from the Economic Development Transportation Fund in order to build a road from its future plant to the nearest highway.[5]

Two points must be highlighted in this case. First, why give so much incentive funding to a company that doesn't need the incentive? The number of water sources large enough to meet Nestlé's needs, with the right mineral components, are rare and valuable. The company's revenues are huge, its U.S. operation bringing in $12 billion in sales and the bottled water sales in 2003 alone generating revenues of over 2.6 billion.[6] Second, the financial concession given to Nestlé in this particular case was "...designated for companies who haven't committed to a location. Nestlé had bought land, dug a well, and built a pumping station long before the grant application [was submitted]".[7]

In Michigan, PBS reported that Nestlé got $10 million in tax abatements to locate there and faces little oversight. The PBS report also raised issues about Nestlé's operation threatening a delicate ecosystem.[8] Based on the latest U.S. Census study of bottled water manufacturing, the 250 water bottling plants operating in the U.S. in 2002 employed only 6,709 people. Of these 250 plants, only 16 employed more than 100 workers. The level of subsidies granted to these bottling plants has yet to be determined.[9] Clearly, the cumulative impact of heavy truck traffic, aquifer depletion, and potential threats to the environment must be measured against massive corporate subsidies and the modest job creation that is linked to the sustainability of aquifers that are being voraciously drained.

So, under what circumstances and conditions should bottled water be produced? In some communities where there are abundant supplies of fresh water, the following terms and conditions are being considered:

- *community control* whereby bottled water production developed in local communities should be owned and controlled by those same communities;

- *sustainable sources,* i.e., making sure the production of bottled water is ecologically sustainable, whether it is extracted from a groundwater spring, aquifer, or tap water system; and
- *recycled containers* so that only recycled and recyclable materials are used, and include a deposit/return process.

Of course, finding terms and conditions under which community-based bottled water production might be more acceptable will require further public discussion and debate. So, too, will the rules that need to be put in place to govern bottled water production. New laws and regulations will be necessary in order to curb the gluttonous practices of the bottled water industry, and to establish terms and conditions for an alternative model for bottled water production.

For these reasons, we have compiled examples of public policies and laws that have been adopted or are being proposed for more effective regulation of the industry. It should be emphasized, however, that these measures alone are not sufficient. More creative and structural changes may be necessary to rein in the Big-Four — and the existing bottled water industry as a whole. The policy and legislative options outlined below will hopefully stimulate imaginative solutions for governing bottled water production and marketing.

What is important now is that the dialogue begins about community-based resistance *and* alternatives to the bottled water industry, and their current models of production. We encourage readers to put forward their own suggestions and proposals for discussion and debate via our website at www.insidethebottle.org .

Industry Responds

When the first edition of *Inside the Bottle* was released in January 2005, the bottled water industry's response was swift. Both the International Bottled Water Association [IBWA] and the Canadian Bottled Water Association [CBWA] issued formal statements on their websites, reacting to the publication of the book. Unfortunately, the commentaries issued by he IBWA and the CBWA did not bear much relation to the contents of the book itself.

In reply, the Polaris Institute responded to both industry associations, saying it welcomed critique and that a public debate about bottled water, as the fastest growing beverage in the North American market, is long over due. However, we noted that the critiques by the IBWA and the CBWA did not appear to be based on a reading of the book, but instead seemed to be mainly a cut-and-paste job taken from previous press releases issued by [them] in response to other commentaries or critiques made by groups and individuals in the past about the bottled industry.

Nevertheless, we felt it was important to reply briefly to the points raised by both industry associations in relation to what we did and did not say in the book itself. It should also be noted that neither the IBWA nor the CBWA represents all of the bottled water industry in North America. Of the Big-Four, for example, they include Nestlé and Danone, but not Coca-Cola and PepsiCo. The following is a synthesis of the statements that Polaris issued in response to the IBWA and the CBWA critiques.

1. Regulated Industry? The IBWA claim that bottled water in the U.S. and elsewhere is governed by an "effective and comprehensive system of federal and state regulations and standards" under the Food and Drug Administration (FDA) simply does not measure up to the facts. In its landmark study, the Natural Resource Defense Council (NRDC) demonstrated that tap water was held to much stricter regulations and standards than bottled water in the U.S.

Indeed, our own review shows a patchwork of regulations across the U.S., with many states adopting FDA regulations, some states developing their own, while other states have no regulations at all. In fact, bottled water produced and sold in the same state does not have to comply with FDA standards. If the FDA standards and regulations were adequate, as the IBWA claims, then why is it that states like Massachusetts, West Virginia, and now Illinois have seen fit to bring in their own, more strict, water safety laws?

Moreover, even if the FDA's measures were adequate, the federal agency lacks the resources required to effectively monitor and enforce its regulations. According to the NRDC report, water bottling plants, for instance, are likely to be inspected once very five or six years, because the FDA does not have sufficient inspectors to do so more often. As well, the NRDC made a series of recommendations designed to strengthen the capacities of the FDA, including: that bottlers be held to the same EPA standards (Environmental Protection Agency) as tap water; that that labs used for bottled water analysis be certified by the EPA or the FDA; and that strict procedures and timelines be followed for microbial and chemical tests along with labelling instructions for consumers to "refrigerate after opening."

Similarly, the CBWA's claim that "bottled water is fully regulated as a packaged food product by Health Canada, through the Food and Drugs Act" does not accord with the facts. In comprehensive studies conducted by Health Canada scientist Dr. Donald Warburton, the conclusions and recommendations emphasized the need for Health Canada to develop "an improved surveillance system for the bottled water industry" — largely because the research showed that the bottled water companies and products studied revealed "poor manufacturing practices." While conducting research for our book, an official from the Canadian Food Inspection Agency told us that, in coming years, inspections of bottled water plants will be carried out less frequently than in previous years: from once every three years to once every four or five years.

Moreover, the model code of conduct advocated by the CBWA is hardly a substitute for government inspections carried out in the public interest. The CBWA code is voluntary within the industry and is not enforceable. Nor are the tests conducted by government-approved labs; and the results of these "unannounced tests" are not made available for closer public or independent scrutiny. Even if the CBWA Model Code was exemplary, it does not apply to two of the four major players in our book, Coca-Cola and PepsiCo, because they are not members.

2. Water Takings? The IBWA completely misrepresents our report when it states: "Claims that the bottled water industry is misusing or depleting the nation's renewable groundwater resources are false and not supported by science." Our book makes no claims about national groundwater depletion by the bottled water industry. We are well aware of the fact that agribusiness and various manufacturing industries put a huge and increasing drain on groundwater resources.

What we do contend, however, is that groundwater drainage must be examined on a watershed-by-watershed basis. When this is done, the bottled water industry becomes a major factor. Take, for example, the case of Nestlé (a prominent member of the IBWA) in Pasco County, Florida, where, despite the fact that the region was hit with serious drought conditions in 2000-01, the company demanded a permit to increase its water takings from 301,000 gallons to 1.8 million gallons per day. Or take the case of Henderson County in Texas, where a Nestlé-owned company began pumping large volumes of groundwater for its Ozarka bottling plant and within four days the landowner's well dried up.

We also note that Nestlé faces class action suits in several states (e.g., Florida, California, Maine, Michigan, and Pennsylvania) not only for watershed depletion, but also, in some cases, for misleading advertising as to where the company's bottled water originates in the first place. The fact that the FDA does not require bottled water companies to name the source of their water takings on their labels allows them to promote their product as "pure, fresh spring water" without specifying where it came from.

Moreover, much of our discussion of water takings is devoted to the lack of laws governing groundwater in the U.S. (compared to surface water), Indeed, what does exist in terms of groundwater laws is a very diverse and confusing patchwork of governance, with the "riparian doctrine" applied east of the Mississippi, the "prior appropriation" doctrine west of the Mississippi, and the "rule of capture" in the state of Texas.

Similarly, the CBWA's statement that "bottled water from groundwater sources represent only 2/10th of 1% of all permitted water users in Ontario" misses the point. Nowhere do we argue that the bottled water industry is the biggest water user in Ontario, or anywhere else. We are well aware that agribusiness and various manufacturing industries are major and growing takers of groundwater resources. What we do contend, however, is that groundwater drainage must be examined on a watershed-by-watershed basis.

When this is done, the bottled water industry becomes a major factor. Take, for example, Danone's water taking practices [which owns and controls 70% of bottled water operations in the province] in the municipality of Franklin near the U.S. border, which became the target of community protests between 1995 and 1998 because the company was draining the local aquifer.

In their critique, both the IBWA and the CBWA cited a study by the Drinking Water Research Foundation, which contends that the bottled water industry takes only a small fraction of groundwater. However, further inquiry revealed that this statement can hardly be claimed as an example of independent and objective research, since the Drinking Water Research Foundation itself is sponsored and funded by over 50 bottled water companies.

3. Water Fees? The IBWA statement that "groundwater resources and usage are not "free to the bottled water industry" is highly misleading. So, too. is the the CBWA claim that "a bottled water company who uses groundwater as their source water does not get the resource for free... the company must pay for everything." Our book shows that the big bottled water companies pay next to nothing for their water takings.

Those companies that use reprocessed tap water, like PepsiCo and Coca-Cola, pay a only a tiny fraction for the water they use compared to the price they sell it for on the market. For example, a 1.5-litre (or 55-ounce) bottle of Coke's brand-name product Dasani sells for $1.20, yet the same amount of water taken from the tap system in New York City would cost 1/100th of a cent [and even lower in Knoxville, Tennessee, at 1/800th of a penny].

Even more astonishing, those companies that use groundwater, like Nestlé and Danone, pay little or no fees for their bottled water takings. If the company takes the water it uses from local groundwater systems like Nestlé and Danone do, then they are required to pay very low rates for permits. In Quebec, for example, where next to half of Canada's exported bottle originates, groundwater takings of over 20,000 gallons per day require a 10-year permit from the government's environment ministry that costs between $1,500 and $4,000, depending on the amount of daily water takings. This is a pittance compared to the revenues generated by the sales of bottled water from these sources.

Unlike other resource industries (e.g., oil, gas, forestry, mining), bottled water companies are not obligated to pay a fee or tax on the extraction of the resource. In fact, the IBWA has been vigorously opposed to any moves by state governments in the U.S. to pass legislation requiring bottled water companies to be taxed at source or having to pay royalty fees on the water they extract.

As with any other resource industry, there are value added costs: not simply elaborate filtering processes, but much more extensive marketing, labelling and packaging costs. But the question is: what value is really added if all that is being done is "turning water into water" in order to sell it?

4. Plastic Containers? The IBWA fails to address our basic critique about the rapidly expanding use of plastic containers by the bottled water industry. Today's skyrocketing sales in bottled water have, in turn, translated into a frightening number of discarded plastic bottles that release toxic chemicals into both groundwater and the atmosphere, thereby contributing to global warming and acid rain.

According to the EPA, plastics are the fastest growing form of solid waste in the country. Between 1995 and 2001, there has been a 56% increase in plastic resins in the U.S. alone. The bottled water industry's share of this plastic resin production has grown so rapidly that it is now estimated to be almost 25%.

What's more, recent peer-reviewed studies have shown that chemicals, including some dangerous contaminants involved in the production of plastic, can migrate from plastic containers into food or beverage products. Better known as chemical leaching, this process is more likely to occur the longer bottled water sits on the shelves.

Equally perplexing is the CBWA's contention in a nationally televised interview that "...plastics used for water bottles are safe. There are no scientific studies linking any disease or consumer harm to the use of PET bottles that we aware of..." Just because one does not know of any scientific studies, however, does not justify the conclusion that the plastics used for bottled water are "safe."

In 1996, the Berkley Plastics Task Force Report reported: "Examples of plastics contaminating food have been reported with most polymers, including styrene from polystyrene, plasticizers from PVC, antioxidants from polyethylene, and acetaldehyde from PET." Furthermore, says the report: "In studies cited in Food Additives and Contaminants, 25 LDPE, HDPE, and polypropylene bottles released measurable levels of BHT, Chimassorb 81, Irganox PS 800, Irganix 1076, and Irganox 1010 into their contents of vegetable oil and ethanol. Evidence was also found that acetaldehyde migrated out of PET and into water."

In our view, however, that more independent scientific studies are needed to properly assess the extent of the damage caused by the use of non-recycled plastic containers.

The beverage industry — especially the bottled water sector — has a relatively poor track record when it comes to recycling plastic containers. According to the Container Recycling Institute, plastic container recycling in the U.S. dropped from 834 to 797 million pounds between 2001 and 2002 alone, which is half the rate achieved in 1995.

We also challenged the CBWA's claim that "...PET bottles are easily recycled and the national recovery rate is about 70%." According to a document entitled *An Overview of Plastic Bottle Recycling in Canada*, prepared for Environment and Plastics Industry Council (EPIC) by C.M. Consulting (August 2004): "Recovery of *plastic bottles* in Canadian provinces varies dramatically based on the bottle type. In 2002, 235,086 tons of plastic bottles were generated and about 84,744 tons were recovered and recycled based on available data. This amounts to a recovery rate of 36% (for all types)."

The information reported by recycling companies themselves indicates that the PET beverage container material collected from the bottled water sector represents a small percentage of the plastics being recycled. One estimate says that 10% of the PET beverage containers are being recycled. In short, this is hardly an impressive record with regards to recycling, given that PET beverage containers are the prime reason why plastics have become the fastest growing component of municipal solid waste.

5. Healthy Hydration? The IBWA misses the point when it tries to dismiss our critique, saying "it's imprudent for critics to discourage people from choosing the consistent safety, quality, and convenience of bottled water for hydration and convenience." We fully agree that filtrated water is the best way for people to meet their hydration needs. But why pay high prices for bottled water when people can satisfy their basic hydration needs through tap water at a tiny fraction of the cost?

If people are concerned about the quality of their tap water, then they can purchase any one of a number of filtration devices for their tap system. And, why buy bottled water in throwaway plastic containers that are environmentally unfriendly? If people want the convenience of carrying their drinking water around with them, they can purchase an environmentally friendly container that can be refilled on an ongoing basis.

Yet the CBWA statement that it and its members "...promote a healthy lifestyle and support the governments across Canada in providing children with healthy food and beverage choices at school" perhaps brings us to the heart of the issue. While we agree with this lofty goal, we disagree with the assumption that bottled water is the healthiest form of hydration, or that it is, by definition, healthier than tap water in this country. In our report, we refer to independent studies conducted at the University of Tuskagee and the Natural Resource Defense Council, plus the Warburton research at Health Canada and a recently completed study by a group of scientists in the Netherlands — all of which reveal startling conclusions about the levels of chemical and bacteriological contaminants in bottled water. Add to this the growing concerns about chemical leaching into the water because of the use of plastic containers, there is more than enough to raise doubts about the health claims of bottled water

In fact, as far as Canada is concerned, we simply do not know what bacteriological and chemical contaminants are contained in bottled water products these days because the tests required do not cover all of the contaminants that need to be detected. Most of the regulations we have in place today for testing date back to 1973, but a great deal has been learned since then about what kinds of microbial and chemical contaminants are harmful to human health. In a Health Canada paper entitled *Why Do the Laws Have to Be Updated?* : http://www.hc-sc.gc.ca/food-aliment/friia-raaii/frp-pra/water-eau/e_rfr_bottle_water.php , it is argued that new laws governing bottled water are needed in Canada to incorporate new scientific knowledge and to bring our regulatory system in line with the *Guidelines for Canadian Drinking Water.* Apart from setting limits on arsenic and lead contents, says the article, Canada's regulations "do not contain specific, detailed parameters for chemical and radiological contaminants in bottled water..."

In their commentaries, both the IBWA and the CBWA praised the "multi-barrier approach" for filtering municipal tap water. In our report, we covered the various techniques used in this approach, including microfiltration, reverse osmosis, distillation, ultraviolet light, and ozone. But one still needs to ask what these processes accomplish. Just take ozone treatment, which is often used to kill bacteria and improve taste. Through this process, calcium chloride is often used containing high levels of bromide that are turned into bromate, a known carcinogen. If the levels of bromate generated in the water exceed the allowable limits, this could pose serious health hazards, depending on the amounts. That's why there needs to be much more stringent public surveillance of the manufacturing practices of the bottled water industry.

Finally, we maintained that, in writing this book, it was not our intention to "use a broad brush to stigmatize an entire industry." Instead, our book identifies 10 critical issues of public concern about the bottled water industry today and outlines some alternative options for ensuring that all people have access to drinking water that is safe, equitable, and sustainable. And we insist that these matters need to be democratically discussed and debated. Moreover, both industry associations ignore a major feature of our report: the increasing concentration of ownership and control of the bottled water industry in the hands of four major corporate players in North America – Nestlé, Coca-Cola, PepsiCo, and Danone. The days when the bottled water market was mainly occupied by dozens upon dozens of small independent operators is rapidly vanishing.

Community Resistance

In most regions of the United States and Canada, the issues outlined in this report have remained largely invisible to the public. In some communities, however, a considerable amount of resistance has been mobilized against the production and sales of bottled water. Following are some mini-profiles of community resistance.

1. Waushara County, Wisconsin: In early 2000, a coalition of community-based groups calling themselves Friends of Mecan Springs organized a campaign to stop Perrier from building a bottled water plant on top of Mecan Springs, Wisconsin.

The Mecan Spring is part of the Mecan River watershed in Waushara County, which is located in east-central Wisconsin, about 70 miles from Madison. Perrier, now part of Nestlé Waters of North America, wanted to drill a well and erect a 250,000 sq.-foot facility on the state-owned property. This would be Wisconsin's largest bulk water bottling plant,[1] an operation designed to pump 500 gallons a minute, 24 hours a day, all year long. The proposed daily extraction of 720,000 gallons a day, or 270 million gallons a year, was estimated to be "five times larger than any other such operations [in the state]."[2]

Mecan Springs was also seen as a natural spawning ground for brook, brown, and rainbow trout. Led by anglers and environmentalists, community residents quickly organized to resist the Perrier project. Realizing that public resistance was likely to mushroom, Perrier promptly announced in February 2000 that it would withdraw from the region and build instead in Big Springs, Adams County, also in Wisconsin. With the support of the then-governor of Wisconsin, Perrier presented plans for building a plant and extracting water in the new location.[3]

In June 2000, communities near Big Springs formed an organization called Waterkeepers of Wisconsin and held referendums opposing the construction of the Perrier plant. The referendums showed overwhelming community opposition to the project. In response, the Perrier spokesperson declared: "The people don't have all the information."[4] This only fanned the flames of resistance. "If that's the company's attitude," replied the Waterkeepers, "[we're] ready to fight. We are going on the Internet, and we're going to the county fairs, to the parades and to the flea markets."[5] The Waterkeepers did just that: they took their campaign to the people of Wisconsin and systematically responded to each of Perrier's allegations.

In August 2000, the Waterkeepers invited a group of groundwater experts to evaluate Perrier's environmental assessment, which had been conducted by the Wisconsin Department of Natural Resources. Their team of experts found the assessment to be flawed because it made improper use of previous groundwater studies, and its tests were inadequate.[6] A member of the Coalition, The Concerned Citizens of Newport sued the Department of Natural Resources "for deciding that the project should be allowed to go forward despite public opposition."[7] In November 2000, the State Governor, who had originally supported Perrier, finally asked the company to leave, saying: "People in Adams County and the Town of New Haven do not want Perrier there, and they've made that crystal clear [...] It's time for them to find a different location."[8]

Two years later, Perrier finally left Wisconsin to relocate to the neighbouring state of Michigan.[9] In January 2004, Perrier's president was quoted as saying: "People were much more receptive in Michigan. We're going to have a very successful operation in another state, which will give the people in Wisconsin an opportunity to see who we are. I don't think that enough people did their homework on who we are."[10]

2. Mecosta County, Michigan: But Nestlé ran into similar community resistance in Michigan. It all began in the fall of 2000 when news broke that Perrier was planning to build a $100 million water bottling plant in either of three locations: Morton Township or Mecosta Township in Mecosta County, located in west central Michigan, about an hour's drive north of Grand Rapids, or in Osceola Township, located in neighbouring Osceola County.

The Nestlé Waters plant was designed to pump as much as 720,000 gallons of water a day, a fact that did not impress the local citizenry.[11] In December 2000, concerned residents formed the Michigan Citizens for Water Conservation (MCWC) to lead the community-based resistance against Nestlé's plans. The community had only found out about the project when a Nestlé's employee gave a presentation to area citizens. The MCWC then discovered that local and state officials were *already* working with the company on a deal. Just as they had in Wisconsin, Michigan officials urged citizens to trust the company.

In Michigan, the initial battle lines were drawn around the zoning changes that would be required at two of the potential sites: Mecosta County and neighbouring Osceola County. The MCWC organized a signature campaign to force local officials to hold a referendum on these proposed changes.[12] In August 2001, referendums were held in both Mecosta and Osceola counties, and rezoning was rejected by a 2-to-1 margin.

Brazilians Challenge Nestlé

São Lourenço is the site of an historic water park of natural springs and mineral waters in the state of Minas Gerais, Brazil.

In 1996, Nestlé sank two wells 162 meters deep into the Primavera aquifer, without legal authorization, and began extracting the mineral water and de-mineralizing its Pure Life brand of bottled water.

When Nestlé got around to obtaining a permit for its water extraction, it was told by Brazil's National Department for Mineral Resources that de-mineralizing the water was illegal under Brazilian law.

In the late 1990s, a citizens' group was organized in São Lourenço to defend the water park and challenge Nestlé. In 2001, the group presented the town's public prosecutor with a petition signed by 3,000 people, expressing concerns that tourists and local citizens were noticing changes in the mineral composition of the springs in the park. While Nestlé blamed these changes on a recent flood, the town's hydrologist confirmed that they were due to the company's water extraction operations.

In 2003, the Brazilian government's mineral resources department outlined the illegal nature of Nestlé's ongoing operations and recommended they be "paralyzed." On March 24, 2004, the company was given 30 days to comply with this order, but refused and took the issue to the Supreme Court, which extended to deadline.

Today, the battle continues, with Nestlé launching a counteroffensive that includes attacks against the citizen group's leading spokesperson, Franklin Fredericks, amid allegations that the company has funnelled money into the community and the government's political party.

At the same time, MCWC organized its own study in which a group of environmental experts countered the claims being made by Nestlé regarding the sustainability of the spring.[13] Throughout the region, the MCWC mobilized concerned residents to participate in the public hearings that were organized by Nestlé and the Michigan Department of Environmental Quality.[14]

In June 2001, the MCWC took Nestlé to court, claiming that the company was violating the "public trust doctrine" in U.S. law.[15] The case emphasized that spring water is part of the riparian stream, and therefore diversion and sale of the resource by Nestlé was unlawful and unreasonable because it would diminish the flow of the stream.

In October 2002, the judge ruled that, while Nestlé had the right to pump water on a "reasonable-use" basis, the company's water takings had harmed, or was likely to harm, the community residents and the environment.[16] Three bands of Native people's also challenged Nestlé in court on the basis that bottling water for export violates the Water Resources Development Act, although that case was dismissed by a federal judge.[17]

In November 2003, the Michigan Circuit Court finally ruled in favour of the MCWC and "...ordered the company that produces Ice Mountain bottled water to halt all water withdrawals in Mecosta County."[18] In December 2003, Nestlé won an emergency reprieve to continue pumping until its appeal of the circuit court ruling had been heard and decided.[19] As of October 2006, the case is still pending in the Court of Appeals, and Nestlé continues pumping the spring water.

3. Pasco County, Florida: Nestlé has also run into public opposition for its spring water takings in Florida. Since 1980, the Crystal Springs in Pasco County, Florida, has been the prime source for the bottling company Zephyrhills, now owned by Nestlé. In 1997, Nestlé wanted to boost its pumping permit for Crystal Springs from 301,000 gallons per day to 1.8 million gallons per day. In response, concerned citizens formed a movement called Save Our Springs (SOS) to stop this expansion.

For most of the 20th century, the actual "Crystal Springs" were privately owned but remained open to the public. Local residents used the springs as a place to gather, picnic, and swim during hot summer days. Then rancher Robert Thomas, the spring's current owner, purchased it in 1975. Originally, Thomas maintained public access to the site, turning it into a park called the Crystal Springs Recreational Park (CSRP), and he also sold water to Zephyrhills. In 1996, however, things changed. Thomas blocked public access to the spring and a year later, on behalf of Nestlé, he requested an increase in the pumping permit for water takings from Crystal Springs.

The Battle of Plachimada

A modern-day drama of David vs. Goliath has been raging in India's southern most state of Kerala. For more than four years, the villagers of Plachimada have been waging a battle to stop the water takings of the global soft drink giant Coca-Cola.

Farmers near the village of Plachimada [pop. 5000] say their water sources have been parched and polluted by the local Coca-Cola plant, which has drilled deep bore holes, drawing up to 1.5 million litres a day. Coke officials have countered these charges, claiming that the company's daily water takings amount to only 500,000 litres and that there are other companies in the region doing the same.

In addition to water depletion, waste sludge from the plant which was supplied to local farmers was found to contain cadmium and lead, which the villagers said resulted in skin disorders.

To protect its local farmers, the panchayat [the village government] denied the Coca-Cola plant access to the local groundwater. In 2003, the State's High Court upheld the panchayat's decision and ordered the company to find other water sources.

In the meantime, the villagers have maintained a 24-hour vigil in front of the gates of the Coca-Cola plant since the spring of 2002, and have organized numerous rallies and demonstrations. Women, in particular, have been at the heart and soul of the Plachimada resistance campaign.

In 2004, a Supreme Court monitoring committee in India also ordered Coca-Cola to retrieve its sludge waste from the farmers' lands and to ensure that people around the plant had access to clean water.

In organizing its campaign, Save our Springs launched its own website, collected names for petitions, and conducted boycott initiatives throughout Pasco County. In concert with the Southwest Florida Water Management District, the SOS filed a lawsuit against Thomas, Nestlé, and several Pasco County councilmen in an effort to stop the changes to the conditions of the permit.

Testifying on the issue before one of the court hearings, a representative of the New York-based Beverage Marketing Corporation stated: "In order for the company to grow, it needs to increase the amount of water it withdraws from Crystal Springs... People want more bottled water, and if Zephyrhills [Nestlé's brand] can't deliver, someone else surely will." He added: "When you have this kind of growth potential, to not take advantage of it is a sacrilege."[20]

In January 1999, a judge ruled in favour of SOS by refusing to grant the six-fold increase in the pumping permit. He stated that Thomas and the company failed to prove the need for the pumping boost and that, since Crystal Springs also feeds the Hillsborough River, one of the main water sources for Tampa Bay, it could worsen a situation made difficult by droughts in the previous years.

As the SOS was savoring its victory, Thomas and Nestlé decided to appeal the ruling, but the Appeal Court rejected Thomas's proposition in a ruling handed down in February 2001.[21]

4. Nottingham & Barrington, New Hampshire: Smaller, independent water companies have also been the focus of community resistance. In May 2000, USA Springs petitioned the Nottingham Planning Board in New Hampshire for a permit to construct a water bottling plant that would extract 300,000 gallons a day from the town's aquifer. The plant was designed to produce bottled water for export. When citizens in Nottingham and nearby communities got wind of the project, they organized a grassroots movement called Save Our Groundwater (SOG).

The State of New Hampshire has some of the most comprehensive laws in the U.S. regarding groundwater takings. As a result, USA Springs was forced to conduct hydrological studies, run pumping tests, and develop measures to reduce the environmental risks associated with pumping, such as aquifer depletion and well contamination. Testing that specific aquifer, however, posed a challenge because it was in bedrock. According to hydrologists, bedrock aquifers "are difficult to appraise and test because of their inherent complex network of water routes."[22]

As the issue intensified in 2002, SOG organized public rallies near the proposed site of the project, convened several public meetings to inform residents of USA Springs' plans, and actively participated in Nottingham's board assembly meetings. The city of Nottingham took USA Springs to court for failing to wait until the city's planning board had made its decision over "the amount of groundwater that can be

Students Challenge Coke

Among the more than 100 activist shareholders who mingled in the crowd of investors at the 2006 Annual General Meeting of Coca-Cola at the prestigious Hotel DuPont in Wilmington, Delaware, were networks of high school and university students.

When Coca-Cola's CEO, Neville Isdell, tried to limit debate and select only pre-planted corporate friendly voices from the audience to speak, a few determined students were able to get to the microphones. Lynette, a high school student, confidently asked the Board of Directors: "I am wondering if the loss of so many consumers, due to Coca-Cola's unethical practices, concerns shareholders?"

Andrea, a university student, also took the mike, challenging shareholders to realize that Coke's reputation was in tatters despite expensive public relations efforts. An increasing number of students, she said, now realize that bottled water is a ruse and are walking away from Coke and not looking back.

Other groups, including Corporate Campaigns: Stop Killer Coke, Corporate Accountability International, the Teamsters Union, India Resource Centre, the Polaris Institute, the International Labour Rights Fund, and the United Students Against Sweatshops raised researched questions about Coke's labour practices in Columbia, Turkey, and the U.S., or about its aggressive water takings in India, and back room role in privatizing water.

But the company's responses were limp and scripted, along with repeated claims that their critics' facts were just simply wrong.

The student activists, however, knew that the residents of Plachimada Kerala in southern India had not been on a peaceful vigil 24 hours a day since 2002 outside of a Coke bottling plant because Coca-Cola has increased its water levels. Similarly, they knew the "choice" to enter into exclusivity and monopoly contracts with little to no meaningful student representation is not a true "choice."

The "bottom line," as they say at shareholder meetings, is that bottling a human right for greater consumer choice, convenience and profit is a message that just doesn't fly.

withdrawn without harming wetlands, lakes, ponds, rivers, and neighbouring private wells."[23] Nottingham officials also tried to stop the company testing activities by restricting the number of water trucks at the site and by reviewing zoning for the site.

In October 2002, the New Hampshire Environmental Services' Wetlands Bureau ordered the bottling company to restore the wetlands affected by the construction of roads and the drilling of wells in the locations where work had already been conducted without permits. Even so, USA Springs continued its pumping tests until the end of 2002. It then issued its findings to state authorities about the environmental impact of the project. According the SOG, the company's report failed to provide sufficiently detailed responses on the key questions raised about the project, such as the proposed withdrawal of water from the aquifer and the effect of large water exports from the region.[24]

In August 2003, the State's Department of Environmental Services formally denied USA Springs' application for a permit, agreeing with the SOG that the company had failed to "explain to the state how it would keep water withdrawals from spreading pollutants found on an adjacent property."[25] When the company appealed this decision in December 2003, the state government reaffirmed the decision not to grant the permit. But the saga continues. On December 29, 2003, the company re-applied for a permit, and in early 2004 proceeded to dig small wells for tests on the site. On July 2, 2004, USA Springs received a permit to pump 307,528 gallons a day. This was promptly challenged in court by the towns of Nottingham, Barrington, and the SOG.

5. McCloud, California: Since 2003, groups in McCloud, a small village of 1,300 on the eastern side of California's Mount Shasta, have been battling the local regulatory body and Nestlé Waters North America over the construction of a huge water bottling facility in the community.

In September 2003, the McCloud Community Service District – the only form of elected government operating in McCloud[26] - went ahead and signed a highly contentious water-supply contract with Nestlé Waters North America. After the contract became public, residents of McCloud and the surrounding area quickly divided into those in favour, who believe that the proposed operation will bring jobs to the region, and those opposed to the plant and the way the contract was negotiated.

The contract entitles Nestlé to 1600 acre-feet of McCloud's spring water per year (or 1.8 million gallons of spring water per day), and the use of unlimited ground water. The contract binds McCloud to its terms for 50 years, while the company holds the option to renew for another 50. It also states that regardless of drought or other shortage, Nestlé can continue to take its maximum draw and should be compensated by the community if the flow is slowed or stopped for any reason.[27]

In addition, the contract: gives the company permission to drill unlimited boreholes; commodifies the resource thus removing local control or protection of the water from laws under NAFTA; gives the water to Nestlé but leaves the legal responsibility for the springs, their infrastructure and water table in the District's hands.[28]

Under the contract the residents of McCloud would have to give all of this to Nestlé and receive only $350,000 a year from the company.

In response to the contract a group called the Concerned McCloud Citizens quickly mobilized and sued the District in Siskiyou County Superior Court. They charged that the contract was rushed through without public participation and that the services district overreached its authority in approving the plant. Don Mooney, lawyer for Concerned McCloud Citizens explained that companies like Nestlé "come in and dangle some money in front of these little towns and get a deal done before there's any kind of public process."[29]

In March 2005, Siskiyou County Superior Court Judge, Roger Kosel, found in the group's favour scrapping the deal saying that the district abused its discretion by not performing a review of the project's environmental impact before signing the contract.[30]

In July 2005, the judge issued his final ruling on the case nullifying the contract in its entirety and directing the District to rescind its approval of the contract with Nestlé.[31] In September 2005, the District and Nestlé appealed the decision.

Since then Nestlé's powerful legal team successfully petitioned to have Kosel recused from the case. They then unsuccessfully pushed for his original ruling to be thrown out.[32]

Nestlé's desire to take water from this area has polarized McCloud and surrounding communities, and caused friction between friends and within families. The issue also highlights how the company is not opposed to using its strength as one of the richest companies in the world to bully a small community into giving up rights to its water for 100 years.

6. Grey County, Ontario: In Grey County, Ontario, an independent bottling company called Artemesia Waters Ltd. was granted a "Permit To Take Water" by the Ministry of the Environment. However, municipal zoning laws for the land where the spring was located stopped the company from storing and transporting water. The company appealed the decision of the municipality, but the county refused to rezone the land.

The Ontario Municipal Board agreed with Artemesia Waters, arguing that, in its opinion, water was a food, subject therefore to the rules governing agriculture. They argued that the planned water taking should be permitted. The OMB also said that, since "water taking" was not a land-use issue, it could not be regulated under the province's Planning Act.

The OMB's decision was promptly challenged by the Grey Association for Better Planning, which argued that the right of local communities to control commercial water takings through their land-use plans—specifically the Official Plan of the County of Grey—had been ignored. They argued that water taking involved land use and that on this issue the Planning Act took precedence over the Ontario Water Resources Act.

As a citizen-based organization, the Grey Association for Better Planning (GABP) was organized in 1989 to work with local residents in developing land-use plans that balanced environmental needs with economic development in the region. Under the Ontario government's Planning Act and 1995 Provincial Policy Statement, community residents were encouraged to participate in land-use planning decisions, which included commercial water takings, through organizations like GAPB.

In November 2001, GAPB appealed the decision of the Ontario Municipal Board in the Ontario Divisional Court. The GAPB appealed on its own, but received support from within the county and elsewhere. Supporters included the Municipality of Grey Highlands, the Water Protection Coalition of South Grey, the Grey County Federation of Agriculture, the Federation of Anglers and Hunters, and the Blue Mountain Ratepayers' Association. Further afield, they were supported by Environment Defence Canada, the Great Lakes Aquatic Habitat and Network Fund, and many other concerned individuals and municipalities across Ontario.

In November 2002, the Ontario Superior Court of Justice ruled in favour of the GAPB appeal, reaffirming the installation of pipes and pumps on land for the purpose of water extraction was a matter of land-use planning, and that, under the Planning Act, communities across Ontario can control commercial water takings. Artemesia Waters at first appealed the decision, but in December 2003 abandoned the appeal.

7. Grafton, Ontario: Community pressure has also had an effect in other communities. Near Grafton, Ontario, CJC Bottling Ltd. was frustrated when the Ontario Ministry of the Environment (MOE) seemed to drag its feet on the granting of a new extraction permit for 180 gallons of groundwater per minute, to be used for export. Community actions by the Concerned Citizens of Northumberland, the local municipal council, and various other agencies were in part responsible for the MOE's cautious approach.

By early 2003, the MOE considered the possibility of permitting 100 gallons per minute (gpm) instead of the requested 180 gpm. In order to reduce the impact on downstream fish habitats, a new plan was reviewed and the MOE proceeded to prepare a draft permit with conditions for further comment.

On Dec. 18, 2003, however, the Ontario government imposed a 12-month moratorium on new or expanded permits for water takings. Prior to this, CJC had partnered with Chesterman company, a bottler of Coca-Cola products based in Iowa. Chesterman entered the bottled water market in 1994 under the name Premium Waters, and had been bottling Port Hope municipal water along with its spring water line.

Meanwhile, the citizens' group had sought to strengthen the hand of the Grafton-area municipal council on new groundwater takings. The Council itself proposed to commission a series of peer review studies to examine the hydro-geological, environmental, and traffic impact of the company's proposed groundwater project. The council's review included public submissions as well as comments from government agencies. CJC's required approval of the cost of the peer reviews was interrupted by the moratorium.

8. Aurora, Ontario: On another front, the exclusive contracts between soft drink giants and school boards are being challenged by students. In Aurora, a small Ontario town north of Toronto, a Grade 8 student used the Freedom of Information Act to compel his school board to disclose details about the vendor contract it had signed with the Pepsi Bottling Group.

The process began when Nicholas Dodds, a 13-year-old public school student, noticed the proliferation of soft drink vending machines in his school and asked what was happening. When he was told the York Region District School Board had signed an exclusive sales contract with the Pepsi Bottling Group, Nicholas asked to see the documents, but was stonewalled. With the help of his father, he filed a Freedom of Information request for a copy of the York-Pepsi proposal and contract. When the requested documents were not disclosed, he filed an appeal and, at the same time, made a similar request for disclosure of the exclusive contract between the Peel District School Board and Coca-Cola.

After submitting several long briefs, 3,000 pages of photocopying, and numerous letters and e-mails, Nicholas's efforts finally paid off. In November 2003, the Information and Privacy Commissioner of Ontario ordered that both the York-Pepsi and the Peel-Coke contracts and proposals be released to the public.[33] The two school boards which, together with Pepsi and Coke, had made their own appeals to the Commissioner resisting the public disclosure request, had them rejected.

In at least 11 states in the U.S., vending contracts between school boards and soft drink manufacturers are accessible by law. This has not been the case in Canada where, until recently, they have been kept secret. Indeed, the first successful challenge came from British Columbia when the student newspaper at the University of British Columbia spearheaded a campaign calling for public disclosure of UBC's exclusive contract with Coca-Cola. In May 2001, the province's Information and Privacy Commissioner ordered both UBC and Capilano College to release the contracts.

But the story of student challenges to Coca-Cola and Pepsi does not end here. Coke has become the target of a student action campaign in at least 70 American universities and colleges, plus a growing number in Canada and elsewhere. The "Stop Killer Coke" campaign is focused on the gruesome murders, kidnappings, and torture of workers and union leaders in Colombia, allegedly resulting from the collusion between Coca-Cola's bottling companies in Colombia and paramilitary security forces.[34]

Taking Democratic Control

When it comes to the question of ensuring safe drinking water, there is no substitute for government. As we have seen, the bottled water industry is certainly one of the most unregulated industries that deals with people's basic health needs. Any move to effectively address some of the issues identified in this book would require exercising democratic control through government intervention .

In discussing regulatory measures, it should be kept in mind that we are dealing with diverse political jurisdictions. Not only are there differences between Canada and the United States in terms of political

systems, but there are also at least three levels of governments wiu..
each country—federal, state or provincial, and municipal—and
sometimes a fourth level, such as county governments in the U.S. and
Aboriginal governments in Canada.

It would be difficult, therefore, to propose regulations that could
apply to each political jurisdiction and/or level of government. Instead,
our objective here is to summarize various legislative and policy initiatives that could be developed and implemented in order to ensure more
effective democratic control over the operations of the bottled water
industry in the public interest. The legislative, policy, and program
initiatives outlined below could be applied at one or more levels of
government in both the U.S. and Canada.

The following set of regulations has been proposed by various
groups working on bottled water issues and, in some cases, has actually
been implemented by some governments. It must be emphasized,
however, that regulating the bottled water industry is not a panacea for
the problems we have been discussing. Even if the main regulatory
measures outlined below were implemented tomorrow, this would not
necessarily mean that the bottled water industry had been brought
under effective democratic control, or that the fundamental issues had
been satisfactorily resolved.

Nevertheless, it is worthwhile to consider the range of actions that
could be undertaken by governments to help communities regain
control of this essential resource.

1. Rebuild Public Tap Water Systems

In its 1999 landmark study, *Bottled Water: Pure Drink or Pure Hype*, the
Natural Research Defence Council was unequivocal in its recommendations: bottled water is not a long-term solution to society's drinking
water needs. At best, concludes the NRDC:

The NRDC cites several compelling reasons to support its
conclusions:

[a] Public Health Concerns: If society shifted to bottled water as
the main source of drinking water, and public systems were therefore
allowed to deteriorate, people would then be exposed to contaminants
when they used tap water for showering, bathing, washing dishes, and
cooking. In other words, tap water must never be allowed to drop below
drinking-level quality or the public health will be at risk.

[b] Social Equity Concerns: If the affluent shift to bottled water
as their primary source of drinking water, and only low-income people

[bottled water] "may be needed as a stopgap measure when tap water is contaminated, rendering the water non-potable [as in the case of a boil-water alert]. In the long run, however, it is far better from an economic, environmental, and public health point of view to improve public drinking water supplies than it is to have a massive societal shift from consumer use of tap water to use of bottled water. We cannot give up on tap water safety."[1]

—Eric Olson, NRDC

are left to drink tap water, this would trigger a downward spiral in the quality of municipal systems, which would put everyone at risk for the reasons stated above.

[c] **Environmental Concerns:** Not only does the excessive use of non-recycled plastic bottles for bottled water harm the environment, but the transportation of water by underground pipes is also much more energy efficient and consumes far fewer natural resources per gallon than the process involved in bottling and transporting water around the country (or the globe).

[d] **Economic Concerns:** Bottled water costs hundreds and even thousand times more than what comes out of the faucet—"costs [that] cannot be easily borne by low-income people and should not be borne by the elderly, the immuno-compromised, or chronically ill people in order to get water that is safe to drink."

The NRDC maintains that it would be better for governments to undertake measures designed to upgrade and improve water services and quality than to have a part of the population shift to bottled water, leaving tap water behind for whoever couldn't afford the alternative. And for those people who claim they dislike the taste and smell of their tap water (due to chlorination decontaminants), the NRDC suggests they consider "placing tap water in a glass or ceramic pitcher in their refrigerator, with the top loose to allow the chlorine to dissipate overnight. Overnight refrigeration in a loosely capped container," says the NRDC, "eliminates the objectionable chlorine taste and odor," while saving money and protecting the environment.

If governments, therefore, are going to develop effective plans to ensure safe drinking water for all, they should begin by making a clear and unequivocal commitment to rebuilding the public tap water systems in both the United States and Canada. Today in the U.S., 85% of all municipal tap water systems are publicly owned,[2] while in Canada it is estimated over 95% are operated and controlled by the public. In some municipalities, aging pipes and other infrastructure for the delivery of drinking and waste water services are in need of major repair or replacement, requiring billions of dollars in new public investment. Yet raising the revenues needed to repair, upgrade, and improve public water systems is a more efficient way to ensure safe drinking water for all than promoting the sale of bottled water that is more costly, polluting, and inefficient.

The proposed Clean and Safe Water Trust Fund Act provides an example of what could be done through national legislation to begin rebuilding public tap water systems.[3] Facing similar gaps between needs and resources for critical national infrastructure, the U.S. Congress has sometimes established trust funds supported by dedicated taxes. As proposed, the Clean and Safe Water Trust Fund would raise $45 billion to be spent on improving tap water systems over a five-year period, between 2006 and 2010, to meet standards required under the U.S. Safe Drinking Water Act. Some $35 billion would be raised through a 5-cent tax on each container of bottled beverages sold, while the remaining $10 billion would come from continued appropriations for these purposes. Although this legislative initiative has its limitations and is by no means sufficient for rebuilding public tap water systems in the U.S., it shows what could be done by establishing a trust fund supported by a designated tax.

2. Control Corporate Water Takings

Various jurisdictions in the United States and Canada have recently adopted regulations to more effectively control water takings. These include changing or improving groundwater laws. The following are some samples.

The State of New Hampshire enacted a new set of laws with regards to groundwater takings, including a set of regulations that pertain directly to bottled water. The New Hampshire laws apply to both source and quality issues. Since New Hampshire is located east of the Mississippi River, it follows the Riparian Doctrine. (For details, check out the following website: http://www.des.state.nh.us/dwspp/bottled.htm)

The New Hampshire law identifies two categories of groundwater withdrawal to be regulated: *minor withdrawals* that are less than 57,600 US gallons per day, and major withdrawals which are withdrawals of more than 57,600 U.S. gallons per day. Minor withdrawals are covered under *Env-Ws 387* and *major withdrawals* are subject to *Env-Ws 388*. Both pieces of groundwater legislation contain rules for prior public notification and community participation.

The permit-granting process is as follows: a preliminary permit application is sought and provided to all municipalities and public water suppliers within the permit area. A public hearing must be held within 30 days of the request followed by a 45-day public comment period. After that, there is an optional pre-testing conference and withdrawal testing, leading to a final report and a technical review. In addition, there is a set of rules [*Env-Ws 389*] specifically governing groundwater sources of bottled water. These rules contain "procedures and standards for the selection of new groundwater sources and for routine monitoring of new and existing groundwater sources of bottled water."

Overall, New Hampshire's rules and regulations with regards to groundwater takings and drinking water quality are fairly comprehensive when compared to those of most other jurisdictions. Moreover, the state provides a useful mechanism on its website for reporting data which is easy to use.

Meanwhile, Washington State has another set of regulations on water takings. Located west of the Mississippi, the State of Washington follows the Prior Appropriation Doctrine. In comparison with New Hampshire, however, Washington has a more limited quota for water withdrawals.

Sometimes referred to as the "scientific ideal," groundwater laws in Washington State require that any withdrawal of more than 5,000 U.S. gallons per day must be subject to a permit application. Emphasis is put on permits for the lowest minimum volume limit. Any request for a new permit must be made public through an approved newspaper for two consecutive weeks. In turn, this is followed by a 30-day protest period. (For more details, check out Washington state's web-site athttp://www.ecy.wa.gov/programs/wr/rights/water-righthome.html.)

In Canada, the Province of Ontario passed a Clean Water Act in December 2006 designed to create a new source water regulatory system. The Clean Water Act aims to create a more preventative approach to protecting Ontario waters by investing regional Conservation Authorities and municipalities with the mandate to produce watershed risk assessments that identify threats to source water.

Under its previous system, Ontario relied mainly on assessments provided by water users (including major water bottling companies) as the basis to approve permits to take water. The new Clean Water Act will invest more powers in the Conservation Authorities to bring water users to compliance with water protection standards as well as divesting the power to provide permits to take water to the municipalities.

It remains to be seen how this new Act will affect companies taking Ontario waters for commercial water bottling. While the Act encourages local communities to take an active role in source water protection, placing the power to grant water licenses in the hands of municipalities creates a situation where well financed commercial water bottlers will be approaching small communities across Ontario to get their water licenses. Currently, many municipalities do not have the skills, experience or resources to protect their waters from bottling companies, who are veterans of the provincial permit process.

Although a community approach to governing water takings is critical, the new legislation allows the Ontario Government to quietly divest themselves of political accountability to the growing opposition against large water takers. With the Province extricating itself from water licensing, bottled water activists now find themselves in a situation where they have to monitor Ontario's 445 municipalities, instead of collectively keeping their eye on one common target, namely, the Ontario Environment Ministry and its permit process. (For details, check http://www.ene.gov.on.ca/envision/water/spp.htm)

3. Ensure Water Quality and Safety

Several states in the U.S. have adopted their own bottled water safety laws that regulate the quality of bottled water. For example, the online version of West Virginia's water safety regulations can be found at http://www.wvdhhr.org/phs/bottledwater/index.asp, and the online text of the Massachusetts regulations are at http://www.mass.gov/dph/fpp/bottledwater.htm . It should be kept in mind, of course, that most U.S. states and Canadian provinces have very few laws for regulating bottled water quality and safety.

Meanwhile, the Illinois State Senate adopted a new bottled water safety bill that came into effect in 2005. Similar to water safety laws in Massachusetts and West Virginia, the Illinois bill is meant to "ensure that the bottled water that Illinoisans are drinking is safe" by giving "the state more regulatory authority over water bottling plants and private water source operators."

Under this new law, the Illinois' Department of Public Health (IDPH) issues permits to bottled water plants and private water source operators, adopts federal regulations pertinent to these establishments, conducts annual inspections, and performs other regulatory functions necessary to assure safe bottled water. The new law also requires the registration of water bottling plants located outside of Illinois that do business within the state. It also gives IDPH the authority to embargo bottled water produced by unlicensed or unregistered establishments. Furthermore, businesses that receive a permit must meet standards for good manufacturing practices, water source, water quality, and labelling. (Information on the Illinois water bill can be found at http://www. illinois.gov/PressReleases/PrintPressRelease.cfm?SubjectID=1&RecNu m=3261.)

In its 1999 report on bottled water, the Natural Resource Defence Council outlined a series of rules that should be adopted by federal agencies for the regulation of bottled water.[4]

The Council suggested governments should:

- require bottlers to retain microbial test results for 5 years, and chemical tests for 10 years, holding them to the same standards as the E.P.A. standards for tap water;
- mandate a bottling date and "refrigerate after opening" statement on labels, in order to inform consumers who seek to minimize the chances of potentially excessive microbial growth and contamination in bottled water;
- require labs used for bottled water analysis to be certified by the E.P.A or the F.D.A.;
- direct that water be tested daily at the plant for microbes, quarterly for chemicals during bottling, and quarterly in bottles after extended storage, especially for chemicals that can leach from bottles and for microbes that can multiply during storage;
- require quarterly reporting of test results to states and the F.D.A., and reporting of acute violations within 24 hours to state and F.D.A. officials; and
- prohibit all sales of water contaminated at levels above F.D.A. standards.

4. Recycle Plastic Water Bottles

As noted above, a few state legislatures have attempted to pass "bottle bills" designed to curb the massive dumping of plastic containers in landfills. These "bottle bills" have been steadfastly resisted by the major bottled water companies, so it is important that environment groups and concerned legislators in both the U.S. and Canada continue their efforts to propose and pass laws curbing the use of these environmentally harmful plastic containers.

In New York State, a "Better, Bigger Bottle Bill" was recently promoted, but it was defeated in the state legislature. The objective was to expand New York's previous bottle bill to include deposits on non-carbonated beverages such as bottled water, iced tea, juice, and sports drinks, and require the beverage industry to return all unclaimed deposits to the state to fund recycling programs and other environmental programs.

The *Bigger Better Bottle* Bill was designed to: protect the environment and increase recycling; prevent litter and make our communities safer and cleaner; reduce waste disposal costs for municipalities and tax-payers; and create new jobs in the recycling and retail industries. (For more details on New York's "Bigger, Better Bottle Bill," check out the following website: http://www.nypirg.org/enviro/bottlebill/bottle billinfo.html)

In other communities, environmental groups continue to push for all-inclusive "bottle bills" that cover non-carbonated beverages such as bottled water. Some proposals call for a mandatory 10-cent return on all plastic beverage containers. (For more information, check out the following websites:

> http://www.bottlebill.org/
> http://www.toolkit.container-recycling.org/)

5. Establish "Right-To-Know" Legislation

As we have seen, one of the more disturbing features of the bottled water industry is the appalling lack of information about the contents of bottled water. As the NRDC Report emphasized, the public has as much right to know about the bottled water they are drinking as they do about the public water supplies in their communities, which are regulated by a state authority.

In the U.S., the Working Group on Community Right to Know and the Public Interest Research Group have been campaigning for the adoption of legislation requiring bottled water companies to provide the following information to the public about their products:

- the level, expressed in whole numbers, of any contaminant found in the water at a level in excess of a health goal plus the fluoride level and sodium level;
- the health goal and allowable level for those contaminants found in the water and noted above, in the same units;
- a statement as to whether the bottler is in substantial compliance with state and federal regulations (based upon an annual certification sent to the state and F.D.A. and not contested in writing by either), and if not, what violations occurred;
- a one-sentence lay-person-readable summary of the health effects associated with any contaminant found at a level in excess of a health goal (taken from model language written by the F.D.A and the E.P.A.);
- a simplified restatement of the EPA/CDC advice to immuno-compromised consumers about the types of bottled water treatment necessary to avoid cryptosporidium contamination, and whether the bottled water meets those criteria;
- the specific water source—e.g., "Philadelphia Public Water System"—and treatment process used (e.g., "reverse osmosis and ozonation");
- an F.D.A. toll-free number for consumers to obtain more information (or a referral to the E.P.A.'s drinking water hotline); and
- the bottler's street address, toll free phone number, and web and email address (if any) for further questions.

For more details, see http://www.crtk.org/detail.cfm?docID=677& cat=drinking%20water. In Canada, the Canadian Food Inspection Agency (CFIA) has produced a policy discussion paper called *Making It Clear: Renewing Federal Regulations on Bottled Water.* For details, check out: http://www.hc-sc.gc.ca/food-aliment/friia-raaii/frp-pra/water-eau/e_rfr_bottle_water_tofc.php.

In this policy document, the CFIA deals mainly with quality standards issues, classification (establishing new "common names"), labelling, and advertising methods. For example, "Making it Clear" itemizes issues directly related to labels, such as those requested in most right-to-know requirements — e.g., what can be called "natural," "pure," or "purified." It also addresses the issue of misleading vignettes (pictures).

Of particular interest, the government's policy would be that a label could depict a geographical feature such as a mountain or waterfall, but only provided that the feature can be seen from the collection point, and the collection point and the depicted geographical feature lie within the boundaries of the same local government unit, or within the boundaries of two separate local government units that are adjacent to one another. If either condition is not met, the label would have to bear a disclaimer, such as "Picture does not reflect the actual source." The disclaimer would have to be printed on the picture itself or immediately beside it. (Source: *Making it Clear Renewing Federal Regulations on Bottled Water: A Discussion Paper.* See p.6.6, Option A.)

It should be noted that some U.S. states, like Massachusetts, do provide public information on bottled water sold in their state, including the bottler's name, location, source, origin, and brands for bottlers within the state, and those from outside the state. For example, check out the Massachusetts information on bottled water at http://www.mass.gov/dph/fpp/bottledwater.htm.

In addition, the exclusivity contracts and proposals for the sale of bottled water in schools, colleges, and universities—plus all other public institutions—need to be subject to right-to-know legislation.

6. Certify Safe Bottled Water Brands

From the consumer standpoint, one way of controlling the quality and safety of bottled water products is to provide an independent and authentic means for certification. In its report, *Bottled Water: Pure Drink or Pure Hype?*, the NRDC made the following set of recommendations on the certification of bottled water:

In light of the poor government regulatory performance, an independent third-party organization such as Green Seal or Underwriters Labs should establish a "certified safe" bottled water program. Criteria for inclusion would be that the water always meets the strictest of all standards, including FDA, IBWA, international (e.g., EU and WHO) and state rules, recommendations, and guidelines; meets all EPA health goals, health advisories, and national primary drinking water regulations; is tested at least daily for microbial contaminants and quarterly for chemicals (monthly if using surface water or other water subject to frequent water quality changes); meets source-water protection criteria; is protected from Cryptosporidium in accordance with EPA-CDC guidelines; is disinfected; and is surprise-inspected twice a year by independent third-party inspectors. The certifying organization should establish an open-docket release of its inspection, testing, and compliance evaluation results. While the current NSF and IBWA seals are intended to provide such a stamp of approval, we believe a more independent and open body imposing stricter standards and making all testing, inspection, and other collected information readily available to consumers (including on the Web), would provide greater consumer confidence in the certification.[5]

Although these recommendations are made with respect to certifying bottled water in the U.S., they apply to the need for bottled water certification in Canada as well.

7. Overhaul Regulatory Agencies and Tools

Finally, the point is often made in various circles that little will be accomplished unless there is a corresponding overhaul of the regulatory agencies and tools at the level of our national governments. These concerns, of course, apply to many public policy issues besides bottled water. Nevertheless, it is worthwhile noting the following recommendations made in the 1999 NRDC Report in this regard.[6]

The F.D.A. rules for bottled water are weak and should be strengthened. If necessary, the F.D.A. should request additional legislative authority to adopt these changes. The FDA should:

- establish standards and monitoring requirements for bottled water no less stringent than E.P.A.'s rules for tap water in major cities, including standards for all microbiological and chemical contaminants,[7] specific and defined water treatment (including filtration and disinfection or strict source-protection requirements), operator-certification requirements, and unregulated-contaminant monitoring rules;
- set strict, up-to-date standards for contaminants potentially found in bottled water; these standards should be at least as protective of public health as the strictest regulations adopted by other authorities so standards should be as stringent as possible for the bottled water industry; and
- establish clearly defined criteria and protections for an "approved source" of bottled water under F.D.A. rules, and require annual state re-evaluation of compliance with these new "approved source" rules, including review of potential contamination problems.

5

ADDITIONAL RESOURCES AND TOOLS

TO FURTHER ASSIST CONCERNED CITIZENS and community groups in developing education and action initiatives on bottled water issues, here are some additional resources and tools.

North American Bottlers' List

The Bottlers' List contains the locations of bottling plants for each of the four majors. A number of U.S. states and some Canadian provinces require bottlers to register the bottling facilities that manufacture products sold in that territory. In order to catalog the highest number of records, different listings were used. This is necessary as products sold in one state, say Maine, are often bottled at different locations but not all locations supply that state. For example, a facility located in North Carolina supplies neighbouring states but would not supply Maine. Thus, this NC plant is not required to be listed on the state's inventory.

The most comprehensive inventory is Massachusetts' Survey of Bottled Water (MA). This particular inventory lists the bottling plant's address, the specific water sources, and the labels bottled. Most other registries only specify the facility's address. Other inventories used are: New York State Certified Bottled Water Facilities (NY), West Virginia Permitted Bottled Water Plants (WV), Alberta's Food Processing Directory for Non-Alcoholic Beverages (AB), Quebec's List of

Distributed Bottled Water (QC) and South Dakota Bottled Water Producers (SD). Polaris Institute research is indicated with a PI.

A "paste-check-add-sort" methodology was used to come up with the current list. That is, the MSBW listings were pasted on a spreadsheet program. Records available on the other inventories were carefully checked and added if lacking from the MSBW inventory. Finally, the records were sorted by major bottlers (4 categories).

INVENTORY	SOURCE		
AB	Food Processing Directory, Non-Alcoholic Beverages	Alberta's Agriculture, Food and Rural Development	www.agric.gov.ab.ca
MA	Survey of Bottled Water Sold in Massachusetts	Department of Public Health, Division of Food and Drugs	www.agric.gov.ab.ca
NY	New York State Certified Bottled Water Facilities	New York State Department of Health, Bureau of Public Water Supply ProtectioServices	www.health.state.ny.us
PI	Polaris Institute	From research conducted by the Polaris Institute	www.polarisinstitute.org
QC	Liste des eaux embouteillés distribuées au Québec	Quebec's Ministère de l'Agriculture, des Pecheries et de l'Alimentation	Requested and electronically sent
SD	South Dakota Bottled Water Producers	South Dakota Department of Environment and Natural Resources, Environmental Services	www.state.sd.us
WV	Permitted Bottled Water Plants	West Virginia Department of Health and Human Resources, Office of Environmental Health Services	www.wvdhhr.org

NORTH AMERICAN BOTTLERS' LIST

CODE	NAME/PLANT ADDRESS	SOURCE(S)	BRAND(S)
COCA-COLA			
AB	Coca-Cola Bottling Company 3851 23rd St. NE, Calgary, AB T2E 6T2	Public Water	Dasani
AB	Coca-Cola Bottling Ltd. 2920 9th Ave. N, Lethbridge, AB T1K 5E4	Public Water	Dasani
AB	Coca-Cola Bottling Ltd. 9621 27th Ave, Edmonton, AB T6N 1E7	Public Water	Dasani
AB	Nothern Bottling Ltd. 10014 102 St, Grande Prairie, AB T8V 2V6	Public Water	Dasani
MA	CCDA Waters, L.L.C. 1 AquaPenn Drive Milesburg, PA	Spring Water from, Bellefonte, PA	Dannon Spring Water Dannon Fluorided Spring Water Enon Springs Products Pure American Products Ritz Carlton Spring Water Vasa Spring Water Walgreens Products Crystal Lake Spring Water Sparkletts Products Publix Spring Water
MA	CCDA Waters, L.L.C. Grand Prairie, TX	Spring and well water from, Kirbyville, TX Keller, TX	Dannon Spring Water Walgreens Drinking Water Walgreens Distilled Water Sparkletts Purified Water Sparkletts Distilled Water Hill Country Spring Water Pure American Spring Water
MA	The Atlanta Coca-Cola Bottling Company Marietta, GA 1091 Industrial Park Drive Marietta, GA USA	Public Water from Marietta, GA	Dasani

CODE	NAME/PLANT ADDRESS	SOURCE(S)	BRAND(S)
COCA-COLA			
MA	Coca-Cola Bottling Company Jacksonville, FL	Public Water from Jacksonville, FL	Dasani
MA	Coca-Cola Bottling Company, Londonderry, NH	Public Water from Manchester, NH	Dasani
MA	Coca-Cola of New York, Inc 59-02 Borden Avenue, Maspeth, NY	Public Water from Valhalla, NY	Dasani
MA	Coca-Cola Consolidated South Atlantic Canners, Bishopville, SC	Public Water from Bishopville, SC	Dasani
MA	Coca-Cola Enterprises Twinsburg, OH	Public Water from Cleveland, OH	Dasani
MA	Coca-Cola Enterprises, Sandston, VA	Public Water from Richmond, VA	Dasani
MA	Coca-Cola Enterprises Washington, PA	Public Water from Pittsburgh, PA	Dasani
NY	The Philadelphia Coca-Cola Bottling Co. 725 East Erie Ave. Philadelphia, PA 19134 (215) 235-8374	Public Water	Dasani
NY	Cameron Coca-Cola Bottling Co. Washington, PA	Public Water	Dasani
PI	Ozarks Coca-Cola/Dr Pepper Bottling Company Springfield, MO	Public Water	Dasani
PI	Sacramento Coca-Cola Bottling Co., Inc. 2200 Stockton Blvd, Sacramento, CA. 95817 916.928.2300 Voice 916.731.5397 FAX	Public Water	Dasani

NORTH AMERICAN BOTTLERS' LIST (cont'd)

CODE	NAME/PLANT ADDRESS	SOURCE(S)	BRAND(S)
COCA-COLA			
PI	Swire Coca-Cola USA Bonneville Production Center of Utah 2269 South 3270 West West Valley City, UT 84119 (801) 816-5450	Public Water	Dasani
QC	Coca-Cola Bottling Embouteillage 1515 46 Ave. Lachine, QC H8T 2N8	Public Water	Dasani
QC	Coca-Cola Bottling 8500 boul. Industriel Tois-Rivières, QC G9A5E1	Public Water	Dasani
QC	Coca-Cola Bottling Co. Brampton	Public Water	Dasani
SD	Coca-Cola Bottling Company 2150 Coca-Cola Lane Rapid City, SD 57702	Public Water	Dasani
DANONE			
MA	Danone Naya Waters, Inc. Mirabel, Quebec, Canada	Spring Water from Mirabel, Quebec, Canada	Naya Spring Water
NESTLÉ S.A.			
MA	Nestlé Waters of North America, Inc Guelph, Ontario, Canada	Spring Water from: Guelph, Ontario Hillsborough, Ontario	Aberfoyle Spring Water Tim Horton's Spring Water Nestle Pure Life Purified Water Sam's Choice Purified Water Simply H2O Berkley & Jenson Purified Water
MA	Nestlé Waters of North America, Inc Breinigsville, PA	Spring water from: S. Coventry, PA New Tripoli, PA Pine Grove, PA Hegins, PA Bangor, PA Strousburg, PA Oakland, MD E. Stroudszburg Well Water from: Breinigsville, PA	Ice Mountain Products Great Bear Products Deer Park Products Nestle Pure Life Purified Water

CODE	NAME/PLANT ADDRESS	SOURCE(S)	BRAND(S)
NESTLÉ S.A. (cont'd)			
MA	Nestlé Waters of North America, Inc Ontario, Canada	Spring Water from: Cabazon, CA	Arrowhead Spring Water
MA	Nestlé Waters of North America, Inc Lee, FL	Spring and Well Water from: Lee, FL	Deer Park Spring Water Nestle Pure Life Purified Water
MA	Nestlé Waters of North America, Inc Hollis, ME	Spring Water from: Hollis, ME Scarborough ME Somerset County ME	Ice Mountain Spring Water Poland Spring Spring Water Deer Park Spring Water Nestle Pure Life Pruified Water Simply H2O Berkley & Jenson Purified Water
MA	Nestlé Waters of North America, Inc Ontario, Canada	Spring Water from: Palomar Mtn., CA Cabazon, CA	Ice Mountain Products
MA	Nestlé Waters of North America, Inc Red Boiling Springs, TN	Spring Water from: Red Boiling Springs, TN Hohenwald, TN Clarksville, GA Blue Ridge, GA Public Water from: Red Boiling Springs, TN Lebanon, TN Lafayette, TN Celina, TN Gallatin, TN	Nestle Pure Life Purified Water Sam's Choice Purified Water Simple H2O Berkley & Jenson Purified Water Deer Park Spring Water Ice Mountain Spring Water Nestle Pure Life Spring Water
MA	Nestlé Waters of North America, Inc Stanwood, MI	Spring Water from: Rodney, MI Well Water from: Stanwood, MI	Ice Mountain Products Nestle Pure Life Purified Water
MA	Nestlé Waters of North America, Inc Houston, TX	Spring Water from Walker County, TX	Ozarka Spring Water

NORTH AMERICAN BOTTLERS' LIST (cont'd)

CODE	NAME/PLANT ADDRESS	SOURCE(S)	BRAND(S)
NESTLÉ S.A. (cont'd)			
MA	Nestlé Waters of North America, Inc Hawkins, TX	Spring Water from: Hawkins, TX	Deer Park Spring Water Ozarka Spring Water Ice Mountain Products Nestle Pure Life Spring Water
MA	Nestlé Waters of North America, Inc Fort Worth, TX	Spring water from: Hawkins, TX Corpus Christi TX Henderson TX	Ozarka Spring Water
MA	Nestlé Waters of North America, Inc Zephyrhills, FL	Spring Water from: Montverde, FL Public Water from: Zephyrhills, FL	Aberfoyle Spring Water Nestle Pure Life Purified Water Deer Park Distilled Water Deer Park Drinking water Simple H2O Berkley & Jenson's Purified Water
MA	Poland Spring Poland, ME	Spring Water from: Poland, ME Scarborough, ME Somerset County, ME	Poland Springs Products Deer Park Products Ice Mountain Products
NY	Nestle Waters of North America, Inc. Hilliard, OH		
QC	Groupe Perrier du Canada Ltée. 3440 Francis-Hughes Laval, QC H7L 5A9		
WV	Nestle Waters of North America, Inc. Calistoga, CA	Spring Water	Calistoga Mountain Spring Water
PEPSICO			
AB	The Pepsi Bottling Group 4815 78th Ave. SE Calgary, AB, T2C 2Y9	Public Water	Aquafina

NORTH AMERICAN BOTTLERS' LIST (cont'd)

CODE	NAME/PLANT ADDRESS	SOURCE(S)	BRAND(S)
PEPSICO (cont'd)			
AB	The Pepsi Bottling Group 11315 182 St. Edmonton, AB, T5S 1R3	Public Water	Aquafina
MA	The Pepsi Bottling Group Harrisburg, PA	Public Water from: Harrisburg, PA	Aquafina
MA	The Pepsi Bottling Group Latham, NY	Public Water from: Latham, NY	Aquafina
MA	The Pepsi-Cola Company Cheverly, MD	Public Water from: Laurel, MD	Aquafina
MA	The Pepsi Bottling Group Johstown, PA	Public Water from: Johnstown, PA	Aquafina
MA	The Pepsi Bottling Group Mississauga, Ontario, Canada	Public Water from: Mississauga, Ontario Brampton, Ontario	Aquafina
MA	The Pepsi Bottling Group Knoxville, TN	Public Water from: Knoxville, TN	Aquafina
MA	The Pepsi Bottling Group Wytheville, VA	Public Water from: Wytheville, VA	Aquafina
NY	Pepsi Americas, Inc. 9300, Calumnet Ave. Munster, IN 46321 (219) 836-6365	Public Water	Aquafina

NORTH AMERICAN BOTTLERS' LIST (cont'd)

CODE	NAME/PLANT ADDRESS	SOURCE(S)	BRAND(S)
PEPSICO (cont'd)			
NY	Pepsi Bottling Ventures, 1900 Pepsi Way Garner, NC 27529 (919)861-8054	Public Water	Aquafina
PI	Lane Affiliated Companies Tucson AZ	Public Water from: Johnstown, PA	Aquafina
QC	TAlex Coulombe Inc. 2300 Jean-Talon Nord Sainte-Foy, QC	Public Water from: Mississauga, Ontario Brampton, Ontario	Aquafina
QC	Pepsi-Cola Canada Ltée. 3700 Boul. Thimens St-Laurent, QC	Public Water from: Knoxville, TN	Aquafina
SD	Pepsi-Cola Bottling Company 777 4th NW Huron, SD 57350	Public Water from: Wytheville, VA	Aquafina
WV	Pepsi Americas 1402 State Road 256 W. Austin, IN	Public Water	Aquafina
WV	The Pepsi Bottling Group 1555 Mack Ave. Detroit, MI	Public Water	Aquafina
WV	PThe Pepsi Bottling Group 2708 Federal Road Knoxville, TN	Public Water	Aquafina
WV	The Pepsi Bottling Group 4532 Highway 67 E Mesquite, TX	Public Water	Aquafina
WV	Pepsi Cola General Bottlers of Ohio Inc. 1999 Enterprises Parkway Twinsburg, OH	Public Water	Aquafina

Additional Corporate Data

In addition to the mini-profiles presented earlier here are additional notes on the big-4 players. These notes are based on more extensive corporate profiles prepared by Richard Girard of the Polaris Institute, which can be downloaded from the Polaris website www.polarisinstitute.org

THE COCA-COLA COMPANY

Organizational and financial information
The Coca-Cola Company employs 50,000 people worldwide and produces close to 400 individual brands.

2006 Financial Data
Coke is ranked 267th on the Fortune 500[1]

	2006	2005
Revenue (billions USD)	$24.08	$23.10
Profit	$5.08	$4.87

Corporate Structure
Coke's corporate structure is broken into 6 operating segments:

GEOGRAPHICAL AREA	% OF REVENUE (2006)
Africa	4.6%
East, South Asia and Pacific Rim	3.3
European Union	14.6
Latin America	10.3
North America	29.1
North Asia, Eurasia and Middle East	16.5
Bottling Investments	21.2
Corporate	0.4
TOTAL	100%

Executive Committee
- **Neville Isdell** – Chair of the Board and Chief Executive Officer
- **Gary P. Fayard** – Executive Vice President and Chief Financial Officer
- **Irial Finian** – Executive Vice President, Bottling Investments
- **Muhtar Kent** – President and Chief Operating Officer
- **Geoffrey J. Kelly** – General Counsel
- **Thomas G. Mattia** – Director, Worldwide Public Affairs and Communications

Coca-Cola executives have historically been awarded incredibly high levels of compensation through salaries, bonuses, and stock options. For example, in 2006, Coke Chief Executive Officer Neville Isdell received $7.5 million in salary and bonuses. Including stock options and awards, pension benefits, deferred compensation and other benefits, Isdell's total compensation reached $32.3 million in 2006.

Board of Directors
- **Herbert Allen** – President and Chief Executive Officer and Director of Allen & Company Incorporated, Contact info: (212) 832-8000
- **Ronald Allen** – Former Chief Executive Officer of Delta Airlines, Contact info: (404) 715-2581, (404) 715-6197
- **Cathleen Black** – President of Hearst Magazines, Contact info: (212) 649-2641
- **Barry Diller** – Chair of the Board and Chief Executive Officer of InterActiveCorp, Contact info: (212) 581-6433, (212) 314-7300
- **Donald Keough** – Chair of the Board of Allen & Company Incorporated, Contact info: (212) 832-8000
- **Donald McHenry** – Professor in the School of Foreign Service at Georgetown University. Owner and President of The IRC Group, Contact Info: mchenryd@georgetown.edu (202) 687-6083
- **Sam Nunn** – Former United States Senator from 1972 through 1996. Contact info: (404) 572-4949, (404) 572-4600
- **James Robinson III** –Co-founder and General Partner of RRE Ventures and Chairman of RRE Investors, LLC. Contact info: (212) 418-5100
- **Peter Ueberroth** – Chair of Contrarian Group. Former Commissioner of Major League Baseball, 1984-1989. Contact info: (949) 720-9646

- **James Williams** – Former Chief Executive Officer of Sun Trust Banks. Contact info: (404) 588-7711

Production

What does the Coca-Cola Company actually produce?
The Coca-Cola Company primarily produces syrups and concentrates that are sold to specific bottlers who are then authorized to distribute the finished product to retailers. Coke also produces and sells a limited number of finished drink products.

The bottling process: 'The Coca-Cola System'
Separate contracts, or bottler's agreements, exist between Coke and each of its bottlers regarding the manufacture and sale of Coke products. The Bottler's Agreements authorize the bottler to prepare designated Coke trademark beverages, package the drinks in authorized containers, and then sell the final product in an identified territory. Bottlers are obligated to purchase all of their concentrates and syrups from the company's suppliers.

Coke has three types of relationships with bottlers: they are either independently owned bottlers, with whom the company has no ownership interest; bottlers that the company has invested in, but has a non-controlling ownership interest; and bottlers that the company has invested in and has a controlling interest. The company makes investments in selected bottling operations in order to bolster production, distribution, and marketing, and to ensure operations are running smoothly. While the company bottles and sells a limited amount of Coke products from company controlled and consolidated bottling operations, most Coke products are produced and distributed by bottling operations not wholly owned by Coke.

According to Coke, in 2005, independently owned bottling operations produced and distributed approximately 25% of the company's worldwide volume, while 58% came from operations where the Coca-Cola Company had investments without controlling interests. Regardless of what Coke says about 'controlling interests' in bottlers, the company, as a 2003 Forbes article reported, "effectively controls them [bottlers] by maintaining big equity stakes and a heavy presence on their boards, and by providing their main source of business. Yet it keeps its stakes in the bottlers below 50%, thereby avoiding getting hit with their piles of debt and any unpleasant liabilities".

Public relations

"Helping people all over the world live healthier lives through beverages" — from Coke's Beverage Institute for Health and Wellness website

Public Relations Initiatives

Coke invests millions of dollars each year to convince the consuming public that their products are tasty, healthy, and life-enhancing. Coke looks to public relations firms, strategic alliances, targeted donations, and the creation of research institutes in order to downplay the risks of tooth decay or weight gain that are a result of consuming their products.

The Beverage Institute for Health and Wellness – In March 2004, Coke created a research institute to counter criticism about the role of soft drinks in the obesity epidemic threatening North Americans. Coke claims that the Institute "will support consumer and health professional education on a variety of topics, such as hydration, sweeteners, micro-nutrient deficiencies, weight management, and physical activity."[2]

Coke's Website – Coke uses its website to highlight many of its strategic programs and initiatives around the world. Many of these programs serve as public relations campaigns to boost the corporation's image. Coke consistently sets up websites designed to respond to any allegations that might harm the company image.[3]

Australian Sports Commission – In September 2004, the Australian Sports Commission released a report on children and sport. The report was funded by Coke, which poured hundreds of thousands of dollars into the research. The report barely mentions dietary intake and its impact on obesity.[4]

American Academy of Pediatric Dentistry – In 2003, Coke donated $1 million to the American Academy of Pediatric Dentistry (AAPD). The Center for Science in the Public Interest, started a campaign to end that partnership on the grounds that the AAPD, by partnering with Coke, was "burnishing the reputation of a company whose products cause tooth decay, obesity, and other health problems in children".[5]

American Council on Science and Health – The American Council on Science and Health (ACSH) is a self-described "consumer education consortium concerned with issues related to food, nutrition, chemicals, pharmaceuticals, lifestyle, the environment, and health."[6] The group is funded by a large number of corporations, including Dow Chemical, Eli Lilly and Shell, all of whom have an interest in presenting their products and operations as harmless. Coke has funded the Council in the past.[7] In 1999, ACSH President Elizabeth Whelan suggested reports claiming that Coke was making European children ill were based on mass hysteria: "Coke should simply announce: 'There is no health hazard at all from our product. It is a figment of your imagination'."[8]

BrightHouse (marketing firm) – Coke's former Vice President of Advertising said that BrightHouse is "fundamental and central to everything that we do on a global basis". What makes BrightHouse noteworthy is the BrightHouse Neurostrategies Institute in Atlanta, which opened in 2001 to undertake research examining how the human brain responds to advertising campaigns.[9] BrightHouse then uses the information to design more effective marketing strategies for its customers. The main centre for this kind of research in the United States is in the neuroscience wing at Emory University in Atlanta, where CEO Neville Isdell sits on the board of trustees. Emory's neuromarketing research is a project of The Neurostrategies Institute. BrightHouse's "thought sciences" website claims that this type of knowledge of the brain will "help establish the foundation for loyal, long-lasting consumer relationships not easily superseded by the competition".[10]

Advertising and Marketing

> In the packaged water business, people pay for a product because they know it is safe, high quality, available, and convenient. When The Coca-Cola Company sells drinking water in its various forms, it is not charging for the water per se, but rather for the value we add to the water to make it a branded beverage.
>
> —from Coca-Cola's website

In 2006, Coke spent $2.6 billion on the production of print, radio, television, and other advertisements. The payoff for such large investments in advertising and branding has helped Coke maintain its position as the world's most valuable brand.[11]

Exclusivity Contracts

A number of schools and universities have begun campaigns designed to terminate these contracts. While campaigns at public schools are usually concerned about health issues, students at a growing list of universities and colleges in Canada, the United States, Ireland, Italy, and the UK are working to end their schools' exclusivity contracts with Coke due to the company's alleged human rights abuses in Colombia.

Many schools have conducted successful campaigns against Coke which have resulted in either:

- the early termination of exclusive contracts;
- the commitment on the part of university administrations and student bodies to not renew existing contracts,
- resolving not to renew contracts or
- the temporary suspension of the sale of Coke products.

As of March 2006, that list includes the following schools: Bard College, New York; Carleton College, Minnesota; College of DuPage, Illinois; Hofstra University, New York; Lake Forest College, Illinois; Macalester College, Minnesota; McMaster University, Hamilton; National College of Art and Design, Ireland; New York University, New York; Oberlin College, Ohio; Oxford University, UK (Wadham, St. John's, St. Hilda's JCR); Roma Tre, Rome, Italy; Rutgers University, New Jersey; Salem State College, Massachusetts; School of Oriental and African Studies (SOAS), UK; Sussex University, UK; Swarthmore College, Pennsylvania; Union Theological Seminary, New York; Trinity College, Ireland; University College, Dublin; Salem State College; University of Guelph — Student Union, Canada; University of Michigan, Michigan, Flint, Dearborn; University of Santa Clara, California.

For updates to this ever-expanding list of schools, please check: http://www.killercoke.org/active-in-campaign.htm

Industry and International Associations

Coca-Cola is aligned with several industry-related groups. The company's involvement with these organizations gives them tremendous power in the formation of legislation favourable to the non-alcoholic beverage industry, and to the corporation itself.

US Council for International Business – The USCIB advocates for US-based corporations with the goal of influencing "laws, rules and policies that may undermine U.S. competitiveness, wherever they may be".

American Beverage Association – Donald R. Knauss, President and Chief Operating Officer of Coca-Cola North America, is on the ABA's board of directors. The Association serves as a liaison between the industry, government, and the public, and represents the industry in legislative and regulatory matters.

Grocery Manufacturers Association – The Grocery Manufacturers Association represents the interests of food manufacturers in the United States. Coke's CEO Neville Isdell sits on the GMA's board of directors.

United Nations Global Compact – Coke became a participant of the United Nations Global Compact in 2006. The Global Compact, a voluntary initiative, is an agreement based on ten principles of human rights, environmental protection, and labour rights designed to promote 'responsible corporate citizenship'. In 2004, EarthRights International stated that the Global Compact "provides little but a public relations cover for global corporate malefactors."[12]

Corporate welfare
In a number of cases Coke has received public money to undertake various projects around the world. Some examples are listed below.

Waste & Resources Action Programme (WRAP): In a major case of corporate greenwashing, WRAP, a Government funded programme in the UK, established to promote resource efficiency, granted Coca-Cola Enterprises £145,000 of public money to carry out trials of redesigned, lighter bottles and to test the use of recycled plastic.[13]

Overseas Private Investment Corporation (OPIC): OPIC provides low-cost financing and insurance to US companies investing in foreign markets. OPIC helped open three separate Coke ventures in Russia with more than $244 million in OPIC Insurance. OPIC backs the company's production and bottling plant in Moscow, its regional distribution center in St. Petersburg, and its soft drink and mineral water bottling plant in Stavropol.[14]

International Finance Corporation (IFC): Coke and its bottlers have received millions of public dollars from the IFC to help finance the company's expansion in the Global South. The IFC is providing $35 - 40 million to South Africa's Coca-Cola Sabco Group (24% of which is owned by Coke) for the expansion of production facilities throughout Southern and Eastern Africa.[15] South Africa is Coke's largest profit and volume country on the continent. The IFC is a member of the World Bank Group.

Environmental Issues

Australia – Coca-Cola Amatil, Coke's main Australian bottler, (Coke has a 34% interest), has come up against fierce resistance from local residence in Gosford, Australia, over its Peats Ridge Springs water bottling plant. Coca-Cola Amatil bought Peats Ridge Springs bottled water company in June 2003. Later that year, Coca-Cola Amatil sought to expand operations and triple the amount of water extracted annually from the local aquifer. In May 2005, the city council rejected the proposed expansion saying they would wait for the results of a report by the Department of Natural Resources on groundwater supplies and the impact of water extraction on the local water system. Instead of waiting for the report Coke responded by taking the city council to the New South Wales Land and Environment Court claiming that their application to increase output from its Peats Ridge plant had already been granted by the Department of Natural Resources and Planning.

In October 2005, the court ruled in Coca-Cola's favour, saying that the company could go ahead with its proposed expansion on a 2-year trial basis with certain restrictions.

In March 2006, the aquifer mysteriously dropped nearly to the point where Coke would have had to stop water bottling entirely. The aquifer was nearing 10 metres below ground level – the point at which the company was required to cease production altogether and contact the Department of Natural Resources under a licence condition. Coca-Cola Amatil corporate affairs manager Alec Wagstaff said that a 'third party' had extracted a huge amount of water, thus impacting the aquifer. Local residents said that Coca-Cola Amatil was to blame for the dropping water levels.

Coca-Cola Amatil immediately applied to the Land and Environment Court to have the 10 metres below ground level condition removed from its license. In response to Coke's move, the Gosford city council said that they would use any legal means necessary to stop the company from changing a key condition of its water extraction license. Coke won its legal battle to change the 10 metre aquifer drawdown limit to 15 metres despite numerous claims by farmers and the city council that the bottling plant is the source of the water scarcity problems. Three hydrogeologists, one acting for Coca-Cola Amatil, one for Gosford Council and one for the Natural Resources Department, agreed on the new 15 metre mark.

India - Coke has had a long and volatile relationship with India. The company began selling its products there during the 1950s, but was kicked out in 1977 for violating India's investment laws. India's Foreign Exchange Regulation Act required multinationals to sell 60% of their equity to an Indian interest. Coke refused, and was forced to leave the country. In 1993, amid a new political and economic climate of liberalized trade and investment policy, Coke was allowed back into the country, where they promptly purchased the leading domestic soft drink brand.[16] Since then, Coke has invested more than $1 billion in India. The company operates 27 wholly owned bottling plants, another 17 franchise-owned bottling operations and the company is keen to expand its presence in a country that offers such a huge market for its products.[17]

Since 2002, Coke has come face-to-face with strong resistance from all levels of Indian society to their ongoing water takings, their polluting business practices, and to the discovery of high levels of pesticides in their products. The fight against Coke has spread to other parts of the country, beginning a movement that could bring about a repeat of the events of 1977.

In August 2005, the Sate of Kerala's Pollution Control Board issued a report that found heavy metal concentrations of cadmium in the sludge and effluent originating from the Kerala plant. The concentration levels were 400-600% above permissible limits. A Supreme Court Monitoring Committee that inspected the plant site and surrounding area found that due to the "operation of the company severe pollution was caused to the drinking water source of a large number of people who are dependent upon well water."[18]

In Plachimada, local farmers watched their wells dry up and crop yields shrink, forcing many to abandon their farms. Despite the region's extended droughts, Coke continued to extract water, while 2000 families in the area were being adversely affected by the lack of water.[19]

In January 2004, the Indian Parliament banned the sale of Coke and Pepsi in its cafeteria after tests found high concentrations of pesticides and insecticides in the colas, making them unfit for consumption.[20] Some samples showed toxin levels 30 times the standard allowed by the EU.

Human Rights

Coke's connections to Nazi Germany

"It is a fact that the soft drinks giant from Atlanta, Georgia collaborated with the Nazi-regime throughout its reign from 1933 to 1945 and sold countless millions of bottled beverages to Hitler's Germany."

—from "Coca-Cola Goes to War", Jones and Ritzman

In 1929, during a period of virulent anti-Americanism, Coke entered Germany with the subsidiary Coca-Cola GmbH. Germany would soon become the company's second biggest market.

Coke's success in Germany during the 1930s, went from sales of 0 cases in 1929 to four million in 1939. So successful was Coke in Germany that while the country was being destroyed in 1944, the company still sold two million cases.[21]

Nazi-collaborator Max Keith was in charge of Coke's German operations. His strategy was to please the Nazis whenever possible and through any means possible.

By 1939, Coke had established itself to such a degree that Keith was appointed to the Office of Enemy Property and was sent to supervise Coca-Cola businesses in Italy, France, Holland, Luxembourg, Belgium, and Norway.[22]

Meanwhile, in the US, the domestic war-time advertising strategy helped transform the Coke brand into a symbol of the United States and made it possible for Coca-Cola to become the American icon that it is today. Unbeknownst to the population in the United States, or to the American soldiers fighting in Europe, their enemy was enjoying the same beverage in Germany with a similar patriotic zeal.[23]

Coke in Colombia

Since 1989, seven union leaders and one plant manager employed at Coca-Cola bottling operations in Colombia have been murdered by right wing paramilitary groups. Hundreds of other Coke workers and their family members have been tortured, kidnapped or illegally detained by these same groups.[24] For Coke, the repression of organized labour helps cut production costs.

There is substantial evidence linking managers of several bottling plants to the paramilitary groups carrying out the attacks. In one case, a plant manager publicly announced that he had ordered the paramilitary to destroy the workers' union SINALTAINAL.[25]

United Steelworkers of America (USWA) lawyer Dan Kovalik has pointed out that "if any of these plants make a mistake in applying Coca-Cola's formula or in delivering Coke, they would be there to correct it, but in cases where they kill union leaders, they do nothing."[26]

The cycle of intimidation and violence towards Coke workers in Colombia continues today. Samples of Coke's Colombian track record include the following:

- On June 3rd 2005, paramilitaries in Barranquilla kidnapped five students who were working with SINALTRAINAL on Coke's environmental record. The students were threatened with death if they ever protested outside a Coke plant again. They were released the same day.[27]
- On April 20th 2004, a number of armed men entered the house of Coke worker and union activist Efrain Guerrero's brother-in-law in Bucaramanga and opened fire at the family. The gunmen killed Guerrero's brother-in-law, Gabriel Remolina, his wife Fanny Remolina and one of their children, Robinson Remolina.[28]
- On November 17th 2004, paramilitaries delivered death threats to the regional headquarters of the CUT (a Colombian labour federation) in Bucaramanga. The letter read as follows:

This threat is directed towards those trade unionists who oppose the governor, the mayor and those private companies who are supporting the policies of the government of Dr Alvaro Uribe Velez. We inform you that we have made a military judgment to force you from the areas under our influence, or to kill you. We will show no mercy to those trade unionists who have initiated legal proceedings against government or private company officials. For this reason we have declared the following as military objectives:

David Florez
Martha Diaz
Teresa Baez
Efraín Guerrero
Carlos Castro
Javier Jiménez
Rafael Ovalle

—Autodefensas Unidas de Colombia (AUC),
Santander.

All of the people mentioned in the letter are members of the CUT. Efrain Guerrero works at Coke's Bucaramanga plant and is the leader of SINALTRAINAL at the facility. This is the second time that Guerrero has received death threats.[29]

Guatemala

Coke has an appalling record of labour abuses in Guatemala dating back to the late 1970s and early 1980s. In 1976, workers at a Coke bottling plant in Guatemala began a nine-year struggle against their employer. During that time, three general secretaries of their union were assassinated while members of their families, friends, and legal advisors were threatened, arrested, kidnapped, beaten, tortured, shot, or forced into exile. After a long battle, with the support of international solidarity campaigns, STEGAC, the Coke workers union, won its fight against the corporation.[30]

Turkey

In November 2005, a lawsuit was filed against Coke charging that managers at the company's bottling facility in Dudullu, Turkey, hired a branch of the Turkish police to beat former plant employees who had joined the union Nakliyat. The former workers – truck drivers and other transport workers - were protesting the firing of close to 100 employees who had joined the union. According to the lawsuit, which was filed by the International Labor Rights Fund, the attacks were designed to coerce and intimidate union members into abandoning their effort to form a union at the Coke facility, and to terrorize the workers into accepting the firing of union activists. Along with Coke, Coca-Cola Export Corp. and Coca-Cola Icecek (Coke's Turkish bottler) were named as defendants in the suit. The ILRF's lawsuit alleges that on May 19, 2005, Coca-Cola Icecek representative Sinan Oksay told workers, "go on working by resigning from the union, otherwise, we as The Coca Cola Company, shall let no members of the union work for us."[31]

Racial discrimination in the workplace
In April 1999, a group of Coke employees filed a class-action lawsuit accusing the corporation of systemic racial discrimination against African Americans. The lawsuit was brought by four current and past employees on behalf of almost 2000 other former and current Coke employees. The class action lawsuit brought together a damning list of improper corporate behaviour including discriminatory evaluations, compensation and promotions, glass ceilings, and glass walls, as well as a higher rate of terminations for black employees.[32] After a long legal battle, a settlement was reached in November 2000, when Coke agreed to pay out a record $192.5 million, the largest settlement in a US race discrimination lawsuit. Despite denying any wrongdoing, Coke agreed to pay $113 million in direct compensation and another $43.5 million towards the elimination of pay disparities.[33]

In 2002, two years after the settlement was reached, the court-appointed panel in charge of monitoring Coke's human resources practices found that minority employees at Coke continued to have issues with fairness in career advancement, pay decisions, and the company's commitment to equal opportunity.[34]

PEPSICO

Organizational and financial information
PepsiCo employs 157,000 people worldwide, and produces dozens of products from its main brands Frito-Lay, Pepsi-Cola, Quaker, Tropicana and Gatorade.

2006 Financial Data
PepsiCo is ranked 175th on the Fortune 500[35]

	2006	2005
Revenue (billions USD)	$35.13	$32.56
Profit (billions USD)	$5.06	$4.07

Corporate Structure

PepsiCo's corporate structure is broken into 4 principal divisions:

SEGMENT	2006 REVENUE (billions USD)	% of total
PepsiCo International	$12.95	37
Frito-Lay North America	$10.84	31
PepsiCo Beverages North America	$9.56	27
Quaker Foods North America	$1.76	5
TOTAL	$35.13	100

Executive Committee

- **Indra K. Nooyi** – Chief Executive Officer, Chair of the Board of Directors
- **Richard Goodman** – President and Chief Financial Officer
- **Albert P. Casey** – Chairman and Chief Executive Officer, Frito-Lay North America
- **Dawn Hudson** – President and Chief Executive Officer, Pepsi-Cola North America
- **Michael D. White** – Vice Chairman of the Board of PepsiCo and Chairman and Chief Executive Officer of PepsiCo International
- **Charles I. Maniscalco** – President and Chief Executive Officer QTG (Quaker Foods, Tropicana, Gatorade)

Board of Directors

- **John F. Akers** – Former Chairman of the Board and Chief Executive Officer, International Business Machines
- **Robert E. Allen** – Former Chairman of the Board and Chief Executive Officer, AT&T
- **Dina Dublon** – Consultant, Retired Chief Financial Officer, JPMorgan Chase
- **Victor J. Dzau, M.D.** – Chancellor for Health Affairs, President & CEO, Duke University Health Systems, Duke University Medical Center
- **Ray L. Hunt** – Chief Executive Officer, Hunt Oil Company and Chairman, Chief Executive Officer and President Hunt Consolidated, Inc.

- **Alberto Ibargüen** – President and Chief Executive Officer, John S. and James L. Knight Foundation
- **Arthur C. Martinez** – Former Chairman of the Board, President and Chief Executive Officer Sears, Roebuck and Co.
- **Indra K. Nooyi** – Chief Executive Officer, Chair of the Board, PepsiCo
- **Sharon Percy Rockefeller** – President and Chief Executive Officer, WETA Public Stations
- **James J. Schiro** – Chief Executive Officer, Zurich Financial Services
- **Franklin A. Thomas** – Consultant, TFF Study Group
- **Daniel Vasella** – Chairman of the Board and Chief Executive Officer, Novartis AG
- **Michael D. White** – Vice Chairman of the Board and Chairman and Chief Executive Officer, PepsiCo International

Production – What does the company produce

Similar to Coca-Cola, much of PepsiCo's revenue from the beverage side of its business comes from the sale of syrups and concentrates to various bottlers. Approximately 10% of PepsiCo's net revenue comes from the sale of concentrates and syrups to the Pepsi Bottling Group (PBG). At the end of 2004, PepsiCo owned approximately 46% of PBG's operations.[36]

I addition to concentrates and syrups, PepsiCo manufactures snack foods and cereal products through its Frito-Lay and Quaker brands.

Public relations

In 2006 PepsiCo spent $1.7 billion on advertising.[37] The company looks to advertising and public relations firms, as well as the formation of strategic alliances and donations to help promote its image and products. Some examples include:

- **Marketing to Teenagers** – In an attempt to attract teenagers to their products, PepsiCo has opened three Pepsi Zone lounges in California, Florida and Illinois. The lounges feature couches, plasma TV screens, video games and computer stations. Everything is free except for the lounge's vending machines which carry carbonated and non-carbonated Pepsi products. PepsiCo will evaluate the effectiveness of attracting young customers before deciding on an expansion plan.[38]

- **False Advertising** – In June 2005, PepsiCo agreed to end its claims that Tropicana orange juice reduces the risk of heart disease and strokes. The move came after the United States Federal Trade Commission (FTC) said there was no scientific evidence to support the statement. Advertisements pushing Tropicana's Healthy Heart brand claimed that drinking two to three cups of the juice a day would lower blood pressure within six to eight weeks. PepsiCo is now prohibited from making similar claims unless they are supported by "competent and reliable scientific evidence."[39]
- **Product Placement** – Paying to have their products appear in movies or television shows is nothing new for companies like PepsiCo. However, when PepsiCo products popped up in one of California Governor Arnold Schwarzenegger's political commercials, product placement reached new limits. In May 2005, a television commercial promoting Schwarzenegger's ballot agenda, featured the Governor in a cafeteria talking to Californians with snack food items spread around the table. Labels for PepsiCo products including Diet Pepsi, Sobe, Cheetos, Ruffles and Sun Chips were all clearly visible along with Arrowhead water, a Nestlé product.[40] PepsiCo donated $20,000 to Governor Schwarzenegger's California Recovery Team during the 2003-2004 election period.[41] In contrast to the Governor's promotion of PepsiCo products in March 2005 he proposed a ban on all junk food in schools. Pepsi was also promoted in Schwarzenegger's movie Terminator 2.[42]

Industry and International Associations
PepsiCo is a member of the following powerful business and industry associations.

US Council for International Business – David Wright, Vice President of Government Affairs at PepsiCo, sits on the USCIB's Executive Board. An example of the USCIB's power comes from early 2003, when the group joined food industry groups and the Sugar Association (the main industry association representing big US sugar producers) in writing to US health secretary Tommy Thompson asking him to push for the withdrawal of a World Health Organization report on healthy eating. The report sets guidelines which say that sugar should only account for 10% of a healthy diet and that soft drink consumption has contributed to the obesity epidemic. Sugar industry associations threatened to use their lobbying power to get the United States Government to withdraw its $406 million funding of the WHO if the report was not withdrawn.[43] The National Soft Drink Association said the reports guidelines for sugar were "too restrictive" and "not based on the best available science".[44]

USA-Engage – PepsiCo is a member of USA-Engage, a broad-based organization representing individuals and corporations who view the US' unilateral economic sanctions imposed on various countries as damaging to the US economy.[45]

National Foreign Trade Council – PepsiCo is a member of the NFTC's Board of Directors. The NFTC is an organization that advocates for the international and public policy priorities of its business members.

American Beverages Association – The Association serves as a liaison between the industry, government and the public, and represents the industry in legislative and regulatory matters. PepsiCo is well represented at the ABA with no less than five representatives on their Executive Board and Board of Directors.

Grocery Manufacturers Association – The Grocery Manufacturers Association is a powerful lobby group that represents the interests of food manufacturers in the United States. Both PepsiCo and the Pepsi Bottling Group Inc. are members of the GMA

Corporate Welfare

Overseas Private Investment Corporation (OPIC): OPIC provides low-cost financing and insurance to U.S. companies investing in foreign markets. Pepsi has been the recipient of millions of dollars in corporate welfare from OPIC.[46] For example, in 1998 OPIC provided Pepsi-Cola General Bottlers with $50 million in political risk insurance for the company's planned expansion into Russia.[47] Pepsi-Cola General Bottlers is owned by PepsiAmericas which is 40% owned by PepsiCo.

International Finance Corporation (IFC): Pepsi and its bottlers have received millions of dollars from the IFC to 'help' finance the company's expansion in the South. In one case the IFC is provided a Russian bottling operation and Pepsi with loans to begin bottling Pepsi products. The Russian company will act as the exclusive Pepsi bottler for Central and Eastern Russia.[48] The IFC is a member of the World Bank Group and states that it "promotes sustainable private sector investment in developing countries as a way to reduce poverty and improve people's lives."[49]

Tax Breaks at home: PepsiCo is listed in 15th position in a 2000 report by the Institute on Taxation and Economic Policy on the top 25 corporate tax break recipients in the United States between 1996 and 1998. PepsiCo received $1.4 billion in tax breaks during this time.[50] The report also states that PepsiCo paid no federal income taxes in 1998.

PepsiCo in India

PepsiCo's operations in India are increasingly coming under fire for water takings and the presence of pesticides in their drinks. While The Coca-Cola Company has received most of the criticism in India over the past few years, local residents and activists are beginning to target Pepsi for equally egregious violations. The following list documents a few of Pepsi's recent problems in India.

March 2005 – Thousand of people demanding the closure of Coke and Pepsi factories in the Palakkad district formed a human chain between Pepsi's bottling plant in Kanjikode and Coke's operation in Plachimada. Protesters included political leaders, students, environmentalists and community members.[51]

January 2005 – Activists from several organizations along with thousands of residents and school children formed a human chain demanding the closure of a Pepsi bottling plant in Mandideep (Bhopal).[52]

December 2004 – Both Coke and Pepsi were ordered by India's Supreme Court to label their products stating the amount of pesticide residues in their soft drinks. The court ruled that consumers had a right to know what they were drinking. Both Coke and Pepsi had challenged the order saying that their products in India were as safe as anywhere else in the world.

October 2004 – PepsiCo was forced to pull an advertisement after child labour activists said the commercial depicted child labour. The ad showed a boy carrying a tray of Pepsi bottles to cricket players on the playing field. The Andhra Pradesh High Court issued an order banning the advertisement saying that no television commercial should be televised "depicting or glorifying child labour."[53]

January 2004 – In January 2004 the Indian parliament banned the sale of Coke as well as Pepsi products in its cafeteria after tests found high concentrations of pesticides and insecticides, including lindane, DDT, malathion and chlorpyrifos, in the colas, making them unfit for consumption.[54] Some test samples showed toxin levels 30 times the standard allowed by the European Union. The conflict began in August 2003 when an independent environmental group, the Centre for Science and the Environment, found that pesticide residue in the drinks were 11 and 30 times higher than the level permitted by the European Union.[55]

Human Rights/Labour Track Record

> "Given the interest in worker rights in Coca Cola production facilities around the world we should not forget the PepsiCo appears to be denying these rights as much if not more systematically in many of its facilities around the world".

—Ron Oswald, IUF General Secretary.

PepsiCo and its affiliated bottlers around the world have a poor labour track record. While many campaigns surrounding The Coca-Cola Company's labour track record, PepsiCo has been able to go about its business outside of the spotlight. Unlike its main competitor where there is a relatively high presence of unions, PepsiCo has effectively avoided or resisted unions. This has left many PepsiCo workers unorganized and voiceless, leaving the stories of abuse untold and the company's practices unchallenged.[56] The following list provides a sample of PepsiCo's labour abuses and the strike actions taken against the company and its affiliated bottlers in the past 5 years.

Argentina
In early 2002, in the wake of Argentina's economic crisis, 52 temporary workers were fired from one of PepsiCo's potato chip factories in Buenos Aires Province. When the workers refused to leave the factory PepsiCo brought in security guards who used force in an attempt to remove the fired workers who are not part of the union. Permanent workers, who are part of a union, quickly organized

actions to resist the mass firing. In response, the company deployed armed security guards to patrol the factory. Other security guards have spied on workers in the lunchroom, while the police tailed unionists' cars in order to intimidate and divide the permanent and temporary workers.[57] The struggle for the rights of temporary workers continues.

Barbados

The Barbados Workers' Union (BWU) took action against Pepsi over the company's refusal to recognize the union and the firing of four employees. The union accused the company of anti-worker and anti-union sentiment and of disrespecting Barbadians.[58] Port workers joined that action by slowing down the handling of Pepsi products. The dispute ended after the company finally recognized the union.

Burma

In January 1997 PepsiCo announced that it would no longer do business in Burma. PepsiCo entered Burma in 1991 only three years after the military took control of the government The company stayed while others like Levi Strauss were leaving due to the country's poor human rights situation and use of slave labour. In 1996, in a New York Times article, PepsiCo's spokesperson at the time, Elaine Franklin, said that PepsiCo was in Burma for the long haul.[59] In April 1996, only months after the New Times article was published, PepsiCo announced that it would sell its bottling plant in Burma citing pressure from a student-led boycott and shareholders who wanted PepsiCo out of the country.[60] It wasn't until January 1997, however, that PepsiCo withdrew its operations from the country. The Student-led boycott of PepsiCo and its products had expanded to over 100 campuses across North America and had a powerful hand in forcing PepsiCo out of Burma.[61]

Guatemala

Sixty six union workers at PepsiCo's Guatemala operations in La Mariposa, were fired in 2002 and replaced by non-union sub-contracted workers with lower wages and benefits. Thirty of the 66 continue to struggle for reinstatement of their jobs and refuse to accept severance payments from PepsiCo.[62] The labour struggle at the La Mariposa plant goes back to 2000 when the previous collective agreement expired. Rather than renewing the agreement, management used bribes and intimidation to induce members to leave the union. In the end, the 66 union members were fired. The company has refused to implement orders from two different courts to reinstate the workers.[63]

India

In 2000 workers at a Pepsi bottling plant in Kanpur India, changed unions from the right leaning Bharatiya Mazdoor Sangh (BMS), who had secured wages just above the paltry minimum wage, to the leftist Centre of Indian Trade Unions (CITU). One month later the plant management fired the union President and its Joint Secretary for an alleged sabotage. Both were nowhere near the area where the alleged sabotage took place. Workers at the factory demanded an inquiry. They eventually became tired of the management's inaction and threatened a one-day strike. In response the management locked out the workers. [64]

Poland

In late December 2004 eight women were dismissed from PepsiCo's Frito-Lay plant near Warsaw after talking amongst themselves about sexual harassment at the plant. For two years women working on the night shift at the plant were allegedly sexually harassed under threat of dismissal. After the women began discussing the harassment, the night shift supervisor and the human resources manager called upon the eight women to resign with compensation or be fired. The workers' union representative was not at work that day. A few days later, the women filed a report of sexual harassment with the Labour Court. Soon after the charges were filed representatives from the union representing the plant workers met with the women's employer hoping to persuade the company to investigate the allegations and reinstate the women. The company refused.

Three of the women claim that they have been victims of sexual harassment while the remaining five substantiate their claims. Two lawsuits have been filed, one under labour law and another under criminal law. After the cases were the filed the supervisor allegedly involved in the harassment was arrested. He however continues to draw his salary from the company and receives legal counsel for his defence.

The International Union of Food, Agricultural, Hotel, Restaurant, Catering, Tobacco and Allied Workers' Associations (IUF), maintains that by refraining from taking the necessary measures to protect its employees from sexual harassment, PepsiCo is in breach of both European and Polish law.[65]

United States

Minnesota – Four hundred workers went on strike at a Pepsi Bottling Group plant in Minneapolis in June 2000 over wages, pension plans, job security and affordable health insurance. As in other strike situations, Pepsi employed scab labour to maintain plant operations. After 12 weeks on the picket lines, the union agreed to a contract with favourable language.[66]

Missouri – In February 2001, 200 bargaining unit members went on strike at two Kansas City area PepsiAmericas bottling operations. The workers struck after Pepsi's final offer on matters involving contract language on insurance benefits and wages was deemed unacceptable. Pepsi brought in managers from operations in surrounding states to continue production.[67] By April of the same year, the strike had not been resolved and Pepsi began hiring permanent replacements, an action that clearly shows their unwillingness to negotiate with organized labour.[68]

New Jersey — In August 2005, approximately 300 loaders, truck drivers, and other members of Teamsters Local 830 in Pennsauken, New Jersey, went on strike over health care issues. The issue surrounds Harold Honickman, the owner of the plant, who asked each worker to pay more than $100 a month for health care coverage. The President of Local 830 commented on the Honickman's request saying that "It's outrageous that the owner of this company would ask our hardworking members to shell out money for health care...The company is claiming it has an economic need, but Honickman is one of the wealthiest people in the United States."[69] Honickman owns a number of Pepsi bottling and delivery plants in Southern New Jersey. He was also on the 2004 Forbes wealthiest Americans list. On September 16 the workers ratified a new four-year contract. The union was able to fight off the company's attempt to force workers to pay for health care coverage.[70]

About 700 drivers, stock clerks, warehouse workers, sales representatives, vending machine repairers and production personnel struck at four Pepsi Bottling Group facilities in Piscataway, Moonachie, Asbury Park and Hanover in June 2001. The workers went on strike over salaries, overtime pay for commission based workers and workshift issues.[71] Workers agreed to a new contract after 7 weeks on the picket lines while Pepsi continued to run operations with managers and replacement workers. No real gains were made for the workers.[72]

In March 2003, Pepsi Bottling Group settled more than eight years of litigation agreeing to pay more than $25 million to workers for overtime they had worked. The case began in 1995 when the State Labour Department fined Pepsi for failing to pay overtime to its customer service representatives at 5 New Jersey facilities. The workers fought Pepsi all the way to the Supreme Court and finally prevailed.[73]

Texas – In November 2002 close to 70 workers at the Pepsi Bottling Group's (PBG) Austin voted to join Teamsters Local 657. The workers voted to unionize when PBG suddenly changed the pay scale from an hourly rate to a commission system which resulted in a pay cut. When the employees sat down with the company to agree on a contract, PBG refused to negotiate. The workers say that management has skipped scheduled meetings and consistently refused to offer anything beyond a contract the union has repeatedly found unacceptable. It is believed that the company is trying to slow down the process until the workers become frustrated with the union and vote to decertify. Workers claim that PBG has withheld pay increases received by nonunion employees at other PBG locations in order to discourage the unionized workers.[74] While PBG claims that they have been bargaining in good faith, the National Labor Relations Board (NRLB), designed to arbitrate labour disputes between unions and management, has filed five complaints against PBG in Austin. A complaint filed by the NLRB indicates that the union's charges of bargaining in bad faith hold water.[75] Regardless of the NLRB's actions, PBG continues to claim innocence. As of September, 2005, there is no update on the situation.

Plant closures

PepsiCo announced in September 2004 that it would be closing four facilities across the United States. The company announced that it would be closing 4 Frito-Lay plants located in Allen Park, Michigan, Council Bluffs, Iowa, Beaverton, Oregon and Visalia, California. The closures will result in the elimination of approximately 780 jobs.[76] The day after the move was announced, the Mayor of Allen Park, Marcy DeGiuli-Galka called the closure a "devastating loss of both jobs and tax base at a time of already high unemployment...This impact will send shock waves not only through Allen Park, but also through Downriver and the state of Michigan."[77]

NESTLÉ

Organizational and financial information

Nestlé employs 250,000 people and claims to have factories or operations in every country in the world. Nestlé boasts a portfolio of hundreds of different brands.

2006 Financial Data

Nestlé is ranked 53rd on the Fortune 500[78]

	2006	2005
Revenue (billions USD)	$80.70	$74.72
Profit	$7.53	$6.55

REGION	2006 (billions USD)	% of total
Zone Europe	21.87	27
Zone Americas	$25.63	32
Zone Asia, Oceania and Africa	$12.65	15
Nestlé Waters	$7.88	10
Other activities (Pharmaceutical products, joint ventures)	$12.63	16
TOTAL	$80.70	100

Corporate Structure

PRODUCT	2006 (billions USD)	% of total
Beverages	$21.32	26
Milk products, nutrition and ice cream	$20.96	26
Prepared dishes and cooking aides	$14.53	18
Chocolate, confectionary & biscuits	$9.39	12
PetCare	$9.40	11
Pharmaceutical products	$5.50	7
TOTAL	$80.70	100

Revenue by product

Executive Board
- **Werner Bauer** – Executive Vice President, Executive Vice President, Chief Technology Officer
- **Peter Brabeck-Letmathe** – Chair of the Board and Chief Executive Officer
- **Paul Bulcke** – EVP: United States, Canada, Latin America, Caribbean
- **Luis Cantarell** – EVP, Zone Europe
- **Francisco Castaner** – EVP, Pharmaceutical & Cosmetic Products, Liason with L'Oréal, Human Resources, Corporate Affairs
- **Carlo Donati** – EVP, Nestlé Waters
- **Richard Laube** – Deputy EVP, President CEO of Nestlé Nutrition
- **Lars Olofsson** – EVP, Strategic Business Units and Marketing
- **Frits van Dijk** – EVP: Executive Vice President (EVP) Zone Asia, Oceania, Africa, Middle East

Nestlé executives have historically been awarded incredibly high levels of compensation through salaries, bonuses, and stock options. For example, in 2005, Chief Executive Officer Brabeck-Letmathe received $11.2 million USD in salary and bonuses.

Board of Directors

- **Peter Brabeck-Lemathe** – Term expires 2007, Chair of the Board, CEO
- **Günter Blobel** – Term ends in 2009, Professor Blobel heads Rockefeller University's Laboratory of Cell Biology, blobel@mail.rockefeller.edu Gunter.Blobel@mail.rockefeller.edu
- **Peter Böckli** – Term expires 2008, Board memberships: Assivalor AG; Doerenkamp-Stifung; Hason Ag; Holler-Stiftung; Manufacturer des Montres Rolex S.A.; UBS AG; Vinetum AG. Böckli is a former professor of business and tax law at the University of Basel
- **Daniel Borel** – Term expires 2009, Chairman of computer hardware company Logitech
- **Jean Rene Fortou** – Term expires 2011, Chairman of the Supervisory Board of Vivendi Universal
- **Edward George** – Term expires 2007, Member of the Committee to the Board and the Remuneration Committee
- **Rolf Hanggi** – Term expires 2009
- **Steven George Hoch** – Term expires 2011, Founder and Senior Partner of Highmount Capital, a U.S.-based investment management firm
- **Naina Lal Kidwai** – Term expires 2011, Chief Executive Officer of HSBC India and Country Head of HSBC Group Companies in India
- **Andreas Koopman** – Term expires 2008, CEO of Bobst Group SA.
- **André Kudelski** – Term Expires 2006, Chair and CEO of Kudelski Group.
- **Jean-Pierre Meyers** – Term expires 2011, Vice-Chair of the Bettencourt-Schueller Foundation
- **Carolina Müller-Möhl** – Term expires in 2009, Müller-Möhl is Chair of the Müller-Möhl group
- **Kaspar Villiger** – Term expires 2009

Production – What does the company produce?

Nestlé has six main international corporate brands: Nestlé; Nescafé; Nestea; Maggi; Buitoni; and Purina. These six brands account for about

70% of the corporation's sales. In addition to the six main brands, Nestlé is involved in the production of a wide variety of products from baby food to pet foods and pharmaceuticals. The company's operational performance is broken into eight product sections: Beverages; Milk products; Nutrition and Ice cream; Prepared dishes and cooking aids; Chocolate and confectionary and biscuits; PetCare; Associated companies; and Pharmaceutical and cosmetic joint ventures.

Its main brands include:

Beverages – Nestlé is one of the world's largest producers of both coffee and bottled water.

- **Water**[79] – Nestlé is responsible for dozens of different brands of bottled water around the globe, some of their main international brands include: Nestlé Pure Life[80]; Nestlé Aquarel[81]; AcquaPanna; Perrier; S. Pellegrino; Vittel; and Contrex.
- **Coffee** – In 1937 Nestlé developed its instant coffee brand, Nescafé. Since then, Nestlé has become one of the big four coffee roasters in the world along with Kraft (Maxwell House), Proctor and Gamble (Folgers), and Sara Lee (Douwe Egberts). These four corporations buy nearly half of the world's raw coffee beans and account for 60% of retail sales in the United States.[82] Some of Nestlé's main coffee brands include: Nescafé; Nesscau; and Nespresso. These brands are linked to dozens of other coffee products that range from instant coffee to single serving coffee beverages to coffee syrup. Nestlé's coffee brands can be purchased around the world.
- **Chocolate/Malt beverage area** – Nestlé's main powdered chocolate and malt drinks are Nesquik and Milo.
- **Ice Tea/Fruit Juice** – Through their Libby's brand, Nestlé bottles a range of fruit juices under the Juicy Juice brand in the United States. Nestlé's ice tea brand Nestea, produces a wide variety of cold tea and powdered beverages.

Milk Products, Nutrition and Ice Cream – This group includes breakfast cereals, ice cream, yogurt, infant formula, energy bars, Ice cream, dairy products and health care nutrition for people under medical care.

Some brand names include: Cereal, Shredded Wheat, Shreddies and Cherrios (UK only); Ice cream, Nestlé, Frisco, Motta, Camy,

Savory, Peters, Häagen Dasz, Mövenpick, Schöller, Dreyer's, Extreme/ Drumstick; Performance nutrition, PowerBar, Nesvita, Neston; Health care nutrition, Nutren, Peptamen, Modulen; Infant nutrition, Nestlé, Nan, Lactogen, Beba, Nestogen, Cérélac, Neslac, Nestum, Guigoz, Good Start; Dairy, Carnation, Coffee Mate, Nido, Nespray, La Lechera, Milkmaid, Gloria, Svelty, Sveltesse, La Laitière; Infant nutrition, Alete (Germany), Baeren Marke (Germany), Beba (Germany), Nestlé Baby, Nestlé Babymilk, Very Best Baby (USA); Health care nutrition, Crucial, Nutren, Peptamen, Glytrol, Modulen, Nubasics.

Pet Care – Nestlé is the world's largest pet food manufacturer. It entered this sector in the 1990s with the purchase of Alpo pet food and then expanded into its present dominant role with the $10.3 billion acquisition of Ralston Purina in 2001. Other Nestlé pet food brands include: Alpo (USA); Beneful (USA); Fancy Feast (USA); Felix (Europe); Friskies (Japan, USA); Go Cat (UK); Gourmet Gold (UK); Mighty Dog (USA); Pro Plan (USA); Purina (5 continents); ONE (USA); Tidy Cats (USA); Vital Balance (UK); Vitalife (Brazil); Winalot (UK).[83]

Chocolate and Confectionary – Nestlé began selling chocolate in 1904 and over the years has expanded its chocolate and candy operations to include the following brands: After Eight; Nestlé Allstars; Baci; Butterfinger; Cailler (Switzerland); Choco Crossies (Germany); Chokito (Hungary); Crunch: Frutips (New Zealand); Kit Kat; Lifesavers (Australia); Lion (Germany); Milky Bar (New Zealand); Negrita (Chile); Nestlé Toll House (USA); Passatempo (Brazil); Perugina (Italy, USA); Powerbar (USA); Rowntrees (UK); Smarties (UK); Wonderball (USA); Wonka (USA).

Prepared Dishes and Cooking Aids – This category includes packaged soups, frozen meals, prepared sauces and flavorings. Nestlé's main brands in this category include: Buitoni (pasta and sauces, Italy); Lean Cuisine (frozen foods); Libby's Pumpkin; Stoufer's; Maggi (soup mix, sauces flavourings); Ortega (USA).

FoodServices – Nestlé FoodServices distributes Nestlé brand foods and beverages to restaurants and food service providers. Some of their products include Coffee machines

Pharmaceutical and cosmetic joint ventures

* **Alcon** – Continuing in their diverse line of operations, Nestlé owns Alcon, a large US pharmaceutical and eye care corporation. Alcon produces drugs, surgical products and consumer eye care products. Nestlé acquired Alcon in the mid-1970s.
* **Galderma** – Pharmaceutical company. Galderma was created in 1981 from a joint venture between L'Oréal and Nestlé. Galderma produces pharmaceuticals for the treatment of dermatological illnesses.
* **L'Oréal** – The cosmetic giant is controlled by French holding company Gesparal, of which 51% is held by the Bettencourt family and 49% by Nestlé.

Public relations

Nestlé knows that its questionable actions, past and present, have put the corporation at a great reputational risk. To combat there reputation problems, they have developed a large public relations machine. The company spends billion of dollars every year on public relations and advertising firms in order to strategically construct their image as an altruistic, caring and health promoting corporation. Nestlé's 2006 annual report states that the company spent 32.50 billion Swiss Francs ($26.73 USD) on "marketing and administrative expenses."[84]

Nestlé also relies on its own publications and website for public relations. The company has a website dedicated specifically to the infant formula question.[85] The site counters every criticism leveled against the company, leaving the public to question the validity of the wealth of information condemning Nestlé's track record. They go as far as providing a link to organizations such as Baby Milk Action and the International Baby Food Action Network (IBFAN). Nestlé has also been known to ask for meetings with groups like IBFAN to discuss infant formula issues and then claim that the two are working together as partners.[86]

Another document posted on Nestlé's website entitled "Nestlé in the Community", describes how the company is committed to the well being of the countries in which they operate. In the document, Nestlé attempts to project a clean image by highlighting their aid projects and financial donations around the world.[87]

Baby Milk Action has published a document exposing Nestlé's public relations machine. The document compares what Nestlé says about the marketing of infant formula, WHO code violations and their ostensible commitment to Africa, with the reality which is Nestlé's intense public relations campaigning.[88]

Advertising and Marketing

Infant Formula[89] *"Those who make claims about infant formula that intentionally undermine women's confidence in breastfeeding are not to be regarded as clever entrepreneurs just doing their job but as human rights violators of the worst kind"* From a speech by Stephen Lewis titled "Malnutrition as a human rights violation: Implications for United Nations-supported programmes"[90]

Along with chocolate, coffee and water, the Nestlé name is probably best known for its unethical marketing of infant formula. According to UNICEF, "If every baby were exclusively breastfed from birth for six months, an estimated 1.3 million additional lives would be saved and millions more enhanced every year". [91] As one of the world's largest producers of artificial baby milk, Nestlé has a hand in this ongoing tragedy. Nestlé knows that once a mother changes from breastfeeding to bottle feeding, she will stop producing milk and not go back. The negative impact of marketing of infant food – which does not contain the natural antibodies found in breastmilk, is expensive, and in some cases is mixed with unsafe drinking water – has been described as commerciogenic malnutrition.[92] In other words, the act marketing of infant formula for the purpose of making money causes malnutrition.

Since 1977, Nestlé's unethical marketing of infant formula has been the target of an international boycott initiated by Infant Formula Action Coalition (INFACT) which was later joined by other organizations to become the Infant Baby Formula Action Network (IBFAN). The successful boycott continued until 1984 when Nestlé finally agreed to implement the World Health Organization's 1981 International Code of Marketing of Breastmilk Substitutes. The boycott resumed, however, in 1988 after numerous code violations by the company were uncovered.[93] The International Code bans all promotion of bottle feeding and sets out requirements for labeling and information on infant feeding.[94]

IBFAN has been documenting Nestlé's numerous violations Code since 1984. In 2004, IBFAN along with a number of other groups, say that Nestlé is continuously violating the International Code. The corporation's interpretation of the Code includes only infant formula and follow on formula, but excludes baby foods, gruels, teas, juices and bottles. Even under this limited interpretation, the company is violating the Code. IBFAN's recent report "Breaking the Rules, Stretching the Rules 2004" reports that Nestlé continues to break the code in a number of countries by: promoting formula to the public; promoting its products at the point of sale; promoting its products in health facilities by giving out free samples and supplies; giving gifts to health care workers; comparing their products to breastmilk; and using misleading text an pictures.[95]

In countries where the International Code has not been adopted and where national codes are inadequate or have expired, Nestlé engages in aggressive and competitive marketing practices. IBFAN says that they "only abide by the code grudgingly when forced".[96] While the profile of the boycott is not as high as it was during the late 1970s and early 1980s, the message about Nestlé's practices is still being heard. In 2004 a UK breast cancer charity refused a 1 million pound promotional deal with Nestlé because of concerns over the corporation's continuing promotion of infant formula in the South.[97]

Industry and International Associations

Nestlé is a member of a number of influential business associations and lobby groups in both the United States and Europe. Their membership in these powerful groups provides the corporation with further links and influence to policy makers in the European Union and in the United States government.

International Food & Agriculture Trade Policy Council (IPC) – Nestlé is a member affiliate of the IPC and Hans Johr, the company's Corporate Head of Agriculture and Assistant Vice President, sits on the IPC's board of directors. The IPC is a strong advocate for the liberalization of trade in the food industry. While the IPC states that its members serve as individuals and do not represent their respective institutions, many of its members are high ranking executives at large multinationals such as Cargill, Monsanto, and Archer Daniels Midland who themselves strongly advocate for further trade liberalization. Along with high powered executives, the IPC members include politicians and World Bank officials.[98] The IPC is funded by Archer Daniels Midland, Cargill, Kraft and Monsanto among others.

US Council for International Business (USCIB) – Nestlé USA is also a member of the USCIB.

Grocery Manufacturers Association – The Grocery Manufacturers Association is a powerful lobby group that represents the interests of food manufacturers in the United States. Nestlé USA is a member. Brad Alford, Chair and CEO of Nestlé USA sits on the GMA's board of directors.

National Confectioners Association – This US based industry association works to advance the interests of its members in the candy industry. The NCA has come under criticism from fair-trade advocates due to its reluctance to encourage its members to use fair trade cocoa in their products.[99] The NCA is a member of the International Confectionery Association.

Chocolate Manufacturers Association – Nestlé is a member of this powerful industry association.

Other Cocoa and Chocolate trade associations looking out for Nestlé's interests include: the Association of the Chocolate; Biscuit & Confectionery Industries of the EU; the Federation of Cocoa Commerce Ltd.; the Cocoa Merchants Association of America; and the European Cocoa Association and the World Cocoa Foundation.

National Coffee Association of the USA – Rob Case, President of Nestlé USA's beverage division sits on the NCA's Board of Directors. In addition to Case, three Nestlé executives sit on the NCA's Government Affairs committee: one on the Market Research Sub-Committee; two on the Public Relations Committee; one on the Scientific Advisory Group; and two on the Technical and Regulatory Affairs Sub-Committee. The NCA rejects claims by groups who see the coffee industry as the cause of low coffee prices and increased poverty among the world's coffee producers.[100]

International Association of Infant Food Manufacturers (IFM) – The IFM represents infant food manufacturers at a number of international agencies including UNICEF, WHO, and the FAO. The IFM is a lobby group protecting the interests of large multinationals like Nestlé.

World Economic Forum (WEF) – As a strategic partner Nestlé contributes resources and support to the WEF in its mission to advance neoliberal economic policies along with the interests of its corporate members. Two thousand political, business and academic elites meet in Davos Switzerland for the WEF's annual meetings. The WEF takes credit for launching the Uruguay Round of the General Agreement on Trade and Tariffs which led to the creation of the World Trade Organization.[101] Nestlé CEO Peter Brabeck-Letmathe is a member of the WEF's Foundation Board and a number of other Nestlé executives are WEF contributors or serve on various boards and committees.

European Roundtable of Industrialists (ERT) – This exclusive group of close to 50 chairpersons and CEOs of some of Europe's largest corporations has been a powerful force in European politics since it was founded in 1983. Nestlé CEO Peter Brabeck-Lemathe's membership in the ERT gives his corporation privileged access to governments and the European Commission. This access gives Nestlé incredible power in shaping the political agenda of the European Union.[102]

United Nations Global Compact – Nestlé became a participant of the United Nations Global Compact in 2004.

Human Rights
Child labour, Chocolate – In all likelihood, at some point the chocolate used to produce such popular candy treats such as Smarties and Kit Kat was produced from cocoa beans that were picked by child slaves or child labourers working in hazardous conditions. Nestlé, along with other chocolate manufacturers purchase much of their cocoa from the Ivory Coast which accounts for over 40 percent of the world's supply. The impact large cocoa multinationals have on economic conditions in the Ivory Coast help produce an environment where child labour is able to flourish. Multinationals using commodity market pricing do not guarantee the minimum price cocoa growers need to cover costs, thus forcing cash strapped farmers to find the cheapest form of labour.[103] A 2002 study quoted by the US State Department's country report on human rights for Cote d'Ivoire, found that between 5,000 and 10,000 children were trafficked to or within the country to work full or part time in the cocoa sector. The study also found that approximately 109,000 (70 percent of which worked on family farms) child labourers worked in hazardous conditions on cocoa farms in the country in what the study described as the worst forms of child labor.[104]

While it is difficult to know for sure if Nestlé's chocolate products contain cocoa produced through child slavery or child labour, a number of NGOs and labour rights groups are continuously putting pressure on Nestlé and other chocolate manufacturers to stop using products sourced from child slavery. Most recently, In July 2005, Nestlé, along with Archer Daniels Midland and Cargill, were sued for using forced child labour. The suit alleges the companies' involvement in the trafficking, torture and forced labour of children who cultivate and harvest cocoa beans which the companies import from different countries in Africa. The lawsuit was filed in a Los Angeles Federal District Court and was brought under two US federal statutes, the Torture Victims Protection Act and the Alien Tort Claims Act.[105] The Washington D.C. based International Labor Rights Fund (ILRF), along with Alabama based civil rights firm Wiggins, Childs, Quinn & Pantazis, LLC, filed the suit on behalf of a class of Malian children who were trafficked from Mali into the Ivory Coast. The lawsuit's background facts state that the defendants "not only purchased cocoa from farms and /or farmer cooperatives which they knew or should have known relied on forced child labor in the cultivating and harvesting of cocoa beans, but Defendants provided such farms with logistical support to do so with little or no restrictions from the government of Cote d'Ivoire."[106]

The lawsuit is in response to the passing of a July 1, 2005 deadline voluntarily set by the chocolate industry known as the Harkin-Engel Protocol. The Protocol was announced in September 2001 by US Senator Tom Harkin, Representative Eliot Engel and large chocolate manufacturers (through the Chocolate Manufacturers and the World Cocoa Foundation) as an attempt to eliminate the worst forms of child labour in the West African cocoa industry. A central part of the Protocol was an obligation by companies to implement an independent and credible system of farm monitoring, certification and verification for their suppliers, to ensure no child labour was taking place. The certification system requires manufacturers to affix labels to chocolate products declaring no child labour was used in their production. The ILRF said in that the chocolate industry failed to establish such a system by the July 1 deadline[107] and that the Protocol is failing to produce any real effective change on the ground.[108]

China – Baby Milk Action reported in 2002 that a Chinese refugee in Australia asserted that she and 130 other prisoners in a Beijing labour camp were forced to manufacture toy rabbits bearing the Nestlé brand name.[109] While Nestlé denied that their products came from forced labour camps, Swiss newspaper Le Temps, found troubling coincidences between the location of a MiQi Toys factory, the company contracted by Nestlé to produce the toy rabbits, and the prison labour camp.[110]

Colombia – Since 1986 ten Nestlé employees who were members of Colombia's Food and Drink Union, SINALTRAINAL have been assassinated or have disappeared.[111] There is no evidence directly connecting Nestlé to the murders, which were most likely carried out by Colombia's paramilitary forces.[112] Nestlé in Colombia has repeatedly been implicated in union busting and a number of cases in recent years indicate a sustained effort by the company to remove SINALTRAINAL's presence from its Colombian operations. After the most recent murder of a SINALTRAINAL leader in September 2005, the union made the following statement regarding the continuing oppression of labour activists in Colombia: "We repudiate this horrendous murder that adds LUCIANO ENRIQUE ROMERO MOLINA to the interminable list of assassinated union leaders in Colombia, [carried out] within the strategy of State Terrorism and through the persecution unleashed by the corporations to exterminate the trade union movement. We condemn once again the government of Álvaro Uribe Vélez and his deceitful 'peace process' with the paramilitary groups, which continue to massacre the unarmed population.

El Salvador – In April 2003, Nestlé employees at the company's instant coffee plant in Ilopango were informed that the plant would be closed due to a production transfer. Employees were offered two months' salary by management who refused to negotiate when the union requested that the terms of the collective agreement be respected until its expiration date at the end of the year. Nestlé promptly closed the factory gates, which housed the union's headquarters, and stated that if employees did not sign the severance agreement it would be forfeited. The union occupied the plant in order to gain access to their office and continue a campaign for a negotiated conclusion. The union campaign and International pressure pushed the local management to the negotiating table at the end of June where the essential demands of the union were met.[113]

France – In November 2003, Nestlé Waters division announced a major shakeup of employment practices at Perrier, expected to impact a quarter of the workforce, after the parent company decided its subsidiary was not making enough money. The French Confédération Générale du Travail (CGT) union, which represents over 80 percent of the workers at the Perrier factory in Southern France, opposed Nestlé's move and forced the corporation to withdraw its restructuring plans.[114] Nestlé threatened to sell the company or move it overseas if the CGT kept obstructing its plans. Finally, in May 2005, after more than a year of disputes, the company and the French unions reached an agreement to cut staff and improve productivity at Perrier. Under the agreement 356 of the 1,650 workers at the Verge'ze factory in Southern France will leave on early retirement packages over the next two years. The French government agreed to finance part of the early retirement program.[115]

South Korea – Demanding an 11.7% pay increase and union participation in management decisions, workers at Nestlé's South Korean operation went on strike.[116] The strike action also came after the company unilaterally transferred 44 employees to a new distribution division, a move that was widely seen as a prelude to subcontracting and layoffs.[117] In August 2003 the company shut its office in Seoul and locked out union workers at its production facility and at warehouse and distribution centres across the country. Nestlé threatened to pull out of the country, violating OECD Guidelines on Multinational Enterprises which prohibit the threat of production transfers as a tool for pressure in the context of union negotiations. A Provincial Labour Relations Committee determined that Nestlé's tactics of refusing to negotiate and threats of moving production out of the country were unfair and illegal, and that the company carried out intimidation and intervention during the negotiations. The Committee instructed Nestlé to enter into negotiations with the union. The negotiated collective agreement established a joint union-management committee and provided for a 5.5 wage increase.[118]

Philippines – Workers at two Nestlé facilities in the Philippines have taken different strike actions against the company since 1997. In both cases there have been violent clashes between the strikers and police along with company security guards.

- **Quezon City, Magnolia factory** – In early 1997, Philippine trade union IBM took strike action after new Nestlé management refused to negotiate with trade unions, dismissed eight union officers along with two union members and then suspended 200 other workers. Employees and supporters organized a permanent protest outside the factory. Incidents of violence took place including the intervention of 300 security guards and 50 police officers.[119]
- **Cabuyao** – In 2002, workers at Nestlé Philippines Cubayo plant went on strike citing unfair labour practice and bargaining. The

union was fighting to include retirement benefits as a collective bargaining issue. In March 2003, the union received a decision from the Philippines Court of Appeals affirming the union's stand that benefits are a mandatory bargaining issue. The Court also ordered Nestlé to return to the negotiating table. In June 2003, plant management had yet to implement the Court's decision. In response 700 workers and supporters attempted to take over the factory, but were violently turned back by 300 security guards and police. Fifty workers and security guards were injured in the clash. [120]

- **Cubayo** – On September 22, 2005, a trade union leader at the Nestlé factory in Cabuyo, Laguna was murdered by unidentified gunmen while on his way home from a picket line at the factory. Diosdado Fortuna headed the Union of Filipino Employees-Drug and Food Alliance which has been on strike since Jan. 14, 2002 in a dispute over bringing retirement benefits within the collective bargaining process, which Nestlé management rejects. Fortuna's wife quickly blamed Nestlé management for his death saying "my husband has no other enemy except Nestlé management."[121] The International Union of Food, Agricultural, Hotel, Restaurant, Catering, Tobacco and Allied Workers' Associations (IUF) called on the government of the Philippines to undertake a full investigation into the murder.[122]

GROUPE DANONE

Organizational and financial information

Groupe Danone employs 89,500 people worldwide. The company has 201 production facilities worldwide, out of which approximately 40% were located in Europe, 45% in the Asia-Pacific region and 15% in the rest of the world. Danone's two largest sources of bottled water, both located in France, accounted for 22% of Danone's total production capacity for water in 2005.[123]

	2006	2005
Revenue (billions USD)	$18.56	$17.40
Profit (billions USD)	$1.88	$1.56

2006 Financial Data

BUSINESS LINE	2006 REVENUE (billions USD)	% of total
Fresh Dairy Products	$10.55	56.4%
Beverages	$5.18	28.0%
Biscuits and Cereal Products	$2.83	15.6%
TOTAL	$18.56	100%

Groupe Danone is ranked 407th on the Fortune 500[124]

Corporate Structure
Executive Committee
- **Franck Riboud** – Chairman and Chief Executive Officer
- **Jacques Vincent** – Vice-Chairman and Chief Operating Officer
- **Georges Casala** – Executive Vice-President, Biscuits and Cereal Products
- **Emmanuel Faber** – Executive Vice-President, Asia-Pacific
- **Antoine Giscard d'Estaing** – Executive Vice-President for Finance, Strategy and Information Systems
- **Bernard Hours** – Executive Vice-President, Fresh Dairy Products
- **Simon Israel** – Chairman, Asia-Pacific
- **Thomas Kunz** – Executive Vice-President, Beverages
- **Philippe-Loïc JACOB** – Company Secretary
- **Franck Mougin** – Executive Vice-President, Human Resources
- **Sven Thormahlen** – Vice President Research & Development

Board of Directors
- **Franck Riboud** – Chariman and CEO, Groupe Danone
- **Jacques Vincent** – Vice Chairman and Chief Operating Officer, Groupe Danone
- **Emmanuel Faber** – Chairman and CEO, Blédina SA
- **Bruno Bonnell** – Chairman of the Board of Directors, Infogrammes Entertainment SA, Infogames Interactive SA, IDRS, Chairman of the Board and Chief Executive Officer, Atari Inc

- **Michel David-Weill** – Associate-Manager: Maison Lazard SAS, Partena (SCS), Partemiel (SNC), Chairman, Lazard LLC, Maison Lazard SAS
- **Richard Goblet d'Alviella** – Director and member of Audit Committee: Suez-Tractebel, Delhaize Group, SES Global
- **Hirokatsu Hikanu** – Chairman, Yakult Life Service Co, Ltd
- **Christian Laubie** – Member, Haut Conseil du Commissariat aux comptes
- **Jean Laurent** – CEO, Crédit Agricole SA
- **Hakan Mogren** – Chairman, Affibody AB, Vice Chairman and Chief Operating: AstraZeneca plc
- **Jacques-Alexandre Nahmias** - Chairman and CEO, Pétrofrance Chimie SA
- **Bernard Hours** – Vice Chairman and Chief Operating, Danonesa Tikvesli Süt Ürünleri Sanayi Ve Ticaret A.S
- **Benoît Potier** – Chairman of Management Board, Air Liquide SA

Production – What does the company produce

Since 1998 the company has focused on three core activities: the production of fresh dairy products, including yogurts, dairy desserts and infant foods; beverages; and biscuits and cereal products.

Advertising and Marketing

In 2006, Danone spent $4.84 billion on what they call 'selling expenses', which includes advertising and promotional expenses, distribution costs and costs relating to the sales force.

Industry and International Associations

Grocery Manufacturers Association – Group Danone's US subsidiary, Dannon Company Inc. is a member of the Grocery Manufacturers Association.

International Association of Infant Food Manufacturers (IFM) – Blédina, Groupe Danone's infant food subsidiary is a member of the IFM, which represents infant food manufacturers at a number of international agencies including UNICEF, WHO, and the FAO. The IFM is a lobby group protecting the interests of large multinationals like Danone.

United Nations Global Compact – Danone became a participant of the United Nations Global Compact in 2003.

CORPORATE WELFARE

In 1995, Danone and the European Bank for Reconstruction and Development (EBRD) formed a 'multi-project facility', a form of financial cooperation, to co-invest in dairy, confectionery and mineral water companies in the EBRD's countries of operations. The EBRD's facility was worth up to $100 million and provides equity financing, on a partnership basis with Danone, for projects in the region.[125]

With this financing from the EBRD, Danone has invested in five projects at production facilities, all owned by Danone, in Russia, Bulgaria, Romania and Poland.[126]

ENDNOTES

INTRODUCTION

1   Conversation between Dr. Joan Davis and Tony Clarke in Zurich, Switzerland, October 30, 2005.

PART 1: THE BOTTLED WATER INDUSTRY

1   Christopher Hamlin, "Waters or Water? – Master Narratives in Water History and their Implications for Contemporary Water Policy," *Water Policy*, vol. 2, 2000, p. 320.
2   Maude Barlow and Tony Clarke, *Blue Gold: The Battle Against the Corporate Theft of the World's Water*, Chapter 6.
3   Ibid.
4   Groupe Danone, "1999 Annual Report," 2000.
5   Anonymous, "Packaging: Anytime, Anywhere: Self-Heating Containers," *Beverage Industry*, Jun. 2004, http://www.bevindustry.com/content.php?s=BI/2004/06&p=14.
6   Jenny Wiggins, NEWS DIGEST, January 6, 2006.
7   Maude Barlow and Tony Clarke, *op. cit.*
8   Anonymous, "Bottled Water Now Number-Two Commercial Beverage in U.S.," *Beverage Marketing Corporation*, Apr. 8, 2004
9   Datamonitor, "Canada—Bottled Water: Industry Profile," Jan. 1, 2003, p. 4.
10 Kathy Noël, "La fontaine de jouvance d'une generation inoxydable," Les Affaires, May 1, 1999, p. 5.
11 For further details see: I.H. Suffet, "Bottled Water," UCLA Department of Environmental Health Sciences, http://www.ioe.ucla.edu/publications/report01/BottledWater.htm.
12 Packaged Facts, "Bottled Water: Compiled From The U.S. Market For Bottled, Enhanced And Flavored Water," Mar. 2004, p. 10-11.
13 Ibid.
14 Ibid.
15 Packaged Facts, *op. cit.*, p. 25.

THE BIG-4 CORPORATE PLAYERS
NESTLÉ

    Nestlé Group, "2006 Financial Statements".
2   Nestlé Group Official Website, http://www.nestle.com/All_About/All+About+Nestle.htm.
3   Nestlé Group Official Website, http://www.nestle.com/All_About/Glance/Introduction/Glance+Introduction.htm.

4   Nestlé Group Official Website, http://www.nestle.com/Our_Brands/Bottled_ Water/Overview/Bottled+Water.htm.

5   Beverage Marketing Corporation.

6   Nestlé Group Official Website, http://www.nestle.com/All_About/Nestle_ Management/Board_Directors/CV/Peter+BR ABECK+LETMATHE.htm.

7   Center for Responsive Politics, Washington, DC at www.opensecrets.org

8   Summary of the WHO code regarding food and milk substitute for children, http://www.infactcanada.ca/Breastfeeding Protection and the International Code (print format).pdf.

9   Infant Feeding Action Coalition (INFACT) Canada, "Nestle WHO Code violations," http://www.infactcanada.ca/obstinat.htm.

10 Arrowhead Water Official Website, https://eservice.arrowheadwater.com/ service/help/environment.aspx.

11 Packaged Facts, *op. cit.*, p. 22.

12 For more details see: http://www.uwec.edu/grossmzc/SCHWARMJ/.

13 Packaged Facts, *op. cit.*, p. 23.

Coca-Cola

1   The Coca-Cola Company Website, http://heritage.coca-cola.com.

2   The Coca-Cola Company, "2006 Annual Report, 10-K Form".

3   Coca-Cola Enterprises, "2006 Annual Report".

4   Anonymous, "Coke to Push Bottled Water Brand in Spain," *Beverage Daily*, Oct. 29, 2002.

5   Nikhil Deogun, "The Really Real Thing: Coke to Peddle Brand of Purified Bottled Water in U.S.," *Wall Street Journal*, Nov. 3, 1998.

6   Scott Leith and Henry Unger, "Water Wars: Coca-Cola and Pepsi Go to Glove in a New Arena," Atlanta Journal-Constitution, Feb. 24, 2002, p. G1.

7   The Coca-Cola Company, "2003 Annual Report".

8   The Coca-Cola Company, "2005 Annual Report".

9   Ibid.

10 Ibid.

11 Richard Girard, "The Coca Cola Company: Inside the Real Thing," Polaris Institute, August 2005, http://www.polarisinstitute.org/files/Coke%20profile%20 August%2018.pdf .

12 Centre for Responsive Politics http://www.opensecrets.org/.

13 C. Surendranath, "The Heat is On in Plachimada," India Resource Center, Apr. 14, 2004, http://www.indiaresource.org/ campaigns/coke/2004/heatison.html.

14 Rama Lakshmi, "Parliamentary Committee Confirms Pesticides in Coca-Cola," *The Washington Post*, Feb. 5, 2004.

15 Center for Science and Environment, press release, "Soft Drinks Still Unsafe...,"

August 2, 2006, http://www.cseindia.org/misc/cola-indepth/cola2006/cola_press 2006.htm.

16   At KillerCoke.org (http://www.killercoke.org/crimes.htm).

17   Anonymous, "Steelworkers to File Lawsuit Against Coke," *Pittsburgh Business Times*, Jul. 20, 2001.

18   H. Unger, "Coke to settle racial suit with $192.5 million deal," *Atlanta Journal Constitution*, November 17, 2000.

PepsiCo

1   PepsiCo, "2006 Annual Report".

2   PepsiCo, "2003 Annual Report".

3   PepsiCo Official Website, http://www.PepsiCo.com/ company/overview.shtml.

4   PepsiCo, "2006 Annual Report".

5   Anonymous "Landmarks of the Week of June 16, 1997" Advertising Age, August 19, 1996 p. 60.

6   Anonymous, "Pepsi's Aquafina Water Nears Full US Distribution," Beverage Digest Aug. 1, 1997, http://www.beveragedigest.com/editorial/970801.html.

7   Aquafina Official Website, http://www.aquafina.com.

8   Packaged Facts, *op. cit.*, p. 26.

9   Beverage Marketing Corporation, 2005.

10   PepsiCo Official Website, http://www.PepsiCo.com/company/directors-commitees.shtml.

11   Center for Responsive Politics, http://www.opensecrets.org

12   United Nations' General Assembly, "Interim report on the situation of human rights in Myanmar," prepared by Professor Yozo Yokota, Special Rapporteur of the Commission on Human Rights, http://www.unhchr.ch/Huridocda/Huridoca.nsf/0/026307f31845840dc125699000591d47/$FILE/N9361495.pdf.

13   In 1996, PepsiCo sold parts of its stake in the Burma bottling venture thus keeping some interests in Burma until 1997.

14   Anonymous, "Coke And Pepsi Responsible For Trashing America. Hurting Taxpayers And Environment," CRI, Apr. 16, 2002, http://www.bottlebill.org/resources/news/newstrashing.htm.

15   Pepsi-Cola North America Official Website, "Our Commitment to the Environment," http://www.pepsiworld.com/help/recycle.pdf.

Groupe Danone

1   Groupe Danone Official Website, http://www.danone.com

2   Groupe Danone 2006 Annual Report.

3   Coke's "2005 Annual Report".

4   Chad Terhune, "Deal and Deal Makers: Suntory and Danone Pool Liquid Assets in

the U.S.," *Wall Street Journal*, Sept. 5, 2003, p. C5.

5   Summary of Birch Hill Equity Partners Inc. Press release Aug. 22, 2006.

6   Anonymous, "Bottled Water Now Number-Two Commercial Beverage in the U.S.," Beverage Marketing Corporation, http://www.beveragemarketing.com/news2.htm.

7   Catherine Ferrier, "Bottled Water: Understanding a Social Phenomenon," World Wildlife Fund, Apr. 2001, p. 4.

8   Anonymous, "Titans Battle Over Water Mart" Apr. 12, 2002, http://adtimes.nstp. com.my/archive/2002/apr12.htm.

9   Beverage Marketing Corporation, 2005.

10   Juan C. Garcia, "Bottled Water in Mexico," *Beverage World*, Apr. 15, 1997, vol. 116, p. 94-112.

11   Groupe Danone Official Website, http://www.danone.com.

12   Lise Dolbec, "La Saga de Franklin," L'Encyclopédie de l'Agora, Volume 6, No. 2.

Global Reach

1   See Emily Arnold and Janet Larsen, BOTTLED WATER: Pouring Resources Down the Drain, Earth Policy Institute, February 2, 2006. See also www.earthpolicy.org/ Updates/2006/Update51.htm).

2   Beverage Marketing Corporation data cited in John G. Rodwan Jr., "Bottled Water 2004: U.S. and International Statistics and Developments," Bottled Water Reporter, April/May 2005, www.beveragemarkting.com/news3e.htm.

3   Leslie T Chang, 'Nestlé Lost Sweet Spot,' The Wall Street Journal, Asian Business News, December 8, 2004. http://72.14.203.104/search?q=cache:ANihCX6C7LYJ: lpc1.clpccd.cc.ca.us/lpc/rgilmore/BUSN40/WSJ_China_Nestle.doc+Nestle+Waters+ in+China&hl=en&ct=clnk&cd=12.

4   Chandra Bhushan, "Bottled Loot: The Structure and Economics of India's Bottled Water industry," in *Frontline* [India's National Magazine] Vol. 23, Issue 7, April 8, 2006.

5   Michael Schwartz, "Bottled Water Conflicts," University of Wisconsin-Eau Claire, USA, Spring 2004.

6   Abid Aslam, "Bottled Water: Nectar of the Frauds?" One World Net, February 5, 2006. Based on the Environment Policy Institute Report, February 2, 2006.

PART 2: ENVIRONMENTAL AND HEALTH ISSUES

1. Water Takings

1   Mandy Burrell, "Polands Spring's Big Break," *Conscious Choice*, January 2004.

2   Co-op America as cited in: Brian Howard, "Message In A Bottle: Despite The Hype, Bottled Water Is Neither Cleaner Nor Greener Than Tap Water," *E-magazine.com*, Sept./Oct. 2003, vol. 14, no. 5.

3   Edward D. Murphy, "Industry and Feds Deny Consumer Right to Know Sources of Bottled Water," *Portland Press Herald*, Oct. 28, 2003.

4   http://www.inspection.gc.ca/english/corpaffr/foodfacts/ bottwate.shtml

5   Brad Willis, "The Problem Facing Florida's Springs," Save America's Water, Oct. 9, 2000, http://www.saveamericas water.com/fl/bwillis100900.html.

6   Department of the Interior, U.S.Fish and Wildlife Service, Water Resources Division, Mountain-Prairie Region, "Water Rights Definitions," http://mountain-prairie.fws.gov/wtr/water_rights_def.htm#RIPARIAN.

7   Colorado Division of Water Resources, "The Prior Appropriation System," http://water.state.co.us/wateradmin/prior.asp.

8   Bruce Lesikar *et a*l., "Questions About Groundwater Conservation Districts in Texas," Texas Water Resources Institute, Texas Cooperative Extension (Texas A&M University System), p. 9, http://twri.tamu.edu/reports/2002/2002-036/2002-036_Questions-Dist.pdf.

9   Texas Water, Water Resources Education, Texas Water Law (Texas A&M University System) at http://texaswater.tamu.edu/waterlaw.texas.htm. See also: Ronald A. Kaiser, "Handbook of Texas Water Law: Problems and Needs," (Texas Water Resources Institute).

10   Peggy Fikac, "High court agrees to hear Ozarka case," *Texas News*, Aug. 26, 1998.

11   Bruce Lesikar et al., *op. cit.*, p.9-10.

12   California Resources Agency, California Environmental Resources Evaluation System (CERES), "California Water Law and Policy: Water Rights in California."

13   Canadian Environmental Law Association, "How is water taking regulated in Ontario?" Resource Library for the Environment and the Law, http://www.ecolaw info.org/ WATER%20FAQs/Water%20Quantity%20and%20Sustainability/ BottledWater.htm.

14   Land and Water British Columbia, Inc. See: http://www.env.gov.bc.ca/wsd/ water_rights/index.html.

2. Transforming Water

1   Coca-Cola Company's Dasani Official Website, http://www.dasani.com/popups/faq01.htm.

2   Felicity Lawrence, "Tap water: It's the Real Thing," *The Guardian*, Mar. 2, 2004.

3   PepsiCo's Aquafina Website, http://www.aquafina.com.

4   Phone communication to Nestlé's Poland Spring's hot-line 866-676-1672.

5   Most Nestlé-owned brands provide few details on treatment processes. Most of them forward to Nestlé Waters North America's website for further information of processes and quality, www.nestle-watersna.com.

6   Larry Hanke, "How do Filters Filter Anyway?" *Water Conditioning and Purification*, Mar. 2002, p. 33.

7   Taken from: Domnick Hunter Group plc, Technical Center: Micro-filtration of Bottled Water, http://www.domnickhunter.com/tech_Centre.asp?chapter =1&section=17_Micro-Filtration-of-Bottled-Water_9.htm&getIndex=false.

8   Domnick Hunter Group, *op. cit.*

9   Joe Gelt, "Consumers Increasingly Use Bottled Water, Home Water Treatment Systems to Avoid Direct Tap Water," *Arroyo*, Mar. 1996, vol. 9, no.1.

10   Bruce Kucera, "The Bottled Water Business: Riding the Tailwind of a Flourishing Industry," *Water Conditioning and Purification*, Oct. 2001, p. 50-52.

11   Felicity Lawrence, *op. cit.*

12   Joe Gelt, *op. cit.*

13   Ibid.

14   Dale Mork, "Ozone in Spring Water: A Bottler's Choice," *Water Conditioning and Purification*, Jan. 2002, p. 38

15   Joe Gelt, *op. cit.*

16   Dale Mork, *op. cit.*, p. 38

17   Joe Gelt, *op. cit.*

18   Dale Mork, *op. cit.*, p. 40.

19   Bruce Kucera, *op. cit.*, p. 53.

20   L. Joseph Bollyky, "A Brief History of the Role of Ozone in Water Bottling," *Water Conditioning and Purification*, Oct. 2001, p. 65.

21   L. Joseph Bollyky, *op. cit.*, p. 62.

22   U.S.Food and Drug Administration, Department of Health and Human Services, 21 CFR Parts 129 and 165, "Beverages: Bottled Water; Technical Amendment," http://www.fda.gov/OHRMS/DOCKETS/98fr/070501a.htm.

23   Barbara L. Marteney and Kristin Safran, "Continually Evolving Regulations: D/DBPs," *Water Quality Product Magazine*, Sept., 2001.

24   L. Joseph Bollyky, *op. cit.*, 2001, p. 40.

25   Carlos David Mogollón, "Viewpoint: Perrier Restricts Ozone Use Awaiting Better Control Options," *Water Conditioning and Purification*, Aug. 2001.

3. Contaminating Water

1   As cited by Erik Olson, *op. cit.* We could not find the exact quote on the IBWA Website (bottledwater.org. However, many IBWA members still use this quote on their websites.)

2   Erik Olson, *op. cit.*

3   Canadian Bottled Water Association Website, http://www.cbwa-bottledwater.org/en/ definitions.htm.

4   Valerie Elliott and Angela Jameson, "Coca-Cola withdraws 'Sidcup tap' water," *The Times*, Mar. 20, 2004, p. 1.

5   The Coca-Cola Company Official Website, http://citizenship.coca-cola.co.uk/pdf/

cr_marketplace_section.pdf.

6   CNN.com, "Coke 'pure' water claim questioned," http://www.cnn.com/2004/ WORLD/europe/03/03/coke.water/.

7   Communication with Paul Kirby, food specialist at the Canadian Food Inspection Agency, May 2004.

8   Donald W. Warburton, "A Review of The Microbiological Quality Of Bottled Water Sold In Canada. Part 2. The Need For More Stringent Standards and Regulations," *Canadian Journal Of Microbiology*, 1993, vol. 39, p. 159.

9   Abua Ikem et al., "Chemical Quality of Bottled Water from Three Cities in Eastern Alabama," *The Science of the Total Environment*, 2002, vol. 285, p. 171.

10   North Carolina Health Department. Available at: http://www.co.gaston.nc.us/ HealthDept/ArsenicFactSheet.HTM.

11   Abua Ikem *et al.*, *op. cit.*, p. 171.

12   Abua Ikem *et al.*, *op. cit.*, p. 172-173.

13   Donald Warburton *et al.*, "A Further Review Of The Microbiological Quality Of Bottled Water Sold In Canada: 1992-1997 Surveys Results," *International Journal Of Food Microbiology*, 1998, vol. 39, p. 22.

14   Ibid.

15   Megan Rauscher, 'High Levels' of Bacteria Found in Bottled Water' November 1, 2004, *Reuters Health*, and Marilyn Chase, "Drinking Water Bottled Water Isn't Always Pure" *Wall Street Journal*, November 2, 2004.

16   Elizabeth Quinn, "Super Oxygenated Water: Is It Better Than Tap Water?" http://sportsmedicine.about.com/cs/nutrition/a/aa022802a.htm.

17   Cathy O'Leary, "Tooth decay blamed on bottled water" *The West Australian Metro*, March 21, 2006.

18   Posted at http://www.psu.edu/ur/NEWS/news/april98sportsmed2.html

19   Elizabeth Quinn, *op. cit.*

20   *Market Place* (television program), Canadian Broadcast Corporation (CBC), aired Feb. 8, 2000, http://www.cbc.ca/consumers/market/files/food/bottledwater/ index.html.

4. Eco-Threatening

1   Berkeley Ecology Center, "Report of the Berkeley Plastics Task Force," 1996, p. 5.

2   U.S. EPA, "Municipal Solid Waste in the United States: Facts and Figures," 2001 and 2002; U.S. EPA, "Characterization of Municipal Solid Waste in the United States: 1998 Update," prepared for by Franklin Associates, 1999.

3   National Soft Drink Association Website, www.nsda.org/softdrinks/History/ history.html.

4   PakIntell LLC, "US PET Beverage Container Market," http://www.plastics news.com/subscriber/fyi.html?id=1061219448.

5   Bart Thedinger, "Your Business Outlook: Strong Growth Ahead for Food and Beverages Bottles," *Plastics Technology*, Feb. 2004.

6   The Freedonia Group. "Beverage Containers: U.S. Industry Study with Forecast to 2007 and 2012," 2003; and American Plastics Council, "Plastic Packaging Resins," www.americanplasticscouncil.org.

7   Harry S. Cole and Kenneth A. Brown, "Advantage Glass! Switching to Plastic is An Environmental Mistake, A Study Documenting the Environmental Advantages of Glass Over Plastic Containers Based on Published Information," Glass Packaging Institute, Sept. 1993.

8   Scorecard.org and National Institute for Occupational Safety and Health, International Chemical Safety Cards.

9   Ibid.

10 M.G. Evandri, P. Tucci and P. Bolle, "Toxicological evaluation of commercial mineral water bottled in polyethylene terephthalate: a cytogenetic approach with *Allium cepa*," *Food Additives and Contaminants*, vol. 17, no. 12, pp. 10371045. At: http://www.mindfully.org/Plastic/Polyethylene/PET-Mineral-Water1dec00.htm

11 William Shotyk, Michael Krachler and Bin Chen, "Contamination of Canadian and European bottled waters with antimony from PET containers," published in the *Journal of Environmental Monitoring* [2006, 8, 288-292] of the Royal Society of Chemistry, 2006.

12 Scorecard.org: http://www.scorecard.org/envreleases/ranking.tcl?tri_id= 29492MCCHMCLEME.

13 U.S. EPA, "Municipal Solid Waste ...," *op. cit.*; U.S. EPA, "Characterization ...," *op. cit.*

14 Berkeley Ecology Center, *op. cit.*, p. 10.

15 International Plastics Task Force, http://www.ecologycenter.org/iptf/index.html.

16 For more details see U.S. Environmental Protection Agency Website, http://www.epa.gov/airmarkets/acidrain/.

17 Bart Thedinger, *op. cit.*

18 The Freedonia Group. "Beverage Containers: U.S. Industry Study with Forecast to 2007 and 2012," 2003. and The Freedonia Group, *op. cit.*

19 See for example, Franklin Associates, "The Environmental Impact of Soft Drink Delivery Systems – A Comparative Analysis (1995 Update)," commissioned by the National Association for PET Container Resources. Available at: http://www.napcor.com/pdf/Env_Impact.pdf.

5. Recycling Record

1   Brian Howard, *op. cit.*

2   Container Recycling Institute, "Report shows plastic bottle waste tripled since 1995," Sept. 2003.

3   Container Recycling Institute. *op. cit.*

4   Container Recycling Institute. *op. cit.*

5   Dave Aftandilian, "Coke's Broken Promise," *Conscious Choice*, Feb. 2000, http://www.consciouschoice.com/2000/cc1302/note1302.html.

6   Jeremy Chan, "Caffeine High, Environmental Low: PEA Protests Pepsi Recycling Policy," *Daily Princetonian*, Feb. 28, 2002.

7   Container Recycling Institute Website, http://www.container-recycling.org/plasfact/PETstraight.htm.

8   Berkeley Ecology Center, *op. cit.*, p. 10.

9   Berkeley Ecology Center. *op. cit.*, p. 9.

10   Society of the Plastics Industry Website, http://www.plasticsindustry.org/outreach/recycling/2124.htm.

11   Container Recycling Institute Website, http://www.container-recycling.org/plasfact/PETstraight.htm.

12   In 2001, Dasani's Take-Home sales have soared by over a 100%.

13   In 2001, Dasani's Take-Home sales have soared by over a 100%. See Andrea Foote, *op. cit.*, p. 36.

14   Jenny Gitlitz and Pat Franklin, "The 10¢ Incentive to Recycle," Container Recycling Institute, Feb. 2004, p. 4.

15   R.W. Beck, "Understanding Beverage Container Recycling: A Value Chain Assessment Prepared for the Multi-Stakeholder Recovery Project," Businesses and Environmentalists Allied for Recycling (BEAR), 2002. See Table ES-1. Available at: http://www.globalgreen.org/BEAR/Projects/index.html#files.

16   Clarissa Morawski, "Who Pays What -An Analysis of Beverage Container Recovery and Costs in Canada 2001-2002," CM Consulting, Jun. 2003.

17   Jenny Gitliz and Pat Franklin, *op. cit.*, p. 11.

18   U.S. Energy Information Administration, EIA Kid's Page, "Recycling Plastics," http://www.eia.doe.gov/kids/energyfacts/saving/recycling/solidwaste/plastics.html.

19   Jenny Gitliz and Pat Franklin, *op. cit.*, p. 3.

PART 3: SOCIAL-ECONOMIC ISSUES

1. Price Gouging

1   Erik Olson, "Bottled Water: Pure Drink or Pure Hype?" National Resources Defense Council (NRDC), Mar. 1999, http://www.nrdc.org/water/drinking/bw/bwinx.asp.

2   For NYC the cost has been established on the water residential meter rate. For Montreal, since there's no unique price, we took the production cost of a cubic meter by the city. In the case of Knoxville, we average the consumption of a four-person household (1 600 L per day = 584 000 L per year) based on the city's tax system.

3   Mel Suffet, "Bottled Water," Department of Environmental Health Sciences, University of California, Los Angeles (UCLA), http://www.ioe.ucla.edu/publications/report01/bottledWater.htm.

4   Canadian Bottled Water Association Official Website, http://www.cbwa-bottledwater.org/en/faq.htm.

5   City of Cleveland (OH), Division of Water, Customer Service: (216) 664-3130.

6   City of Marietta (GA), Marietta Water, http://www.city.marietta.ga.us/Water/feesservices.htm. Based on the second level rate: consumption between 18 000 and 980 000 gallons.

7   Knoxville Utilities Board, Water Division, "Schedule A—Water Service Charge." Available at http://www1.kub.org/newsite/index.shtml.

8   *Bottled Water Web*, http://www.bottledwaterweb.com/pricescan.jsp.

9   As cited in Hillary Chura, "Water War Bubbling Among Top Brands," *Advertising Age*, Jul. 7, 2003, vol. 74, no. 27.

10   Hillary Chura, *op. cit.*

11   Betsym McKay, "Coke Strays From The Real Thing—Investors Fret That Bottled Water, Other Beverages Don't Quench Their Thirst For Soft-Drink Profit," *Wall Street Journal*, Oct. 29, 2002, p. C1.

12   Chad Terhune, *op. cit.*

13   Andrea Foote, "What Price Water?" *Beverage World*, Apr. 15, 2002, p. 36.

14   Andrea Foote, *op. cit.*, p. 36.

15   Andrea Foote, *op. cit.*, p. 40.

16   Ibid.

17   Based on our estimates: Gas prices ranging from a low of $0.454/liter to a high of $0.603/liter and bottled water commonly sold between $1.00 and $1.50 in single-serve packages (All prices in US dollars).

2. Marketing Schemes

1   Research communication, American Water Work Association, May 2004, 1-800-926-7337.

2   Kathy Noël, *op. cit.*

3   Frank Greve, "Is Bottled Water Worth The Price?," *Knight Ridder Newspapers*, May 19, 1998.

4   Catherine Ferrier, *op. cit.*, p. 18.

5   Kent Phillips, "Why Water?" *Beverage World*, Sept. 2000, p. 66.

6   Catherine Ferrier, *op. cit.*, p. 18.

7   Henry R. Hidell III, "Water: The Search for a Global Balance," *Bottled Water Reporter*, Jun./Jul. 1995, p. 53, as cited in Erik Olson, *op. cit.*, see Ch. 2, note 47.

8   Sandra, Eckstein, "Water: Nothing To It For Bottled Variety," *The Atlanta Journal-Constitution*, Apr. 9, 2004.

9   Email communication with Paul Hawken, figure from company documents 21/10/2004.

10   Packaged Facts, *op. cit.*, p. 26.

11   "Some 20% of consumers drink tap water exclusively in casual dining restaurants and 17% drink it in family restaurants," in David F. Gallagher, "Word for Word/Deep Water: 'Just Say No to H20' (Unless It's Coke's Own Brew)," *New York Times*, Sept. 2, 2001.

12   See http://www.commondreams.org/headlines01/0902-02.htm to find what was on Coke's website before Aug. 2001.

13   Kenneth Hein, "Hey, Kids! Here's The New, Cool Drink: Bottled Water," *Brandweek Magazine*, June 2006.

3. Manipulating Consumers

1   For Canada: Presse Canadienne and Léger Marketing, "Perception et comportement des Canadiens vis-à-vis de l'eau potable-Rapport," Léger Marketing, Sept. 2001. and For United States: U.S. EPA, "Analysis And Findings Of The Gallup Organization's Drinking Water Customers Satisfaction Survey," commissioned by the U.S. Environmental Protection Agency's Office of Groundwater and Drinking Water Satisfaction (OGWDW), Aug. 6, 2003, p. 4.

2   Packaged Facts, *op. cit.*, p. 21

3   From "Canadian Consumer Water Quality Survey" (1995 and 2000), as cited by Vic Adamowicz, et al., "The Value of Good Quality Tap Water: Preliminary Results from Pilot Testing of Online Survey," Faculty of Social Science, Brock University.

4   From "US Consumer Water Quality Survey" (1999 and 2001), as cited by Vic Adamowicz *et al.*, *op. cit.*

5   For more details on the question see: Joe Gelt, *op. cit.*, and Anonymous, "Water, Water, Everywhere: Bottled Water Market in the U.S.

6   U.S. EPA, "Analysis and Findings of the Gallup ...," *op. cit.*, p. 5.

7   The News and Observer, March 28, 2006, http://www.newsobserver.com/150/story/422751.html.

8   Sandra Eckstein, "Water: Nothing To It For Bottled Variety," *The Atlanta Journal-Constitution*, Apr: 9, 2004.

9   Sandra Eckstein, ibid.

4. School Contracting

1   D. Keough, "Soft Drink Companies' Deals with Schools Raise Concerns," *Plain Dealer*, January 18, 1999.

2   Jim Metrock, "Commercialism: Who is indebted to whom?" *Urban Advocate*, Council of Urban Boards of Education, an affiliate of the National School Board Association, Summer 2003, p. 2. See: 2003, p. 2. See: www.nsba.org/cube.

3   Alex Molnar, "No Student Left Unsold: The Sixth Annual Report on Schoolhouse Commercialism Trends, 2002-2003," Commercialism in Education Research Unit (CERU), Education Policy Studies Laboratory, Arizona State University, Oct. 2003, p. 13. Available at: http://edpolicylab.org.

4   Alex Molnar, *op. cit.*

5   Partners in Education, "Partnerships 2000: A Decade of Growth and Change," National Association of Partners in Education, 2001, p.17, Chart 1C.

6   See CCSP's Website at www.corpschoolpartners.org and CSPI's newsroom: Center for Science in the Public Interest, http://www.cspinet.org/new/200209252.html.

7   CCSP Website: Members of the Council, http://www.corpschool.partners.org /members.shtml.

8   Gary Ruskin, "The Fast Food Trap: How Commercialism Creates Overweight Children," *Mothering,* Issue 121, Nov./Dec. 2003.

9   Heather Jane Robertson quoted in, "How Grass Roots Beat Deep Pockets," *Teacher News Magazine*, Apr. 1999.

10   Dan Blake, "How Grass Roots Beat Deep Pockets," *Teacher News Magazine*, Apr. 1999.

11   Jane Meinhardt, "Pepsi contract called for crystal-ball readers," *Tampa Bay Business Journal*, Jun. 2, 2003.

12   Pamela Griner Leavy, "Pepsi Sweetens Pot for Hillsborough Schools," *Tampa Bay Business Journal*, Aug. 30, 2002.

13   Pamela Griner Leavy, "Schools ready to pop top on soft drink vendor contract," *Tampa Bay Business Journal*, Mar. 7, 2003.

14   Pamela Griner Leavy, *op. cit.*, "Pepsi…".

15   "Challenging McWorld, Second Edition," Canadian Centre for Policy Alternatives, 2005, p. 37.

16   Ontario Secondary School Teachers' Federation (OSSTF), "Commercialization in Our Schools—Executive Summary," http://fr.osstf.on.ca/www/abosstf/ampa01/ commercialization/execsum.html.

17   Debbie Field et al., "Open Letter to Toronto District School Board Trustees," *Food Share*, Jun. 2004, http://www.foodshare.net/school03.htm.

18   Anna White, "Coke and Pepsi are going to school," *Multinational Monitor*, Jan. 1999, http://www.essentialaction.org/spotlight/CokeSchool.html

19   Anna White, ibid.

20   Anna White, *op. cit.*

21   Karolyn Schuster, "Locking up revenue … or locking out choice? Exclusive brand contracts," *Food Management*, Feb. 1998, vol. 33, no. 2, p. 35.

22   "Campus Exclusivity: Dasani or Aquafina. Coca-cola or Pepsi. What choices do your really have? A look inside exclusivity contracts," Polaris Institute, 2006, p 3.

23   Communication with D. Matovic 6/21/2005.

24   Karolyn Schuster, *op. cit.*, p. 35, citing Julaine Kiehn, campus dining services director of the University of Missouri-Columbia.

25   National Education Association (NEA), "Protecting Public Education from Tax Giveaways to Corporations: Property Tax Abatements, Tax Increment Financing, and Funding for Schools," NEA Research Working Paper, Mar. 2003, p. vii.

26   Jon Bricker, "McGill ends negotiations with Coca-Cola," *The McGill Daily*, Mar. 27, 2001.

27   Ai Lin Choo, "Coke deal made public," *The Ubyssey*, Aug. 1, 2001.

28   Jeanne Corriveau, "Bris d'un contreversé contrat d'exclusivité —L'UdeM poursuit Pepsi," *Le Devoir*, Nov. 5, 2002.

29   Jeanne Corriveau, "Pepsi veut rouvrir le contrat d'exclusivité avec l'UdeM," *Le Devoir*, Nov. 6, 2002.

30   David M. Herszenhorn, "New York Picks its Beverage, for $166 Million," *New York Times,* Sept. 10, 2003.

31   David M. Herszenhorn, *op. cit.*

5. Water Privatizing

1   Both Suez and Veolia Environment owned their own HOD (Home/Office Delivery) subsidiaries until the early 2000s.

2   In March 2006, RWE announced that it would pursue an Initial Public Offering in the US for shares of American Water.

3   National Environmental Education and Training Foundation/Roper Starch, "The National Report Card on Safe Drinking Water," NEETF, July, 1999.

4   Culligan Water Conditioning of Laredo Website, http://www.culliganlaredo.com/ bottled_water_faq.htm#q1.

5   *Bottled Water Web*, http://www.bottledwaterweb.com/ municipal.html.

6   David A. McDonald, "Water Pricing and the Poor," *Alternatives*, Spring 2003, vol. 29, no. 2, p. 20.

7   American Water Works Association (AWWA), "Utility's bottled-water offer a 'win-win' situation," *E-Mainstream*, Dec. 1999, http://www.awwa.org/communications/ mainstream/archives/1999/December/ms12bottled.cfm.

8   See Decisions of the Regional Council of the Regional Municipality of Peel, http://www.region.peel.on.ca/council/ decisions/2004/04_01_2004.htm.

9   Biksham Gujja, Richard Holland and Catherine Ferrier, "From the Tap or Bottle: Protecting the Source is Cheaper," *Water Conditioning & Purification*, October 2001, p. 56-60.

10   AWWA, "Funding gap for drinking water infrastructure 'is real and is big," AWWA News Release, Apr. 29, 2004.

11   IBWA, 2001 Annual Report, "Winning Through Teamwork," p. 4, http://www.bottledwater.org/public/annual01.pdf .

12   IBWA, *op. cit.*, 2001, p. 4.

13   Texas Water Development Board, "Proposed Constitutional Amendment: Proposition 19," http://www.twdb.state.tx.us/publications/newsletters/waterfortexas/wftfall01/art4.htm.

14   Texans for Public Justice, "Perrier Sells A Drought Solution : Water Bottlers Funded Passage Of $2 Billion In TX Water Bonds," Lobby Watch, Nov. 19, 2001, http://www.tpj.org/Lobby_Watch/waterbonds.pdf.

Part 4: RESPONSE AND RESISTANCE

Summing Up and Moving On

1   IBWA 46th annual convention and trade show: Program Schedule and BevExpo conference grid http://www.bottledwater.org/public/conv2004/schedule/.

2   First Global Bottled Water Congress 4-6 October, 2004, Evian-Les-Bains, France Main Conference Programme.

3   Ibid.

4   Ibid.

5   Joan Hughes, "Water Fallout," *Florida Trend*, September 2003, p. 36.

6   Richard Girard, Nestlé Corporate Profile - www.polarisinstitute.org.

7   *op. cit.*

8   For further details on the Big Rapids Case see the transcription of a PBS report by Fred de Sam Lazaro available at: http://www.pbs.org/newshour/bb/environment/julydec02/water_fight_12-31.html.

9   US CENSUS, *Bottled Water Manufacturing: 2002*, Manufacturing — Industry Series, August 2004, p. 3.

Community Resistance

1   Anonymous (Associated Press), "Perrier Wants to Bottle Wisconsin Water," reprinted from the *Milwaukee Journal Sentinel*, Dec. 18, 1999, http://www.wsn.org/issues/Perrier.html.

2   Will Fantle, "What Price for Bottled Water? Perrier's 2 plans highlight groundwater concerns," Wisconsin Stewardship Network, Mar. 21, 2001, http://www.wsn.org/water/Perrierstory.html.

3   Tom Vanden Brook, "Thompson works to find a home for Perrier," *Milwaukee Journal Sentinel*, Feb. 23, 2000, http://www.jsonline.com/news/metro/feb00/water24022300a.asp.

4   Peter Maller, "Perrier isn't deterred by bottling plant votes," *Milwaukee Journal Sentinel*, Jun. 14, 2000, http://www.jsonline.com/news/state/jun00/water15061 400a.asp.

5   Ibid.

6 Waterkeepers of Wisconsin, "Experts Say Perrier Environmental Assessment Flawed," Press Release, Aug. 11, 2000, http://www.wsn.org/water/WOW Perriernews.html

7 Meg Jones, "Perrier sued over test wells," *Milwaukee Journal Sentinel*, Oct. 18, 2000, http://www.jsonline.com/news/metro/oct00/water19101800a.asp.

8 Jo Sandin and Steven Walters, "Thompson sends Perrier packing," *Milwaukee Journal Sentinel*, Nov. 22, 2000, http://www.jsonline.com/news/state/nov00/water23112200a.asp.

9 Kevin Murphy, "Nestlé Waters won't develop Big Spring site," *Milwaukee Journal Sentinel*, Sept. 17, 2002, http://www.jsonline.com/news/state/sep02/80699.asp.

10 Dan Egan, "Bottler taps into trouble in Michigan," *Milwaukee Journal Sentinel*, Jan. 30, 2004, http://www.jsonline.com/news/state/jan04/199128.asp.

11 Anonymous (Associated Press), "Osceola County clears path for Perrier plant," *Detroit News*, Feb. 22, 2001.

12 Anonymous (Associated Press), "Dispute erupts over Perrier water," *Detroit News*, Jan. 30, 2001.

13 MCWC, Press Release, May 8, 2001, http://www.savemiwater.org/news/Press%20Releases/PR01.05.08.pdf.

14 Francis X. Donnelly, "Bottled water fight grows," *Detroit News*, May 20, 2001.

15 James Prichard, "Production begins at western Michigan water-bottling plant," *Detroit News*, May 11, 2001.

16 Anonymous (Associated Press), "Judge's ruling in lawsuit favor water bottler," *Detroit News*, Nov. 2, 2002.

17 Anonymous (Associated Place), "Lawsuit against bottler rejected," *Detroit News*, Jun. 6, 2002.

18 James Prichard, "Judge orders halt to Ice Mountain bottling," *Detroit News*, Nov. 25, 2003.

19 Hugh McDiarmid Jr., "Ice Mountain gains a reprieve," *Detroit Free Press*, Dec. 17, 2003.

20 Cary Davis, "Expert: Perrier Should Get Water Because It Sells," *St. Petersburg Times*, Sept. 25, 1999, p. 2.

21 Cary Davis, "Owner Of Springs Seeks Court's Help To Sell Water, *St. Petersburg Times*, Mar. 25, 2000, p. 11.

22 Terry Date, "Water Expert Try To Alley Concerns Over Proposed Bottling Plant In Nottingham," Jul. 18 2001, http://premium1.fosters.com/2001/news/july/18/ro0718c.htm.

23 Anonymous, "Nottingham Selectmen Sue To Stop Testing USA Springs," Sept. 16, 2002, http://premium1.fosters.com/2002/news/sept_02/sept16_02/news/ro0916c.asp.

24 Terry Date, "Questions Raised About Impact Of USA Springs Water Tests," Jan. 6,

2003, http://premium1.fosters.com/2003/news/feb_03/feb_06/news/ro_0206g.asp.

25 Anonymous, "USA Springs' Nottingham Permit Denied," Aug. 13, 2003, http://
premium1.fosters.com/2003/news/aug_03/august_13/news/reg_nh_0813e.asp.

26 Josh Indar, "Drinking Problem," Sacramento New And Review, August 18, 2005.

27 Read the contract: http://www.mccloudwatershedcouncil.org/docs/signed_
nestle_agreement.pdf.

28 McCloud Watershed Council website, http://www.mccloudwatershedcouncil.org/

29 Quoted in Josh Indar, *op cit.*

30 Brian Melley, "Judge Nixes Town's Spring Water Deal with Nestlé," The Associated
Press, March 23, 2006.

31 Deborra Clayton, "Judge Voids Entire Nestlé Contract," Mt Shasta News, July 27,
2005.

32 For updates on this situation please go to the McCloud Watershed Council website:
http://www.mccloudwatershedcouncil.org/.

33 The rulings and contracts can be accessed at http://aci.on.ca/~saublent/school/
vending.html.

34 http://www.killercoke.org/crimes.htm.

Taking Democratic Control

1 Erik Olson, "Bottled Water: Pure Drink or Pure Hype?" National Resources Defense
Council (NRDC), Mar. 1999, http://www.nrdc.org/water/drinking/bw/bwinx.asp.

2 Tim Holt, Untapped Market. http://www.greatlakesdirectory.org/mn/
012604_great_lakes.htm.

3 www.win-water.org/.

4 Olson, *op. cit.*

5 Ibid.

6 Ibid.

7 Ibid.

Part 5: ADDITIONAL RESOURCES AND TOOLS

1 "World's largest corporations," *Fortune*, Vol.154, Issue 2, July 24, 2006.

2 Coca Cola Company Press Release, "Coca-Cola Unveils Plans For Institute
Dedicated To The Role Of Beverages In Healthy Lifestyles," March 1, 2004, http://
www2.cocacola.com/presscenter/nr_20040220_beverages_healthy_lifestyles.html.

3 The Coca Cola Company Website, http://www2.coca-cola.com/citizenship/
critical_global_resource.html.

4 "Health studies increasingly funded by food companies," Transcript from the
Australian Broadcasting Corporation, PM, Broadcast September 6, 2004,
http://www.abc.net.au/pm/content/2004/s1193417.htm.

5   Center for Science in the Public Interest Press Release, "Pediatric Dentists Accused of Selling Out to Coke," March 4, 2003, http://www.cspinet.org/new/ 200303041.html.

6   American Council on Science and Health Website, http://www.acsh.org/about/ index.html.

7   Gumbel, A., "The man who ate McDonalds," *The Independent*, June 19, 2004

8   Thurston, S., "Coca Cola: Struggle in Europe," *Atlanta Journal and Constitution*, June 22, 1999.

9   Burne, J., "A Probe Inside the Mind of the Shopper," *Financial Times*, November 28, 2003.

10 BrightHouse Neurostrategies Group Website, http://www.thoughtsciences.com

11 The Coca-Cola Company's 2006 Annual Report, 10-k.

12 "Joint civil society statement on the Global Compact and corporate accountability," June 23, 2004, http://www.earthrights.org/news/ngogcstatement.shtml.

13 "Coca-Cola gets pounds 145,000 to make greener bottle," *The Guardian*, March 16, 2006.

14 Overseas Private Investment Corporation, http://www.opic.gov/.

15 International Finance Corporation Website, http://ifcln001.worldbank.org/IFCExt/ spiwebsite1.nsf/d7e0de183d3bf4c685256eac004b7e90/5bf0e454deff12b585256b9d00 529cd6?OpenDocument.

16 Multinational Monitor, "Backwash: Coke Returns from India Exile," An Interview with George Fernandes, July August 1995, Vol. 16, No. 7&8

17 Ranjith, K.R., "Holy Water From the West," Altermedia: Thrissur, 2004, p. 48.

18 "Shut down, PCB tells Plachimada cola," *New India Press*, August 20, 2005.

19 Ranjith, K.R., "Holy Water From the West," Altermedia: Thrissur, 2004, 58.

20 Srivastava, A., "Coke with Yet Another New Twist: Toxic Cola," India Resource Center, January 31, 2004, http://www.indiaresource.org/campaigns/ coke/2004/coketwist.html.

21 Jones, E., Ritzman, F., "Coca-Cola Goes to War," http://xroads.virginia.edu/ ~class/coke/coke.html.

22 Ibid.

23 Ibid.

24 http://www.killercoke.org/crimes.htm.

25 Complaint filed against The Coca Cola Company in the United States District Court Southern District of Florida, page 19, http://www.laborrights.org/projects/ corporate/coke/index.html.

26 Lobe, J., Coca-Cola to be Sued for Bottlers' Abuses, Inter Press Service, July 20, 2001, http://www.commondreams.org/cgi-bin/print.cgi?file=/headlines01/0720-01.htm.

27 "The people vs Coke," Colombia Solidarity Campaign, http://www.colombia solidarity.org.uk/cocacolacampaign/peoplevscoke.html.

28 Communique between SINALTRAINAL and the Colombia Solidarity Campaign, April 20th, 2004, http://www.colombiasolidarity.org.uk/UA%20Apr-Jun%2004/UA04.04.20.html.

29 "Bucaramanga: More death threats against Coca Cola worker and trade unionists," Colombia Solidarity Campaign press release, November 17, 2005, http://www.colombiasolidarity.org.uk/UA%20Oct-Dec%2004/UA04.11.22.html.

30 For more information on this case please refer to, Gatehouse M., Reyes, M.A., "Soft Drink Hard Labour: Guatemalan Workers Take On Coca-Cola," London: Latin American Bureau, 1987.

31 International Labor Rights Fund, Tortured Turkish workers complaint, http://www.laborrights.org/projects/corporate/index.html.

32 United States District Court Northern District of Georgia, Civil Action No. 1-98-CV-3679, http://www.essentialaction.org/spotlight/coke/complaint.html#IV.

33 Unger, H., "Coke to Settle Racial Suit with $192.5 Million Deal," *Atlanta Journal Constitution*, November 17, 2000.

34 Day, S., "Anti-Bias Task Force Gives Coca-Cola Good Marks, but Says Challenges Remain," *New York Times*, September 26, 2002.

35 "World's largest corporations," *Fortune*, Vol.154, Issue 2, July 24, 2006.

36 PepsiCo's 2005 annual report on 10-k.

37 PepsiCo's 2006 annual report on 10-k.

38 Goodison, D., "Pepsi Zone fun lounges target teens at malls," *The Boston Herald*, August 10, 2005.

39 "PepsiCo to drop Tropicana ad claims," *Financial Times*, June 3, 2005.

40 "Branding campaign finance," *Los Angeles Times*, June 3, 2005.

41 California Secretary of State, http://cal-access.ss.ca.gov/Campaign/Committees/Detail.aspx?id=1009318&view=contributions&session=2003.

42 "Governor Schwarzenegger sells junk food in political ads for corporate donors," The Foundation for Taxpayer and Consumer Rights press release, May 25, 2005, http://www.consumerwatchdog.org/pr/?postId=4485&pageTitle=Governor+Schwarzenegger+Sells+Junk+Food+In+Political+Ads+for+Corporate+Donors.

43 Boseley, S., "Sugar industry threatens to scupper WHO," *The Guardian*, April 21 2003

44 National Soft Drink Association Press Release, "World Health Organization Report Contains Crucial Recommendations for More Physical Activity," March 4, 2003, http://www.nsda.org/about/news/2003%20Releases/WHOreport.html.

45 Bruno, K., Vallette, J., "Halliburton's Destructive Engagement," Earth Rights International, September 2000, http://www.earthrights.org/pubs/halliburton.shtml.

46 Danaher, K., "50 Years is Enough: the case against the World Bank and the International Monetary Fund," Boston: South End Press, 1994.

47 Platt, G. "Sonnet Financial Web service provides access to discount foreign exchange," *Journal of Commerce*, April 8, 1998.

48 International Finance Corporation Website, http://ifcln1.ifc.org/ifcext/agribusiness. nsf/Content/SelectedProject?OpenDocument&UNID=2F571EC90DB93E1E8525688 E007A600B.

49 International Finance Corporation Website, http://www.ifc.org/about

50 McIntyre, R.S., Coo Ngyuen, T.D., "Corporate Income Taxes in the 1990s," Institute on Taxation and Economic Policy, 2000.

51 "Thousands form Human Chain for Closure of soft drink units," *The Hindu*, March 30, 2005.

52 "Human chain formed against Pepsi, Coke," *Hindustan Times*, January 20, 2005.

53 "Pepsi ad 'Glorifying' child labour off air," *The Economic Times*, October 9, 2004.

54 Srivastava, A., "Coke with Yet Another New Twist: Toxic Cola," India Resource Center, January 31, 2004, http://www.indiaresource.org/campaigns/coke/2004/ coketwist.html.

55 Dhillon, A., "Soft-drink giants lose pesticide legal battle," *South China Morning Post*, December 9, 2004.

56 "PepsiCo: Union-Busting, Trashing Rights…and Buying Danone," International Union of Food, Agricultural, Hotel, Restaurant, Catering, Tobacco and Allied Workers' Associations (IUF) press release, July 21, 2005, http://www.iuf.org/cgi-bin/ editorials/db.cgi?db=default&ww=1&uid=default&ID=422&view_records=1&en=1.

57 Koppel, M., Green, R., "Workers organize resistance to mass firings in Argentina," *The Militant*, Vol.66/No.31, August 19, 2002.

58 Burnham, L., "Pressure on Pepsi," *The Daily Nation*, September 20, 2002.

59 Mydans, S., "Pepsi courts Myanmar, preferring sales to politics," *The New York Times*, February 22, 1996.

60 Matthews, J., "Pepsi to sell Burma plant, citing protests," *The Washington Post*, April 24, 1996.

61 Matthews, J., "Pepsi to pull out of Burma," *The Washington Post*, January 27, 1997.

62 "Demand Reinstatement of Guatemala Pepsi Workers," International Union of Food, Agricultural, Hotel, Restaurant, Catering, Tobacco and Allied Workers' Associations (IUF) Press Release, May 18, 2004.

63 "Protest Violations of Union Rights at PepsiCo Guatemala!," International Union of Food, Agricultural, Hotel, Restaurant, Catering, Tobacco and Allied Workers' Associations (IUF) Press Release, January 31, 2003.

64 Prashad, V., "'Just Say No to PepsiCo': So Say 101 Indian Workers," www.zmag.org, May 13, 2000, http://www.zmag.org/Sustainers/Content/2000-05/13prashad.htm.

65 "Sexual Harassment in Poland: PepsiCo Still Refuses to Accept Responsibility," International Union of Food, Agricultural, Hotel, Restaurant, Catering, Tobacco and Allied Workers' Associations (IUF) press release, July 20, 2005, http://www. iuf.org/cgi-bin/dbman/db.cgi?db=default&uid=default&ID=2194&view_ records=1&ww=1&en=1.

66   Duffy, C., "Teamsters at Pepsi Score Contract Gains," *The Militant*, Vol.64/No. 65, September 18, 2000.

67   Heaster, R., "Union on strike at Pepsi plants," *Kansas City Star*, February 22, 2001.

68   Heaster, R., "Pepsi seeks new employees after union rejects contract," *Kansas City Star*, April, 5, 2001.

69   "Pepsi workers on strike in Southern New Jersey," Teamsters press release, August 15, 2005, http://www.teamster.org/05news/hn_050815_1.htm.

70   "New Jersey Teamsters Approve New Pepsi Contract," Teamster press release, September 20, 2005, http://www.teamster.org/05news/hn_050920_3.htm.

71   The Associated Press, "Pepsi workers picket at four bottling facilities," June 2, 2001.

72   Diamond, M., "New Jersey Pepsi Drivers Agree to Contract, End Strike," July 19, 2001.

73   Diamond, M., "Pepsi Bottling Group Settles Overtime Pay Dispute with New Jersey Drivers," *Asbury Park Press*, March 13, 2003.

74   Proctor May, R., "Pepsi brings union fight to city council," *The Austin Chronicle*, May 6, 2005.

75   Ibid.

76   "PepsiCo Q3 Revenue Growth Over 6% and Operating Profit Up 11%," PepsiCo press release, September 30, 2004, http://phx.corporate-ir.net/phoenix.zhtml?c= 78265&p=IROL-NewsText&t=Regular&id=621144&.

77   Gallagher, J., "Frito-Lay dumps jobs," *Detroit Free Press*, October 1, 2004.

78   "World's largest corporations," *Fortune*, Vol.154, Issue 2, July 24, 2006.

79   For locations and addresses for Nestlé Waters' regional offices around the world visit the following website: http://www.nestle-waters.com/en/Menu/NWToday/ FactsFigures/Implantation#.

80   This product is available in Canada, USA, Mexico, Brazil, Argentina, South Africa, Saudi Arabia, Jordan, Egypt, Lebanon, Turkey, Russia, Uzbekistan, Pakistan, China, Thailand, and the Philippines.

81   This product is available in Belgium, France, Portugal, Spain, Switzerland, Italy, Hungary, Austria, Germany, Luxembourg, and Finland.

82   Innes, L., "Brewing Misery: The Third World and the Politics of Coffee Production," *Z magazine*, October 2001.

83   Nestlé's website, http://www.nestle.com/Header/Internet_Directory/Brand+ Category/Internet+Directory+Brand+Category.htm?BrandCategory=Petcare

84   Nestlé's 2006 Financial Statements.

85   http://www.babymilk.nestle.com.

86   Baby Milk Action Press Release, "Nestlé claim to be working with the IBFAN Africa coordinating office is untrue," October 24, 2001, http://www.babymilkaction.org/ press/press24oct01.html

87   Nestlé publication, "Nestlé in the Community," http://www.nestle.com/NR/

rdonlyres/632AD11A-7DA2-490F-8434-F15A5D39ADCA/0/Community_English.pdf

88 "The Nestlé Public Relations Machine Exposed," IBFAN, Baby Milk Action, http://www.babymilkaction.org/pdfs/nprmeprint05.pdf.

89 For more information on Nestlé's continued violations of the WHO code and a complete history of the company's track record concerning infant formula please visit the following websites: Baby Milk Action http://www.babymilkaction.org/ International Baby Food Action Network, http://www.ibfan.org/ Infant Feeding Action Coalition, http://www.infactcanada.ca/InfactHomePage.htm.

90 Lewis, S., "Malnutrition as a human rights violation: Implications for United Nations-supported programmes," Keynote Speech at the Administrative Committee on Coordination/Subcommittee on Nutrition (ACC/SCN) Symposium on the Substance and politics of human rights: Approach to food and nutrition policies and programmes. Geneva, 12-13, April 1999.

91 United Nations Children Fund, http://www.unicef.org/nutrition/index_breastfeeding.html.

92 Baby Milk Action, http://www.babymilkaction.org/pages/history.html.

93 Ibid.

94 Baby Milk Action, http://www.babymilkaction.org/regs/thecode.html

95 International Baby Food Action Network, "Breaking the Rules, Stretching the Rules 2004," http://www.ibfan.org/english/pdfs/btr04.pdf.

96 Ibid.

97 Frith, M., "Breast Cancer Charity Rejects Pounds 1m," *The Independent*, May 6, 2004.

98 http://www.agritrade.org/.

99 Franklin, S, "Youths Taste Protest at Candy Trade Show," *The Chicago Tribune*, June 8, 2004.

100 Reuters, "US coffee groups dispute Oxfam on poor farmers," September 26, 2002.

101 New Internationalist Magazine, "The Naked Lobbyist," New Internationalist, No. 347, July 2002.

102 Ibid.

103 "The Cocoa Industry in West Africa: A history of explanation," Anti Slavery International 2004, http://www.antislavery.org/homepage/resources/cocoa%20report%202004.pdf.

104 Cote d'Ivoire, Country Reports on Human Rights Practices – 2004, United States Department of State, February 28, 2005, http://www.state.gov/g/drl/rls/hrrpt/2004/41599.htm.

105 "Human Rights Watchdog and Civil Rights Firm Sue Nestlé, ADM, Cargill, for Using Forced child Labor," International Labor Rights Fund Press Release, July 14, 2005, http://www.laborrights.org/press/cocoa_pressrel_071405.htm.

106 United States District Court Central District of California,

http://www.laborrights.org/projects/childlab/FinalCocoa-Complaint_Jul05.pdf

107 Ibid.

108 "May 2005 Report – Child Labor in Agriculture," International Labor Rights Fund Report, May 2005, http://www.laborrights.org/projects/childlab/cocoa_childlabor_update_May05.pdf.

109 Babymilk Action, *Boycott News*, Issue No. 31, 2002, http://www.babymilkaction.org/pdfs/bn31.pdf.

110 Koller, F., "Mise en cause par une ancienne prisonnière chinoise, Nestlé introduit une clause contre le travail forcé," *Le Temps*, April 13, 2002

111 SINALTRAINAL website, http://www.sinaltrainal.org/Textos/martires.htm

112 Higginbottom, A., "Nestlé in Colombia," *Morning Star*, December 28, 2002

113 International Union of Food, Agricultural, Hotel, Restaurant, Catering, Tobacco and Allied Workers' Union (IUF), Press Release, "Positive Result at Nestlé El Salvador – Conflict Ends in Negotiated Solution," July 8, 2003.

114 Townsend, A., "Nestlé Threatens to Sell Perrier as Dispute with Workers Grows," *The Independent on Sunday*, March 21, 2004.

115 Arnold, M., "Closure threat ends Nestlé Water impasse," *Financial Times*, May 4, 2005.

116 Chi-Yon, S., "Nestle Korea Shuts Down Main Office Due to Strike," *World News Connection*, August 26, 2003.

117 International Union of Food, Agricultural, Hotel, Restaurant, Catering, Tobacco and Allied Workers' Union (IUF), Press Release, "Negotiated Agreement Ends Lengthy Conflict at Nestlé Korea," November 28, 2003.

118 Ibid.

119 http://www.hartford-hwp.com/archives/54a/038.html.

120 *Philippine Daily Inquirer*, "50 Workers, Guards Injured in Plant Clash," June 25, 2003

121 "Nestlé union leader murdered," *Inquirer News Service*, September 23, 2005.

122 "Nestlé Philippines Union Leader Murdered – Government Must Act Now!", International Union of Food, Agricultural, Hotel, Restaurant, Catering, Tobacco and Allied Workers' Associations press release, September 26, 2005, http://www.iuf.org/cgi-bin/dbman/db.cgi?db=default&uid=default&ID=2330&view_records=1&ww=1&en=1.

123 Groupe Danone 2005 annual report on 20-F.

124 "World's largest corporations," *Fortune*, Vol.154, Issue 2, July 24, 2006.

125 "EBRD to help Danone improve central and east European Food Industry," EBRD press release, March 29, 2006, http://www.ebrd.com/new/pressrel/1995/26mar29.htm.

126 "EBRD ups investment in Russia's Danone operations," EBRD press release, August 2, 2004, http://www.ebrd.com/new/pressrel/2004/112aug2.htm.